TESTING THE
FIELD OF VISION

TESTING THE FIELD OF VISION

DOUGLAS R. ANDERSON, M.D.

Associate Professor of Ophthalmology, Bascom Palmer Eye Institute,
University of Miami School of Medicine, Miami, Florida

With **243** *illustrations*
Illustrated by **Leona M. Allison**

The C. V. Mosby Company

ST. LOUIS • TORONTO • LONDON   1982

MOSBY

A TRADITION OF PUBLISHING EXCELLENCE

Editor: Eugenia A. Klein
Assistant editor: Kathryn H. Falk
Manuscript editor: Karen Gamble
Design: Jeanne Bush
Production: Margaret B. Bridenbaugh

The C.V. Mosby Company
11830 Westline Industrial Drive, St. Louis, Missouri 63141

Library of Congress Cataloging in Publication Data

Anderson, Douglas R.
  Testing the field of vision.

  1. Perimetry. I. Title. [DNLM: 1. Perimetry.
2. Vision disorders—Diagnosis. 3. Visual fields.
WW 145 A546t]
RE79.P4A53   617.7'5   81-14045
ISBN 0-8016-0207-6   AACR2

AC/CB/B 9 8 7 6 5 4 3 2   01/A/095

Like every author, I am indebted to my parents, sisters, wife, children,
teachers, friends, colleagues, pupils, bosses, assistants, patients from whom
"clinical experience" is gained, critics, academic heroes of the past,
those who helped in preparation of the illustrations and manuscript,
and the readers who are motivated to buy, borrow, or steal a copy of this book.
If you are any of these, there is a special way in which this book is
dedicated to you, with thanks.

Preface

This manual concentrates on the principles of performing a good visual field examination and is intended for anyone who will perform visual field testing clinically. It is derived from a series of lectures given at the Bascom Palmer Eye Institute, first organized into a perimetry course in August, 1974, and subsequently given in part in a variety of other educational settings. Although the emphasis is on quantitative projection perimetry as performed with the Goldmann perimeter, both the theory and the application are also relevant to the tangent screen and to any other type of visual field testing apparatus.

Although the subject of this book is the applied technique of performing a high-quality visual field examination, enough theory is given so that the reader can understand the basis of the techniques. This understanding will allow the reader to modify the technique to fit the type of disease under consideration, the constraints of time, the equipment available, and the special problems posed by specific patients. Most important is the ability not only to use the projection perimeter or tangent screen but also to know when and how to use various other instruments and techniques introduced later in the book. Flexibility in the artful use of several techniques based on the understanding of basic principles is what makes the difference between a high-quality diagnostic test and a mediocre one.

The approach in this book is that of learning one step at a time. Especially at the beginning of the book, a chapter with a small amount of theory is followed by a chapter on practical techniques, which is followed by more theory and then more practical application, and so on. Simple basic concepts and techniques are presented first, and the reader who is already knowledgeable may be disturbed that important details are not filled in until later in the book. However, the aim is to provide a sequence of learning from the beginning, assuming no prior knowledge: certain important details simply cannot be assimilated until more basic concepts are mastered completely. Knowledgeable readers who are using this book to refine their knowledge should at least skim through the first chapters to be sure they understand the perspective that forms the basic building blocks that are the foundation for the later chapters.

This book is designed to be used for individual reading or self-teaching, perhaps supplemented by some guidance from a more experienced person. It is also designed for use as a textbook for perimetry courses (see Appendix A). Whether this book is used for self-teaching or in a formal, complete course, the practical exercises and some of the outside reading assignments are important for beginners if they are to assimilate the information in each chapter and be prepared for subsequent chapters.

Douglas R. Anderson

Contents

CONTENTS

Appendixes

TESTING THE
FIELD OF VISION

CHAPTER 1

Introduction

Before describing the methods for testing the visual field, we must first consider what the field of vision is.

THE VISUAL FIELD

With our eyes directed straight forward, we pay attention to and see the details of the object at which we are looking. While looking at an object, we are able to detect the presence of other objects above, below, and to the sides of the object of regard—though we may not be able to discern the details or even to say what the objects are.

> **FIG. 1-1. Field of vision of the right and left eyes.** Note that the fields of view of the two eyes overlap. Over a broad area objects are seen by both eyes but objects to the extreme right or extreme left are seen only by one eye. In this way the field of view with both eyes open is greater than with either eye alone. (Illustration by George E. Schwenk.)

To see for yourself that you can not discern details of an object without looking right at it, have a person stand 2 feet to the side of a visual acuity chart. Look at his face, and see if you can read the letters (the details of the chart) while your eyes are directed at the person's face.

When an object in our peripheral vision catches our attention, perhaps because it is moving or flashing, we reflexly turn our eyes toward it so that we can see its details and identify it. Visual function, then, includes both the ability to detect the presence of objects in a field of vision and the ability to discern the details of an object as we look directly at it. Without either component of visual function, we are handicapped.

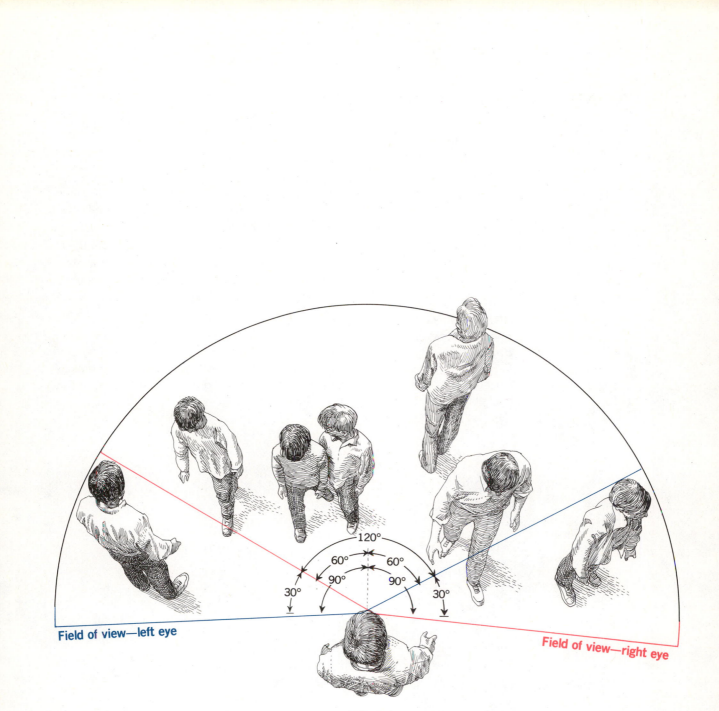

FIG. 1-1

BOUNDARIES OF THE VISUAL FIELD

The boundaries of the field of vision, measured in degrees from the point of fixation (the object at which the eye is directed) are approximately:

60 degrees superiorly (above)

75 degrees inferiorly (below)

100 degrees temporally (to the right for the right eye, to the left for the left eye)

60 degrees nasally (to the left for the right eye, to the right for the left eye)

The extreme boundary of the visual field could be determined by bringing a large object around the head from behind an individual who is looking straight ahead and determining when the object first becomes visible to him. If a disease state has contracted the peripheral boundary of the visual field, it may be necessary to bring the object quite far around before it is seen.

FIG. 1-2. The limits of the average normal visual field.

A, Upward and downward limits.

B, Temporal and nasal limits.

C, Plot of the limit of the field of vision of the right eye. Note that the field is standardly plotted on the field diagram "as the patient sees it"—the border of his visual field to the right is plotted to the right on the field diagram.

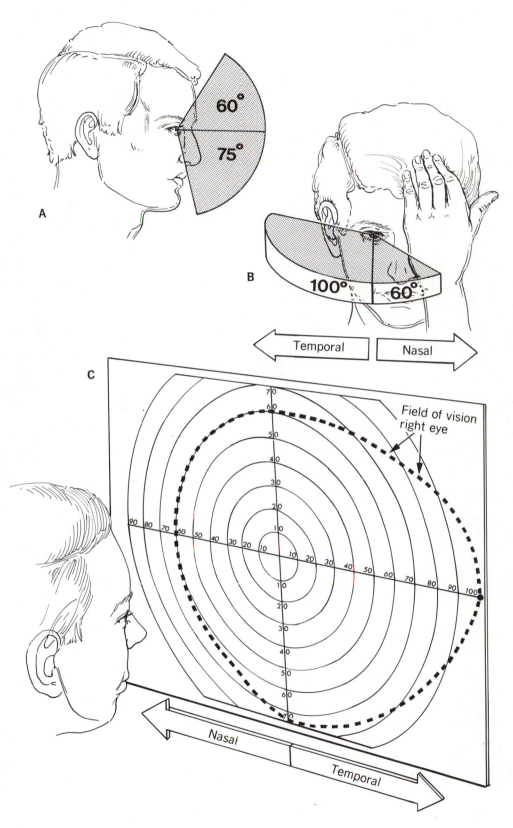

A

B

Temporal   Nasal

C

Field of vision
right eye

Nasal   Temporal

FIG. 1-2

VISUAL CHARACTERISTICS WITHIN THE VISUAL FIELD

Determining the outside boundary of the visual field is one aspect of testing the visual field but is not really the aspect that is of greatest diagnostic importance. More important is the fact that within the boundaries every point in the visual field has a certain characteristic of visibility.

For example, as already noted, the ability to discern details (i.e., visual acuity) is greatest at the point of fixation. Clinically, we ask the patient to look at letters in order to determine the visual acuity of the point of fixation in terms of the smallest letters that can be identified when the person looks directly at the letter (Fig. 1-3, A).

If we wished, we could determine the visual acuity at all other points in the visual field by having the person look at a certain spot, placing a letter chart at selected locations (e.g., 10 degrees to the nasal side), and determining the smallest letter that can be correctly identified (Fig. 1-3, B). We could do this for many points scattered throughout the visual field (e.g., 10 degrees temporally, 10 degrees superiorly, 20 degrees nasally, 30 degrees nasally) and thereby document or quantitate the functional ability (or visual acuity) in each region of the field of vision in that individual. It would be found that the acuity is best at the point of fixation and becomes less and less as the chart is placed farther from fixation.

FIG. 1-3. Determining visual acuity.
A, Usual method, which determines visual acuity at the point of fixation.
B, Hypothetical method for testing visual acuity 10 degrees from fixation.

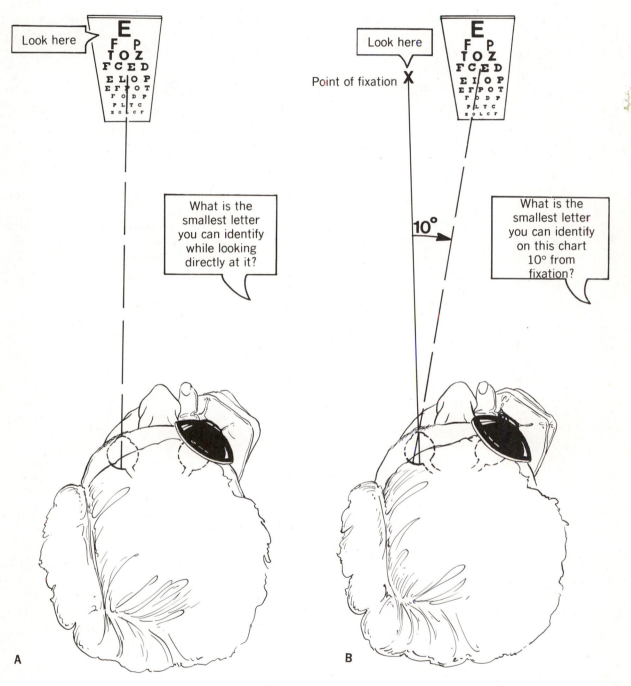

FIG. 1-3

In clinical practice, we do not quantitate the functional ability within the visual field in terms of the smallest letters that can be identified. Instead we quantitate the visual field in terms of the weakest white spot that can be seen in each region of the field. With the tangent screen technique of field testing (p. 44), these test stimuli consist of white beads or discs of standard diameters (e.g., 1 mm, 3 mm, 5 mm, 10 mm). With projection perimeters (p. 22), the stimuli typically consist of projected white spots that can be adjusted in both size and intensity.

It is important to know what factors enter into the visibility of a white spot:

APPARENT SIZE (DIAMETER OR AREA) OF THE SPOT is an important factor. The apparent size depends on the real size and the distance of the spot from the eye. Thus a 3-mm spot 1 meter from the eye is equivalent to a 6-mm spot that is 2 meters from the eye or a 1-mm spot that is ⅓ meter from the eye. With the Goldmann perimeter, the distance is fixed at 30 cm and relative visibility relates to the real size of the spot. With the tangent screen, which can be used at varying distances, both the size of the spot and the distance are considered.

INTENSITY OF THE SPOT is important, too, in a reciprocal relationship with size such that two spots may be roughly equivalent visual stimuli if one is ½ (0.5) log unit more intense but half the diameter (one-fourth the area) of the other. The exact relationship of size and intensity is different in different parts of the visual field.

BACKGROUND ILLUMINATION is the third factor to which we pay special attention in quantitative perimetry. The background is important because a stimulus of certain intensity will be less visible against a light background than it will be against a dark background. The background intensity also determines the degree of light or dark adaptation of the retina (photopic, mesopic, or scotopic), which of course influences whether dim stimuli are seen.

OTHER FACTORS are also important. These include color, movement of the stimulus, duration of the stimulus, attentiveness of the person, and refractive state of the eye. Throughout most of the field, a moving stimulus is somewhat more visible than a nonmoving one. The duration of a stimulus is important for a brief flash (e.g., 0.01 second vs. 0.02 second), but duration does not change the visibility of a stimulus after a certain critical time—approximately ⅓ second or longer. After this critical time, duration does not matter because maximum temporal summation has occurred.

VISUAL THRESHOLD: DEFINITION

Every point within the visual field has a visual threshold, defined as the weakest test stimulus that is just visible in that location under the specific test conditions.

Also visible at each location are all test stimuli that are stronger (larger or more intense) than the threshold stimulus. Such a stimulus, stronger than the threshold stimulus, is a *suprathreshold stimulus*.

An object is *not* seen if it is weaker (smaller or less intense) than the threshold stimulus—that is, if it is an *infrathreshold stimulus*.

> Visual field testing—which is what this book is all about—is the testing of visual threshold throughout the field of vision, not simply a determination of the extreme outside boundary of the visual field.

METHODS FOR DETERMINING VISUAL THRESHOLD
Static threshold perimetry

For visual field testing, the patient's eyes should be held in a steady position by having him look at a specific point—the "fixation target" or "point of fixation." At some other place within the field of vision is presented a spot stimulus of light and the patient communicates whether or not he can see it.

With a typical projection perimeter, e.g., the Goldmann perimeter, this would be a projected spot of white light of a selected size and intensity on a background of a certain standard intensity. Keeping the size of the spot and the background illumination the same, and starting with the spot too dim to see, the examiner successively increases the spot intensity until the patient reports that he can see it. The dimmest stimulus that can be seen is recorded as the threshold stimulus for that location in the field.

FIG. 1-4. Diagram of the visual field within 40 degrees of fixation. The visual threshold at twenty locations was tested with five different stimuli (*A*, *B*, *C*, *D*, and *E*). At each location is indicated the weakest stimulus seen, i.e., the threshold at that location.

Note the similarity between recording the weakest white spot that is visible (determination of visual threshold) and recording the smallest letter that can be identified (determination of visual acuity).

In *static threshold perimetry*, then, a location is chosen and the stimulus is presented in that location without moving it. The stimulus is increased in intensity (or size) until it becomes visible, determining the visual threshold in that location (as in Fig. 1-4). This process is repeated at other points.

It is also noteworthy that *D* represents a weak (dim) stimulus and *E* is the weakest. Wherever stimulus *D* is visible as a threshold stimulus, stimuli *A*, *B*, and *C*, being stronger, are also visible. They are suprathreshold stimuli for that location. In the places marked with a *C* the two stronger stimuli, represented by *A* and *B*, would also be visible and would be suprathreshold stimuli for that location. The weaker stimuli, represented by *D* and *E*, would not be visible, meaning that they are infrathreshold (subthreshold) for that location. In the center portion of the field, near the point of fixation, the eye is very sensitive, able to see the weakest stimulus. However, toward the periphery of the field, stronger illumination is needed for the stimulus to be seen.

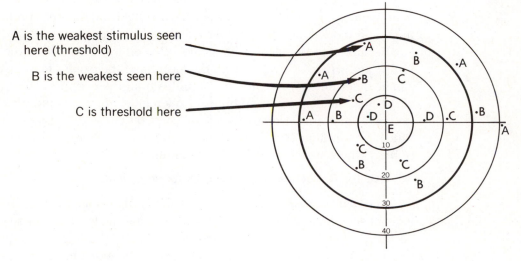

A is the weakest stimulus seen here (threshold)

B is the weakest seen here

C is threshold here

FIG. 1-4

Kinetic threshold perimetry

The line connecting all points where C is the threshold is called the *isopter* for stimulus C.

FIG. 1-5, A. The isopter for stimulus C.

It is an important characteristic of an isopter that the stimulus for that isopter (stimulus C in this instance) is not seen anywhere outside the isopter, since everywhere outside the isopter the stimulus is infrathreshold. The C stimulus is, however, seen everywhere inside the region surrounded by the isopter, being threshold at the line and suprathreshold closer to the center. It is important to note that near the isopter the stimulus is threshold and that the stimulus becomes more and more suprathreshold for locations closer to fixation.

Because the isopter is a boundary between a region where the stimulus is visible and where it is not visible, the location of the isopter for a given stimulus can be determined by moving the stimulus from the periphery toward the center of the field. As long as the stimulus is in a region where it is infrathreshold it will not be seen, but it becomes visible as soon as it crosses the isopter, where it is a threshold stimulus. It remains visible after it enters the region surrounded by the isopter, where it is a suprathreshold stimulus.

FIG. 1-5, B. Determining the isopter for stimulus C.

In *kinetic perimetry,* then, a selected stimulus is moved from an area where it is not seen toward an area where it is seen and the location where the stimulus becomes visible is recorded, as just described (Fig. 1-5, *B*). This process is repeated from all directions toward the center (fixation) until the isopter can be drawn by connecting the points where the stimulus first became visible. Several isopters can be drawn by repeating the process with several stimuli of differing intensity or size.

FIG. 1-5, C. The isopters for *A, B, C,* and *D*. Note that the weak stimulus *D* is seen only inside the region enclosed by its isopter, a small area near fixation, the most sensitive part of the field. In contrast, a stronger stimulus such as *B* is seen over a larger area, the area enclosed by its isopter.

Thus:

> Kinetic perimetry—A *stimulus is chosen*, and the location where it is threshold is determined.
>
> Static perimetry—A *location is chosen*, and the stimulus that is threshold is determined.

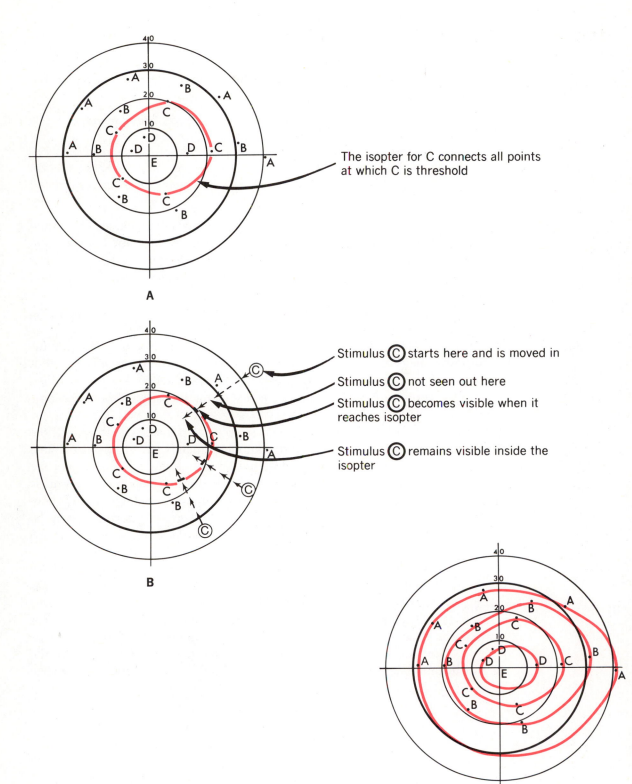

The isopter for C connects all points at which C is threshold

Stimulus Ⓒ starts here and is moved in

Stimulus Ⓒ not seen out here

Stimulus Ⓒ becomes visible when it reaches isopter

Stimulus Ⓒ remains visible inside the isopter

A

B

C

FIG. 1-5

13

MERIDIONAL STATIC THRESHOLD PERIMETRY

Rather than perform static threshold determinations at scattered points in the visual field, it is often useful to determine threshold at points along one of the meridians. The results can be represented as a graph.

FIG. 1-6. Static threshold perimetry performed along an oblique meridian. In this case it is performed from the upper nasal quadrant, through the point of fixation, into the lower temporal quadrant. The points where threshold was tested are indicated on the field diagram and the thresholds at some of these points are indicated by letters *A, B, C, D,* or *E.* The results are also indicated on the graph, which shows greatest sensitivity at the point of fixation.

Note that visual threshold is determined only at the points that are tested and not at any other places within the field of vision. Thus in the static cut shown in Fig. 1-6 the visual threshold is not known for any points in the lower nasal or upper temporal quadrants but only for the positions along the line where visual threshold was tested.

The same is true of kinetic perimetry. The threshold is known only along the isopter at those points where the stimulus first becomes visible.

The threshold is not known in the region outside the isopter. The stimulus was intrathreshold along the path while the isopter was being approached, but one does not know how much intrathreshold, i.e., one does not know how much stronger the stimulus must be at various points along the path in order to become visible.

Similarly, the threshold is not known in the region inside the isopter. If the stimulus is moved even further inward, it should remain visible if the visual field is normal. However, the perimetrist does not actually know whether or not the field is normal and the stimulus is indeed visible within the isopter, as it normally should be, unless the stimulus is actually placed inside the isopter and the patient is asked if, in fact, it is visible. Moreover, even if the examiner determines that the stimulus is visible everywhere inside the isopter, one does not know how much dimmer the stimulus can be made and still be seen.

Thus, in both kinetic perimetry and static perimetry, the threshold is known quantitatively only at the spots where the patient indicates that the object is visible. The number of places tested with either method depends on the time available to do the field testing. Given a practical limit on the number of places where the threshold can be determined in the time available, the diagnostic value of the information depends on whether the examiner has chosen wisely the places within the field where such quantitative information is obtained. We shall see this principle applied later (p. 118).

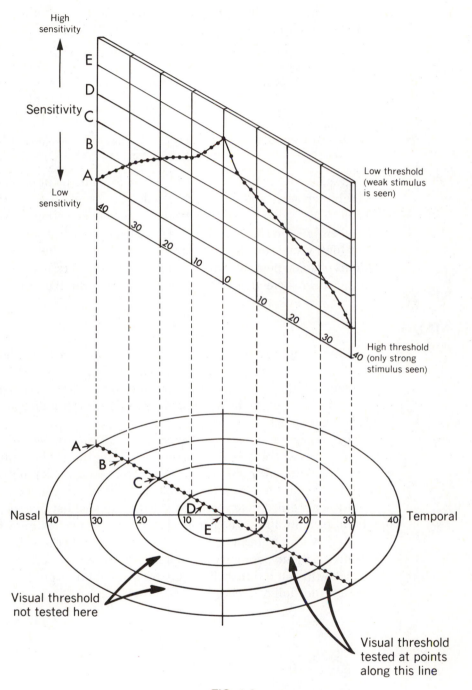

FIG. 1-6

HILL OF VISION

The "island of vision", or "hill of vision," is a three-dimensional graph of visual sensitivity. The horizontal axis represents location in the visual field. The altitude of the hill (vertical direction) at any location represents the visual sensitivity at that location.

FIG. 1-7. "Hill of vision." The hill (graph) is highest where dim, small objects of low contrast are visible. The hill is lower where the object must be more intense or larger or have more contrast in order to be seen.

The hill of vision can be represented as a contour map (isopter plot) representing horizontal slices through the hill, as is usual for kinetic perimetry. It can also be represented as a vertical slice of the hill (profile plot), as is usual (but not always) in static perimetry.

"Sensitivity" is the inverse of "threshold." The point of fixation in the center is highly sensitive and has low threshold in the sense that a very weak stimulus is visible. Thus, a low visual threshold means high sensitivity to light. Inversely, the peripheral regions have a high threshold because only a strong stimulus is visible. This high visual threshold means a low sensitivity to light. The hill of vision and graphs of static perimetry are in terms of sensitivity rather than threshold, so that the most sensitive areas of the field show up as the highest points on the graph.

SUMMARY

Every point in the visual field has a certain visual threshold, defined as the weakest stimulus that is visible in that location. Visual field testing consists of determining the visual threshold (or the inverse, visual sensitivity) at selected points throughout the field of vision, as well as determining the outside boundary of the field of vision.

In *kinetic* perimetry a selected *test stimulus is moved* until it crosses its isopter, the location where the stimulus is the threshold stimulus. In *static* perimetry, a *stationary test stimulus* in a given location is intensified (or enlarged) until it is seen, thereby determining the visibility threshold at that location.

Either method determines the visual threshold at one location, the location where the stimulus is just barely visible. By repeated testing with various stimuli the threshold is determined at several locations. The results are most often recorded in kinetic perimetry as isopters representing a contour map of the "hill of vision" or in static threshold perimetry as a graph or profile representing a slice through the "hill of vision."

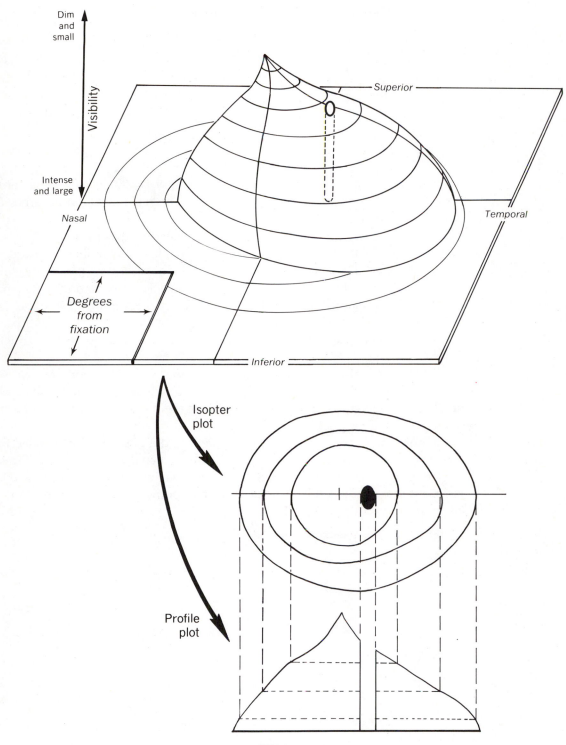

Dim
and
small

Visibility

Intense
and large

Nasal

Superior

Temporal

Degrees
from
fixation

Inferior

Isopter
plot

Profile
plot

FIG. 1-7

17

CHAPTER 2

Anatomy and function

THE EYE

The wall of the eye has three layers. The outer layer consists of the cornea, which is clear, and the sclera, which is white. The region where the cornea and sclera join is called the limbus.

The second layer is the uveal tract, which has three parts—iris, ciliary body, and choroid. The iris has an opening, the pupil, and the root of the iris inserts into the ciliary body. The ciliary body lies within the anteriormost part of the sclera and contains the ciliary muscle, which is responsible for changing the shape of the lens. This allows the eye to focus on objects at varying distances, or to *accommodate*. The ciliary body also produces aqueous humor. The third part of the uveal tract is the choroid, which lies under the retina and provides nutrition to the outer retina.

The retina is the innermost layer of the ocular wall. The retina receives and detects the light that has been focused into an image by the optics of the cornea and lens. Visual impulses are transmitted from the retina to the brain by the optic nerve.

Within the eye, the lens lies directly behind the pupil. It is suspended from the ciliary body by zonular fibers, and as already noted, the lens shape (accommodation) is controlled by muscles in the ciliary body. In front of the iris and lens is the anterior chamber filled with aqueous humor. Behind the lens is the vitreous cavity filled with vitreous humor.

FIG. 2-1. Cross section of the eye.

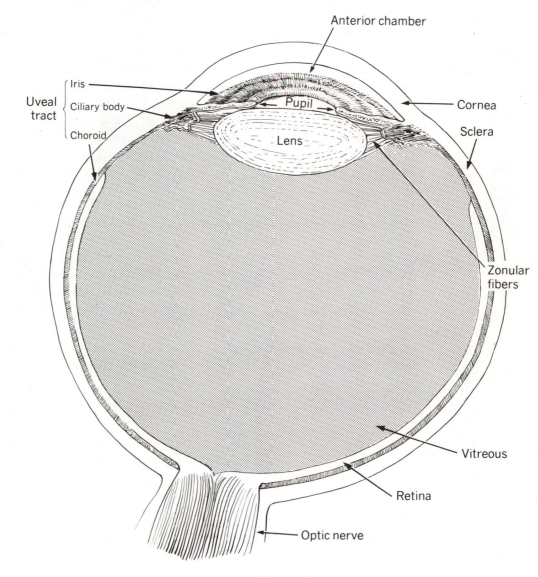

Anterior chamber

Iris

Uveal tract

Ciliary body

Choroid

Pupil

Cornea

Lens

Sclera

Zonular fibers

Vitreous

Retina

Optic nerve

FIG. 2-1

CORRESPONDENCE OF RETINA AND VISUAL FIELD

Every point in the retina corresponds to a certain direction in the visual field. For example, the fovea at the very back of the eye corresponds to the point of fixation. The fovea is centered in the macula, a part of the retina specialized for sharp vision and for color discrimination. This area of the retina can discern detail, allowing one to read very small letters, and also has the highest sensitivity for detecting the stimuli used for visual field testing. Points in the peripheral retina, near the ciliary body, correspond to points in the peripheral visual field.

Because the image formed by the optics of the eye is upside down and backward, just as in a camera, the image is reversed so that the nasal retina sees objects in the temporal visual field and vice versa. Also, points in the upper (superior) retina correspond to objects in the lower (inferior) visual field and vice versa.

From all points in the retina, the visual information is converted to nervous impulses. These are collected by nerve fibers that course along the inner surface of the retina toward a spot 10 to 15 degrees on the nasal side of the fovea, a little above the horizontal. Here the nerve fibers collect together to become the optic nerve, which exits from the back of the eye and courses toward the brain. At the spot where these nerve fibers bundle together, which is called the optic nerve head or the optic disc, there is necessarily an opening through the retina to allow the exit of the nerve fibers into the optic nerve. Because light cannot be detected where there is an opening in the retina, there is a corresponding location in the visual field 10 to 15 degrees from fixation where stimuli are not seen. This location in the visual field is called the physiologic blind spot. Because the optic nerve leaves from the nasal side of the eye, the blind spot is in the temporal portion of the visual field.

FIG. 2-2. Diagram of the left eye. In this view the eye is seen from above to show the relationship between retinal location and visual field location.

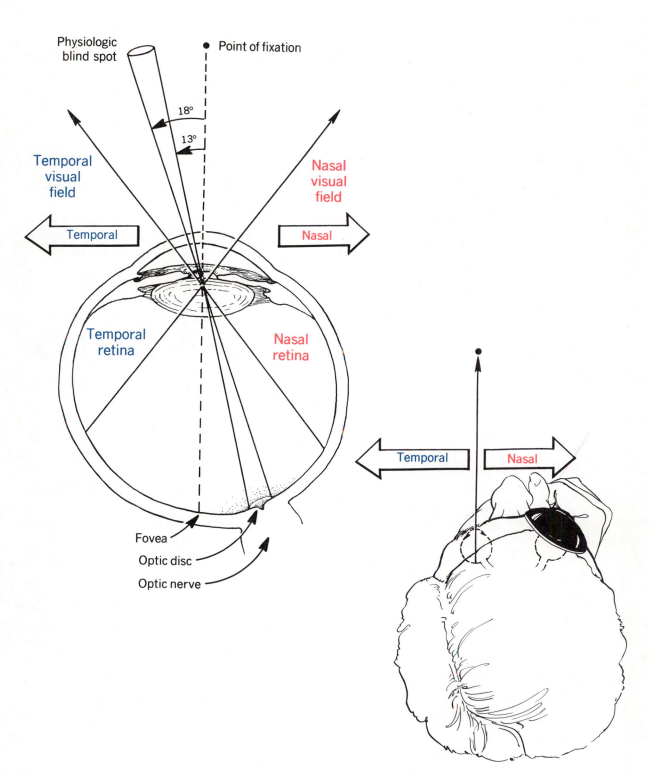

Physiologic blind spot

Point of fixation

18°

13°

Temporal visual field

Nasal visual field

Temporal

Nasal

Temporal retina

Nasal retina

Fovea

Optic disc

Optic nerve

Temporal

Nasal

FIG. 2-2

21

CHAPTER 3

Goldmann perimeter

Many modern perimeters for testing the visual field, whether manual or automatic, consist of a hemispheric bowl evenly illuminated inside. The patient looks at a central fixation point while test spots of light of various sizes and intensities are projected at various places within the bowl and the patient communicates whether or not the spot is visible. The most common type of bowl perimeter is the Goldmann perimeter.

FIG. 3-1. The bowl perimeter.

There are several models of the Goldmann perimeter, all very similar, made by several manufacturers (including Haag-Streit Co., Topcon Inc., and Marco Equipment, Inc.). To be described here is the Goldmann perimeter 940 made by Haag-Streit Co.

Beginners now learning to use the perimeter should consult the instructions provided by the manufacturer. The instructions will include the method for changing the light bulb and the fuse.

CARE OF THE PERIMETER

The inside of the bowl must stay clean and evenly white, without smudges, scratches, or pencil marks. Therefore, do not touch the inside of the bowl with anything except the brush used to clean it. Also, never hold a pencil that might inadvertently mar the surface when you are placing the lens holder in position or when you are removing it (see p. 98). Do not allow the lens holder to scrape against the side of the bowl when inserting or removing it.

If it will be longer than an hour before the next usage, and especially overnight, place a dust cover over the perimeter. A soft brush that looks like a shaving brush is provided for dusting out the inside of the bowl as needed. This brush is not for use on the outside of the perimeter because it may pick up oil or grease. The outside of the perimeter must be kept dusted, of course, but with something else.

A special cleaning compound is available for cleaning the inside of the bowl about once a year; depending on usage and care. Rarely, the inside of the bowl may need repainting by the manufacturer's service representative.

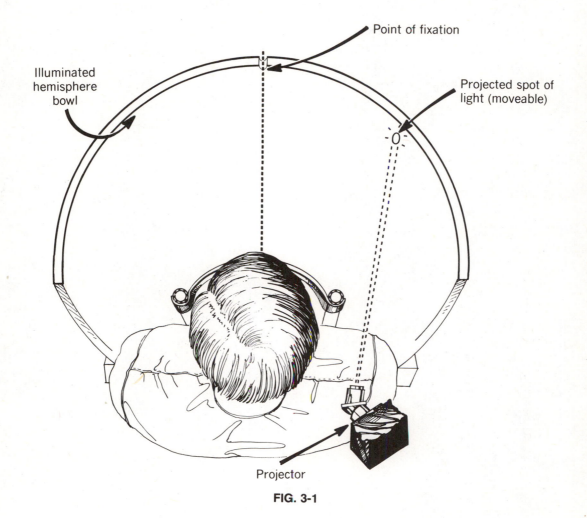

Point of fixation

Illuminated hemisphere bowl

Projected spot of light (moveable)

Projector

FIG. 3-1

INSERTION AND ALIGNMENT OF PAPER

There are two knobs to loosen the chart plate. When these are given half a turn it is possible to insert the paper into a narrow slit. At the bottom of the chart paper are four short vertical lines near the center. One of these is taller than the others and in line with the vertical meridian passing through the center of the circular chart. This taller mark should be placed exactly within the V-notch in the frame at the bottom. The paper should also be level with the two lateral V-notches. Then the knobs are turned back in order to hold the paper in place.

FIG. 3-2. Inserting the field chart into the Goldmann perimeter.

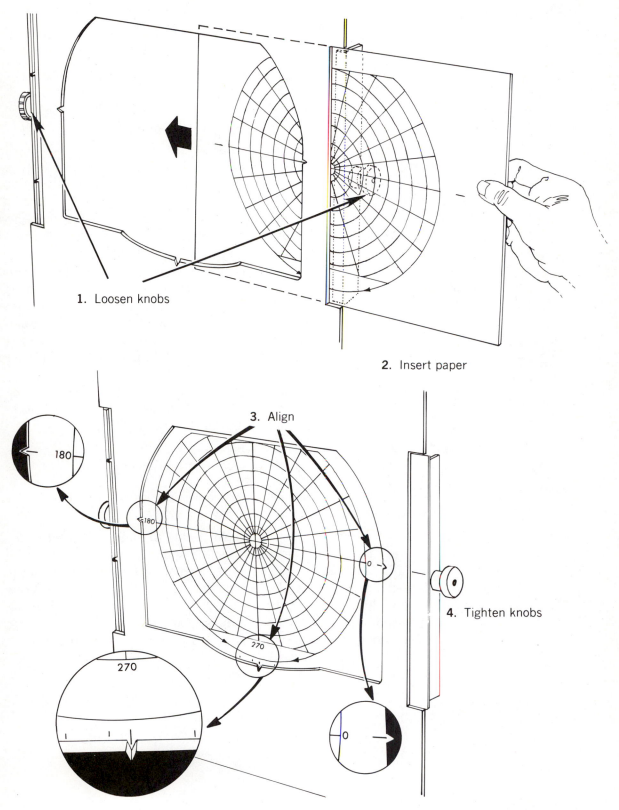

1. Loosen knobs

2. Insert paper

3. Align

180

180

270

270

4. Tighten knobs

0

0

FIG. 3-2

25

CONTROL OF THE PROJECTED LIGHT STIMULUS

On the back of the perimeter is a set of levers to control the size and intensity of the projected test stimuli.

FIG. 3-3, A. Controls for the size and intensity. The three levers provide control of:
Size: 0, I, II, III, IV, and V (V is the largest)
Intensity (coarse adjustment, 0.5 log unit steps): 1, 2, 3, and 4 (4 is the brightest)
Intensity (fine adjustment, 0.1 log unit steps): a, b, c, d, and e (e is the brightest)

Recent models have an extended range of intensity by means of an additional lever with major jumps (2 log units) in intensity. The single-bar setting is 2 log units dimmer and the double-bar 4 log units dimmer than the setting with no bar, which is the most intense.

With all the levers pushed to the right, the stimulus is the largest and brightest possible. With all the levers pushed to the left, it is the smallest and dimmest possible.

Size I is the standard size test stimulus used and perimetry is performed with stimuli of various intensities. The larger sizes are used *only* when the most intense stimulus of size I (I-4e) is not adequate and a stronger stimulus is required. Similarly, size 0 is used only when a weaker stimulus is needed than can be obtained with size I and all the intensity filter levers to the left. This sometimes happens on instruments without the extended range of intensity (see p. 178 for further details).

The stimulus is turned on and off during visual field testing with a knob at the right side of the perimeter near the bottom. The knob can be twisted clockwise and counterclockwise and can also be depressed or elevated.

FIG. 3-3, B. Control to turn the stimulus on and off.
Left, When the knob is twisted to one position, the stimulus is on when the knob is depressed and off when the knob is released.
Right, When the knob is twisted to the alternate position, the stimulus is off when the knob is depressed and on when the knob is released.

With rare exceptions, during visual field testing the knob is placed in the position that requires it to be depressed for the stimulus to be on. The main exception is during calibration of the instrument, when one wants the stimulus to be on without the need to hold the knob down. So that the operator can know whether the stimulus is on or off, there is a tiny aperture, the stimulus indicator, below the plate with the levers to control the size and intensity of the stimulus. Light is visible through the aperture when the test stimulus is on but the aperture is dark when the test stimulus is off.

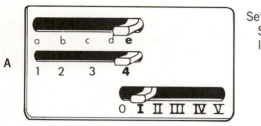

Set at
Size I
Intensity 4e

FIG. 3-3

The position of the stimulus inside the bowl is controlled by the pantograph handle. With the handle on the left side of the field chart, the projected stimulus will be inside the bowl to the patient's left.

FIG. 3-4. The pantograph handle.
A, When to the left, the pantograph handle will cover somewhat more than the left half of the field (unshaded portion) but cannot go beyond a curved line to the right of the vertical meridian on the field chart.
B, To test the right half of the field, the pantograph handle must be passed to the other side by moving the pantograph handle carefully around the bottom of the visual field chart.
C, After passing the handle along the pathway indicated by arrows on the field chart, the right half of the field can be tested.

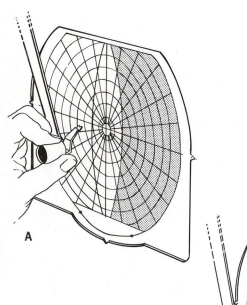

A

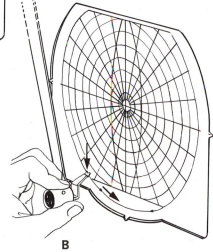

B

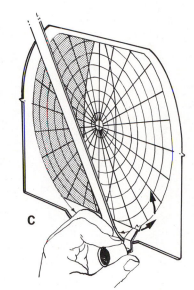

C

FIG. 3-4

29

POSITIONING THE PATIENT

Only one eye is tested at a time and the other eye is covered. The perimeter comes with a translucent white occluder designed to provide the theoretical advantage of avoiding dark adaptation of the covered eye. It will then be ready for visual field testing when the testing of the first eye is completed. This was deemed important because visual field testing is performed under light-adapted (photopic) conditions. However, in actual practice if a black patch is used as an occluder, the eye becomes light-adapted again rather promptly when uncovered.

When the eye not being tested is covered and the patient's chin and forehead are in the appropriate position, the head can be positioned up and down as well as right and left with the large chin rest control knobs at the bottom of the operator's side of the perimeter. The operator can determine by looking through the telescope when the eye is centered. The image of the patient's eye will be upside down. The telescope can be focused by pulling the eyepiece in and out. When the telescope is focused, a reticle is visible that is subdivided in millimeters for the purpose of measuring the diameter of the patient's pupil. If the patient's eye is not in focus while the reticle is in focus, it usually means that the patient's head is not fully forward against the forehead rest.

When the patient's eye is positioned, he can see a small fixation point in the center of the bowl. Every beginning perimetrist should position his head in front of the fixation point to see that it is actually a small mirror mounted on a small pillar reflecting light from the light bulb above the patient's head. A larger mirror can be positioned behind the small mirror with a lever at the base of the telescope on the operator's side. The larger mirror is for patients with poor vision who cannot see the small one. The small one should be used whenever possible for more accurate fixation and for better control of accommodation.

FIG. 3-5. Controls for centering the patient's position.

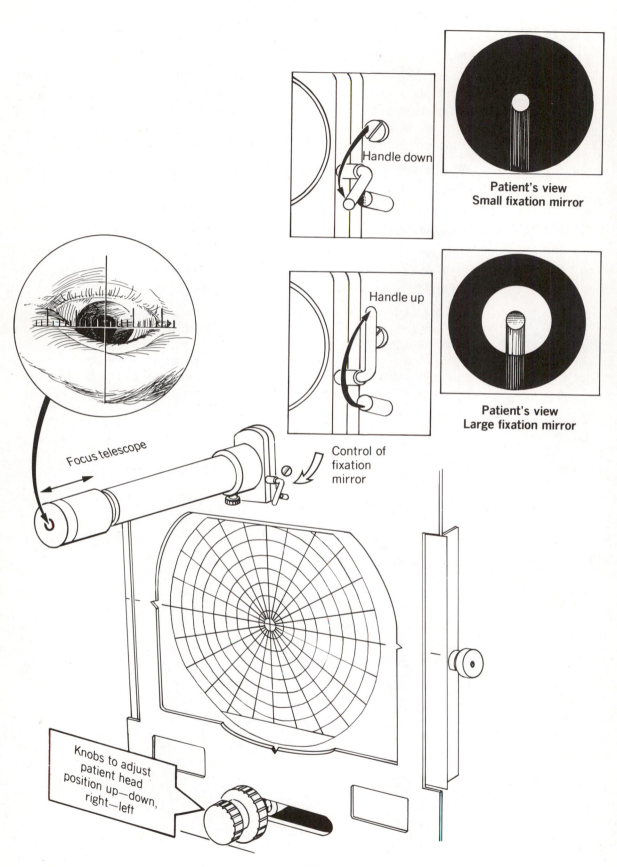

Handle down

Patient's view
Small fixation mirror

Handle up

Patient's view
Large fixation mirror

Focus telescope

Control of
fixation
mirror

Knobs to adjust
patient head
position up—down,
right—left

FIG. 3-5

LEVELING THE PERIMETER

The perimeter should be leveled. When the perimeter is level, the projection arm, when released by the operator, will automatically (by gravity) come to rest in the port at the side of the perimeter bowl. This prevents the patient from hurting himself or damaging the projector arm by sitting back at the end of the test and bumping his head on the extended projector arm. It also prevents harm to the projector arm from people walking by when the perimeter is not in use.

FIG. 3-6. Leveling controls. Two knobs control the feet and on the left side is a spirit level.

CONTROL OF ILLUMINATION FOR THE OPERATOR

Provision is made for the operator to see because the test is performed in a darkened room. Light bulbs inside the machine illuminate the field chart from behind and light shines on the table through adjustable panels.

FIG. 3-7. Light for the operator. On the side of the perimeter to the operator's left there are two rheostats. The one closest to the operator controls the intensity of the light behind the chart paper. On the two sides of the perimeter beneath the chart paper are sliding metal door panels that can be opened in varying degrees to allow some of the light behind the chart to fall on the examiner's side of the table to see the pencils and anything else on the table.

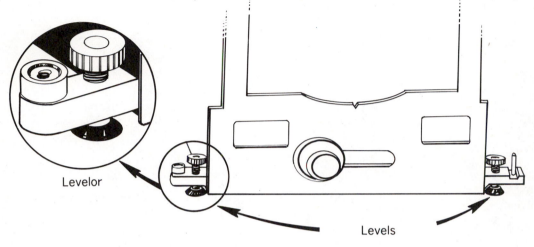

Levelor

Levels

FIG. 3-6

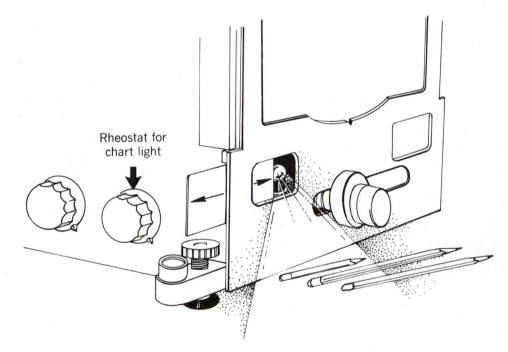

Rheostat for
chart light

FIG. 3-7

CHAPTER 4

Plotting isopters kinetically

In this chapter the method of plotting normal isopters with the Goldmann perimeter is described; however, the principles and sequence can be adapted by the reader to any other visual testing apparatus. The beginning perimetrist should first attempt the sequence on a volunteer with normal sight, at the same time becoming acquainted with the mechanics of the instrument.

FIG. 4-1, A. The levers are set to the desired stimulus size and intensity. For example, I-2e is appropriate for a person with normal sight. The knob of the shutter switch is turned such that the projected stimulus comes on when the switch is depressed but is off when the switch is not depressed (see p. 26).

The eye not to be tested is covered. The head is positioned so that the uncovered eye is properly centered in front of the fixation target by looking through the telescope and adjusting the large knobs near the bottom of the perimeter to move the head sideways or up and down. The pupil size is noted and recorded on the chart. All room lights are turned off and the door of the room closed to prevent any stray light.

FIG. 4-1, B. Projecting the stimulus. With the left hand, the operator moves the position of the test stimulus until it is near fixation (e.g., at 5 degrees). The shutter switch is depressed with the right hand, which is holding the pencil, to make sure that the patient is able to see the object when it is turned on. A mental note is made of the approximate reaction time from when the stimulus is turned on to when the subject responds by pushing the buzzer.

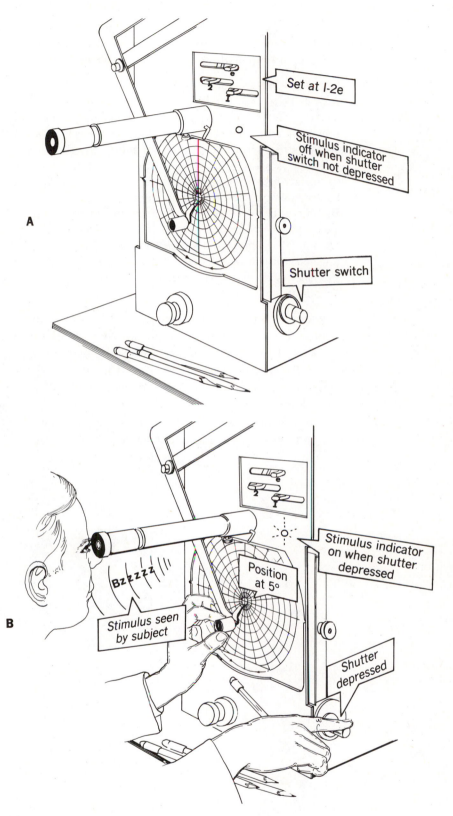

FIG. 4-1

After confirming in this way that the test object is visible near the center of the field, the examiner lifts the right hand off the shutter switch so that the projected spot is turned off.

FIG. 4-2. Plotting isopters kinetically.

A, With the left hand, the pantograph handle is moved to the peripheral portion of the field (e.g., 60 degrees). The projected stimulus is turned on by depressing the shutter switch with the right hand. There should be a wait of about 1 second (or twice the subject's reaction time) to be sure that the object is not seen at the periphery of the field. If it is seen at 60 degrees, a weaker stimulus such as the I-1e is used. It is necessary to make sure that this weaker stimulus is visible at the center of the field before turning attention once again to the periphery of the visual field.

B, After waiting 1 second to make sure that the object is not visible at the periphery, the examiner moves the stimulus inward at a speed of about 3 to 5 degrees per second. The stimulus is kept on continuously by holding the shutter switch in a depressed position with the right hand. As the object is moved toward the center, the examiner looks through the telescope at the patient's eye to make sure that it maintains fixation.

It is important to be looking at the eye just prior to the patient's response to make sure he is maintaining fixation at the very instant he responds. If it happens that he looked away momentarily toward the object and then responded that he saw it, that response must be ignored. It is no good for the examiner to look at fixation after the patient responds. The patient may have looked at the object and responded and by the time the examiner looks through the telescope the patient may have regained his proper fixation. The examiner would not realize that the patient had looked away for a split second.

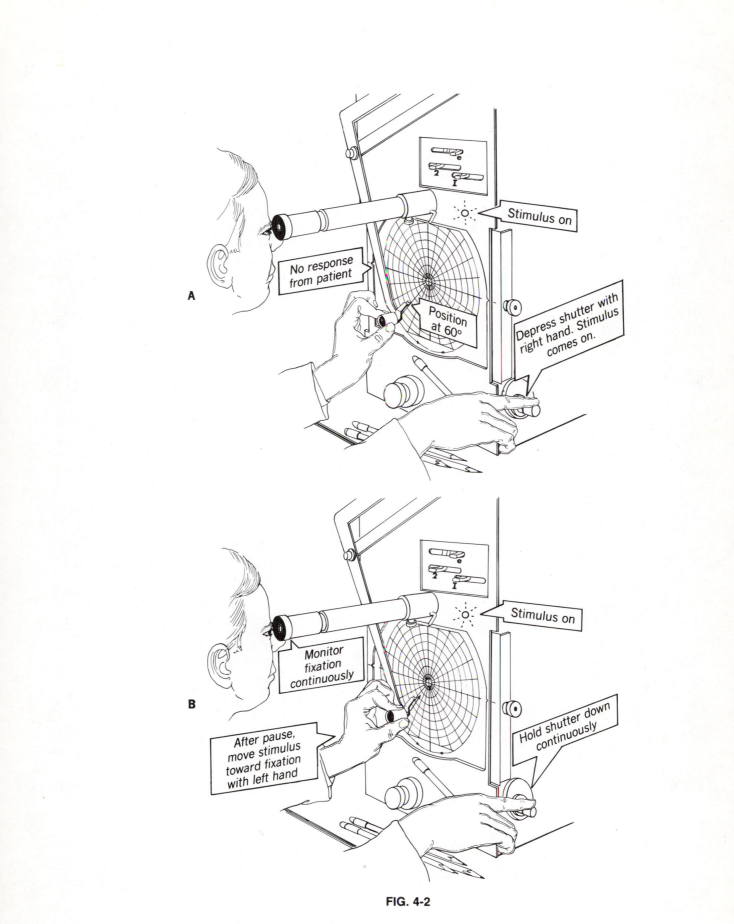

FIG. 4-2

FIG. 4-3. Plotting isopters kinetically, cont'd

A, As soon as the subject responds without having shifted fixation, the operator stops moving his left hand.

B, The operator then lifts his right hand off the shutter knob, which turns off the stimulus.

C, The pencil in the right hand is used to mark the position at which the object became visible.

From the perspective of the subject, the sequence of events is that the test object becomes visible, he responds, and the test object disappears.

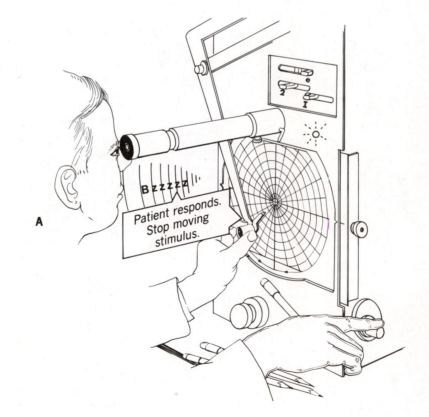

FIG. 4-3

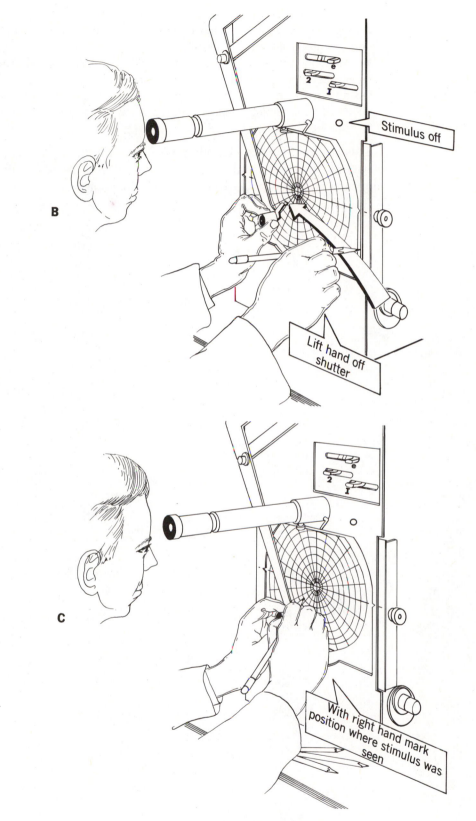

FIG. 4-3, cont'd

39

FIG. 4-4. Plotting isopters kinetically, cont'd

A, Next, with the left hand the projected stimulus is moved outward by 10 or 15 degrees and shifted to an adjacent meridian.

B, The shutter is again depressed with the right hand. After a 1-second wait to be sure the object is not visible, it is moved toward the center. If the stimulus is seen before it is moved, turn it off, move it more peripheral, and start again. When the subject responds, the right hand releases the shutter switch and marks the position where the stimulus became visible.

This process is repeated around the entire circumference. The perspective of the patient repeatedly is that the stimulus is seen, he responds, the stimulus disappears, and he waits for the next stimulus to appear.

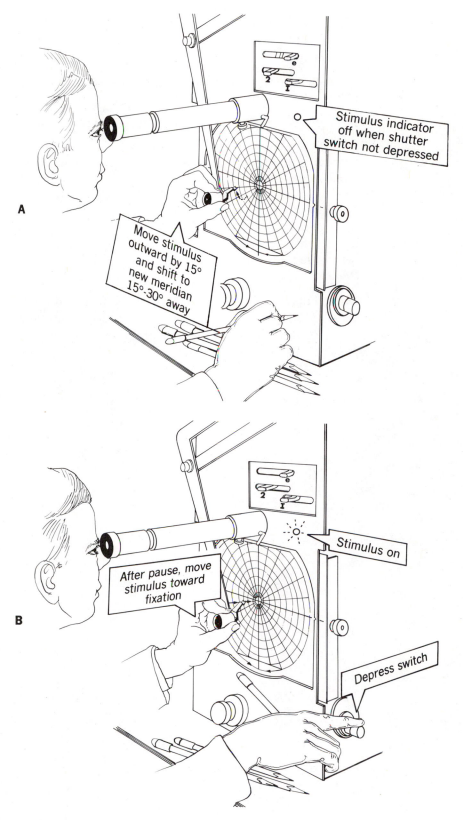

FIG. 4-4

When the I-2e threshold points are completely plotted, a line is drawn connecting all of the dots. Then the test stimulus is set at I-4e and the entire procedure is repeated.

FIG. 4-5, A. Plotting a second isopter. The isopter for I-2e is completed and the plotting of the I-4e isopter is being started.

After this is completed, the entire procedure is repeated testing the subject's other eye.

FIG. 4-5, B. The field diagram. Each field diagram should be completely labeled with:
Name of patient—first and last
Date—including year
Evaluation of the quality of the test (p. 179)
Name of perimetrist
Size of pupil
Stimuli used
Eye tested

Other information that should always be recorded on each field diagram is the visual acuity, lenses used, and which isopters were tested with lenses (see Chapter 10). Sometimes the intraocular pressure is also given on the field chart (see also pp. 68, 96, and 179).

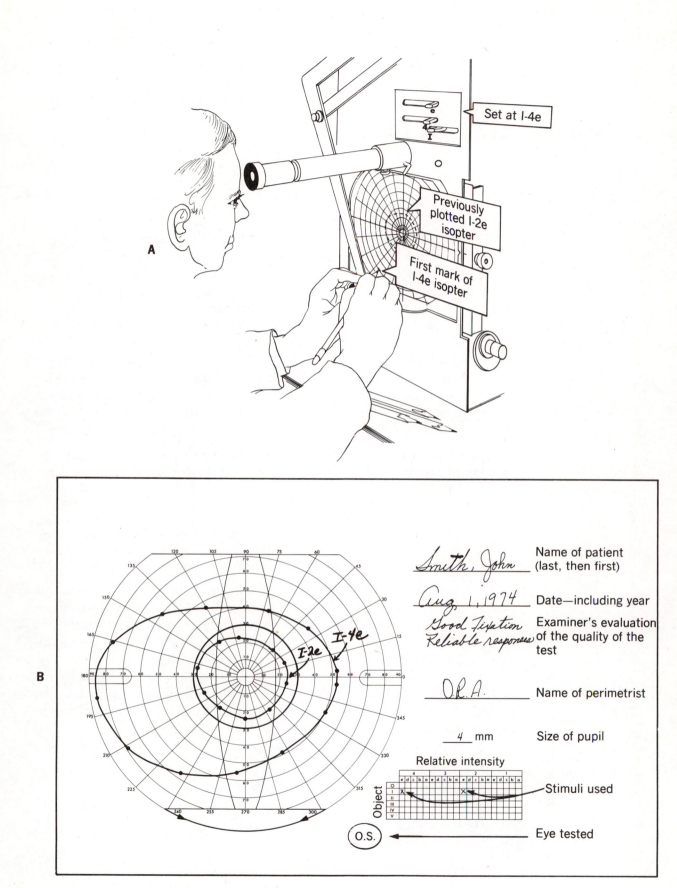

FIG. 4-5

CHAPTER 5

Tangent screens

The tangent screen is a classic method of visual field testing that employs a large black or gray panel. The classic stimuli are discs or spheres, "test objects," mounted on wands that are black. Projected spots of light (the Auto-Plot*) or self-illuminated stimuli (the Lumiwand†) are also used. In plotting several isopters, the stimuli are not varied in intensity. The variables are size of the object (1 mm, 2 mm, etc.), color (white, red, etc.), and distance of the screen (1000 mm, 2000 mm, etc.). When a 1-mm white test object is used at 1 meter (1000 mm), the isopter is labeled "1w/1000," which is more or less equivalent to an object twice the size at twice the distance (2w/2000). Almost always the test objects used are white and the testing distance is 1 meter and only the size is varied. When a 2-meter distance is used, it must be remembered that the circle on the screen representing 30 degrees at 1 meter is a 15-degree circle for 2 meters.

FIG. 5-1. Using the tangent screen. To plot an isopter, the patient is instructed to look at the fixation spot at the center of the screen and the examiner moves the test object from the edge of the screen toward fixation. The patient reports when the test object first becomes visible. It is important that the patient is reporting when he first sees the white test object, not when he first sees the wand. The examiner monitors fixation directly by watching the patient's eyes. The examiner should watch the patient's eyes, not the wand, while moving the wand. In this way, the examiner can know that the patient's eye is steadily fixed at the instant when he reports seeing the stimulus.

The principles of visual field testing with the tangent screen are the same as with a projection perimeter: cover one eye, move the stimulus from the periphery to the center, and so on. The manner by which the principles of field testing can be applied to testing with the tangent screen are usually obvious and are specifically explained only occasionally (pp. 74, 107, 136, and 250).

The tangent screen is flat, and no matter how big, it would not come around to the client's side to test as far as 90 degrees. With the usual method, only the central 30 degrees is tested; fortunately, the central field is diagnostically more important than the periphery.

---

*Bausch & Lomb, Inc.
†Jenkel-Davidson Optical, San Francisco, California.

ADDITIONAL READING

For more on use of tangent screens see the following book.

Harrington, D.O.: The visual fields: a textbook and atlas of clinical perimetry, ed. 5, St. Louis, 1981, The C.V. Mosby Co.

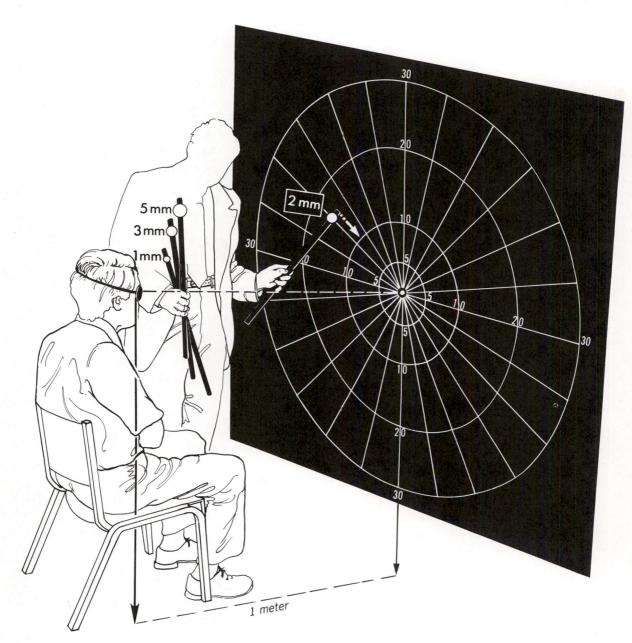

FIG. 5-1

CHAPTER 6

The normal visual field

In the more central region of the field, one can normally see smaller and dimmer objects (weaker stimuli) than one can see in the peripheral visual field. Hence the I-2e test stimulus can be seen over a certain area, but a more intense test stimulus, such as the I-4e, can be seen over a larger area. The area within which each test stimulus is seen is bounded by the "isopter" for that stimulus and can be mapped on a chart.

FIG. 6-1. A normal visual field. For progressively stronger stimuli, the area surrounded by the isopter is progressively larger. Eventually, however, the absolute periphery of the visual field is reached, and the field does not extend beyond the absolute periphery no matter how large or bright the test stimulus becomes. Each isopter plotted here is 0.5 log unit more intense than the previous. Each step, e.g., from I-1a to I-1b, to I-1c, to I-1d, to I-1e, to I-2a, to I-2b, is 0.1 log unit more intense. Five such steps, e.g., from I-1e to I-2e, add up to 0.5 log unit.

The region inside the I-3e isopter is not equally sensitive everywhere. For example, in the region where the I-1e stimulus is visible (inside the I-1e isopter), the I-3e stimulus is at least 1.0 log unit more intense than necessary for it to be seen (i.e., it is at least 1.0 log unit suprathreshold) because I-1e is visible and the I-3e is 1.0 log unit more intense than the I-1e. Similarly, in the region between the I-2e and I-1e isopters, the I-3e is 0.5 to 1.0 log units suprathreshold because the I-3e stimulus is 0.5 log unit more intense than I-2e and 1.0 log unit more intense than the I-1e.

It should be noted that the apparent brightness of a stimulus relates to how much more intense than threshold it is. Thus the I-3e appears dim just inside the I-3e isopter where it is just barely suprathreshold and the I-1e appears dim just inside its isopter; however, the I-3e appears bright inside the I-1e isopter, where it is at least 1.0 log unit more intense than the threshold.

Another feature of the normal field to note is that the isopters are not round but bulge toward the temporal side and are flattened superiorly. This means that visual sensitivity is less (i.e., depressed) superiorly compared to inferiorly. Thus, I-3e is threshold at 40 degrees superiorly, but the dimmer stimulus I-2e is threshold at 40 degrees inferiorly. Similarly, I-3e is threshold at 50 degrees nasally but the weaker stimulus, I-2e, is threshold at 50 degrees temporally.

Isopter plot

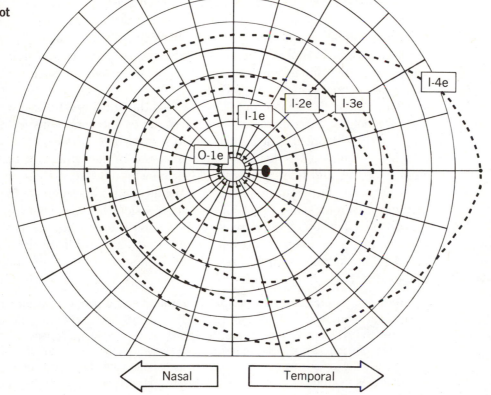

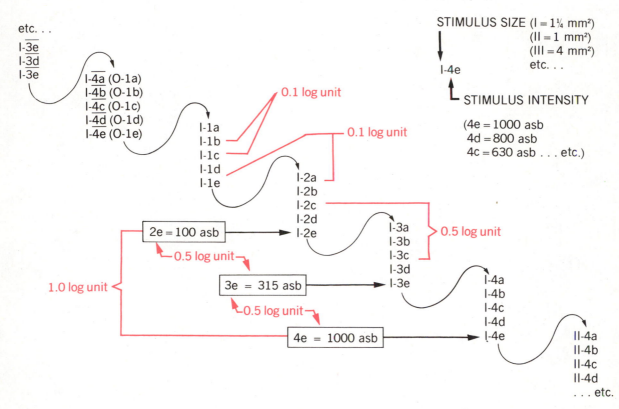

FIG. 6-1

In kinetic perimetry, the stimulus is moved from a region where it is infrathreshold (invisible), across a boundary where it is threshold (barely visible), into a region where it is suprathreshold (easily visible). The point at which the stimulus first becomes visible is the place where the stimulus is threshold. The line connecting the points where the stimulus first became visible is a line connecting points with equal visual sensitivity.

Thus, along the isopter for I-1e, the visual threshold is I-1e. Likewise, I-2e is the threshold at the isopter for I-2e. At points in the zone between these two isopters the threshold is a light intensity somewhere between I-1e and I-2e, which is to say that I-2e is visible but I-1e is not. In the same way, between the isopter for I-2e and I-3e the threshold is somewhere between these two.

After several isopters are plotted, the points along a meridian could be plotted on a graph to represent a profile of the "hill of vision" because visual threshold is known at each isopter. Of course, static perimetry is the technique used to obtain a profile plot in actual practice, but a profile derived from kinetically determined points is shown here to emphasize the equivalence of an isopter plot and a profile plot (see p. 16).

FIG. 6-2. Isopter plot of a normal visual field and a profile plot along the horizontal meridian. Each isopter plotted here is 0.5 log unit more intense than the previous. When the isopters are far apart, the 0.5 log unit intensity change in the threshold occurs gradually as one passes away from fixation along the meridian, and this is a flat region in a profile plot. When the isopters are close together, the threshold changes more rapidly as one passes along the meridian between the two isopters, and this corresponds to a steep slope in the hill of vision. Thus, the steepness of slope corresponds to the distance between two isopters that differ in intensity by a specific amount.

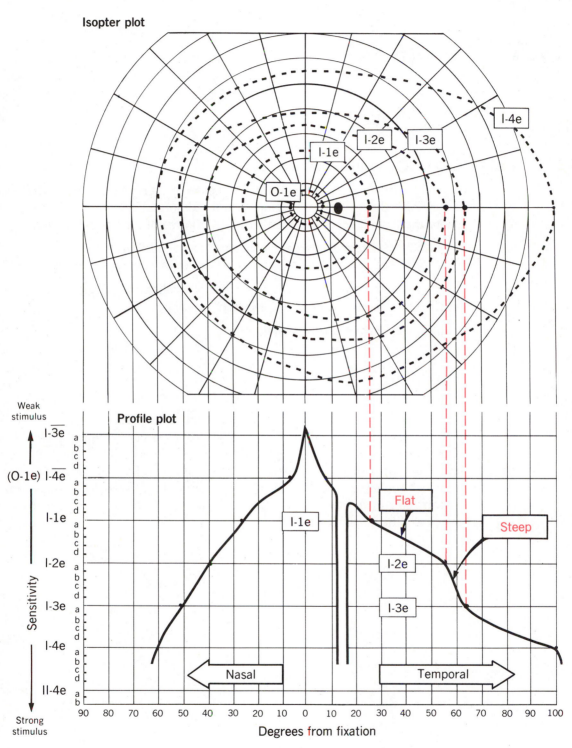

Isopter plot

O-1e
I-1e
I-2e
I-3e
I-4e

Weak stimulus

I-3ē
(O-1e) I-4ē
I-1e
I-2e
I-3e
I-4e
II-4e

Sensitivity

Strong stimulus

Profile plot

I-1e

Flat

Steep

I-2e

I-3e

Nasal

Temporal

90 80 70 60 50 40 30 20 10 0 10 20 30 40 50 60 70 80 90 100

Degrees from fixation

FIG. 6-2

49

CHAPTER 7

Scotomas

THE NATURE OF SCOTOMAS: THEORY

It is normal for a test stimulus to be seen everywhere within the region bounded by the isopter. A "scotoma" is an abnormal region within the isopter where the test object is *not* seen—that is, an area of relative blindness.

FIG. 7-1. Scotoma: an area of reduced visual sensation. The area within the scotoma is less able to see test objects than the region surrounding the scotoma.

Scotomas are abnormal except for the physiologic blind spot. They may be described or named according to location, size, and shape.

FIG. 7-2. Examples of scotomas.
A, Central scotoma—involving fixation.
B, Centrocecal—joining the blind spot to fixation.
C, Paracentral scotoma—near fixation, within 20 degrees.
D, Arcuate (Bjerrum's) scotoma—a curved scotoma above or below fixation.

The boundary of a scotoma is essentially an isopter separating a region where the stimulus (I-2e in this case) is not seen from a region where the stimulus is seen. The isopter marking the boundary of a scotoma differs from the usual isopter in that it encloses an area where the stimulus (I-2e) is *not* seen, whereas the usual isopter encloses an area where the stimulus *is* seen. To avoid confusion we can refer to the former as "the I-2e boundary of a scotoma" and the latter simply as "the isopter for I-2e."

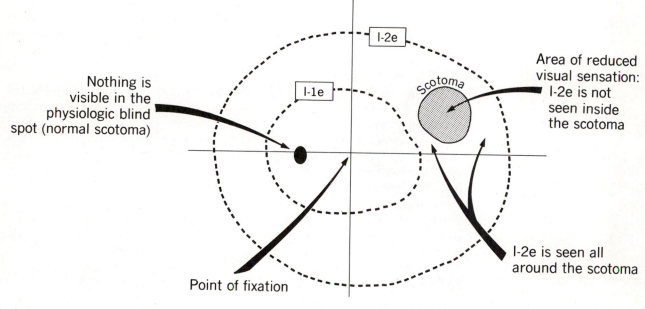

Nothing is visible in the physiologic blind spot (normal scotoma)

I-2e

I-1e

Scotoma

Area of reduced visual sensation: I-2e is not seen inside the scotoma

I-2e is seen all around the scotoma

Point of fixation

FIG. 7-1

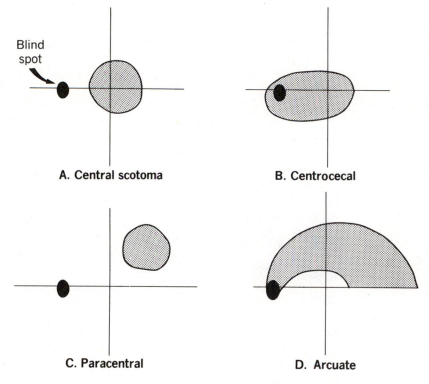

Blind spot

A. Central scotoma

B. Centrocecal

C. Paracentral

D. Arcuate

FIG. 7-2

QUANTITATING SCOTOMAS: THEORY

In characterizing a particular scotoma, it is not enough to describe the location, size, and shape. The depth and the slope of its boundary should also be described.

FIG. 7-3. Depth of scotomas.

A, TO DETECT THE SCOTOMA, a spot where the test object *is not* visible must be found. Indeed, the main feature of a scotoma is that a certain test stimulus is not visible that should be visible.

TO DETERMINE THE DEPTH of a scotoma is to reverse the question and to ask what *is* visible. Or, stated differently, to determine the depth of a scotoma is to determine the visual threshold within the scotoma.

B, If the stimulus must be made only slightly more intense or larger for it to be seen, the scotoma is termed "shallow." If the stimulus must be made *much* more intense to be seen, the scotoma is termed "deep." If the strongest available stimulus on a certain visual field apparatus is not seen, the scotoma is termed a "maximal luminosity scotoma." If no conceivable stimulus is visible, the scotoma is "absolute." Hence, we can qualitatively speak of the depth of a scotoma as shallow, deep, maximal (for this instrument), or absolute. The physiologic blind spot is an absolute scotoma.

NOTE: One cannot determine visual threshold at a location by determining that a stimulus is *not* seen any more than one can determine visual acuity by determining that the 20/20 letters are not seen. The fact that a stimulus is not seen where it should be seen simply uncovers the presence of an abnormality and the next step is to determine what *is* seen.

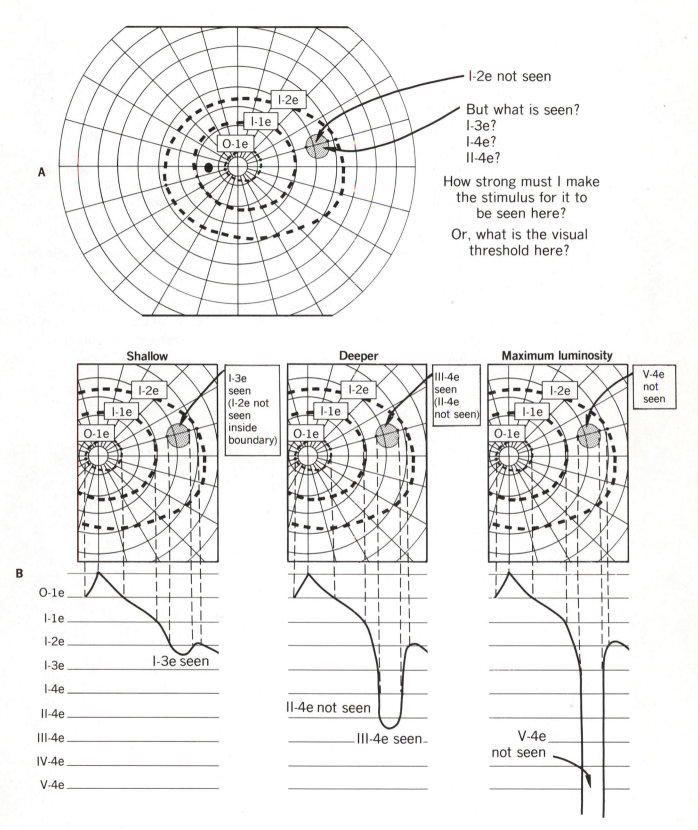

A

I-2e not seen

But what is seen?
I-3e?
I-4e?
II-4e?

How strong must I make
the stimulus for it to
be seen here?

Or, what is the visual
threshold here?

O-1e   I-1e   I-2e

B

Shallow

O-1e   I-1e   I-2e

I-3e
seen
(I-2e not
seen
inside
boundary)

Deeper

O-1e   I-1e   I-2e

III-4e
seen
(II-4e
not seen)

Maximum luminosity

O-1e   I-1e   I-2e

V-4e
not
seen

O-1e
I-1e
I-2e
I-3e ____ I-3e seen
I-4e
II-4e ____ II-4e not seen
III-4e ____ III-4e seen
IV-4e
V-4e

V-4e
not seen

FIG. 7-3

53

FIG. 7-4. The slope of the boundary.

A, A scotoma with a sloping margin. The visual threshold changes gradually between the boundary and the deepest part of the center.

B, In contrast, the visual threshold is very different just inside the boundary, compared to just outside the boundary in a scotoma with a steep wall (right). The depth of the two scotomas illustrated is the same, with II-4e being the threshold stimulus for both.

The meaning of the terms "sloping" and "steep" is apparent from the profile plots of the two scotomas with the same depth but differing margins.

In the plot of a scotoma, the boundary line for each stimulus encloses the region within which that stimulus is *not* seen. Naturally, the boundary lines for stronger stimuli enclose smaller regions than the boundary lines for weaker stimuli (the opposite of the usual isopters, which enclose regions where the stimulus *is* seen).

Just as with usual isopters (see Fig. 6-2), a sloping contour of the profile is represented by isopters separated one from another, whereas a steeper contour is represented by isopters crowded together.

Not all scotomas are as simple as the ones shown. An arcuate scotoma, for example, may be of different depth in various places within the scotoma. Moreover, one side may have a steep margin whereas the opposite side may have a sloping margin.

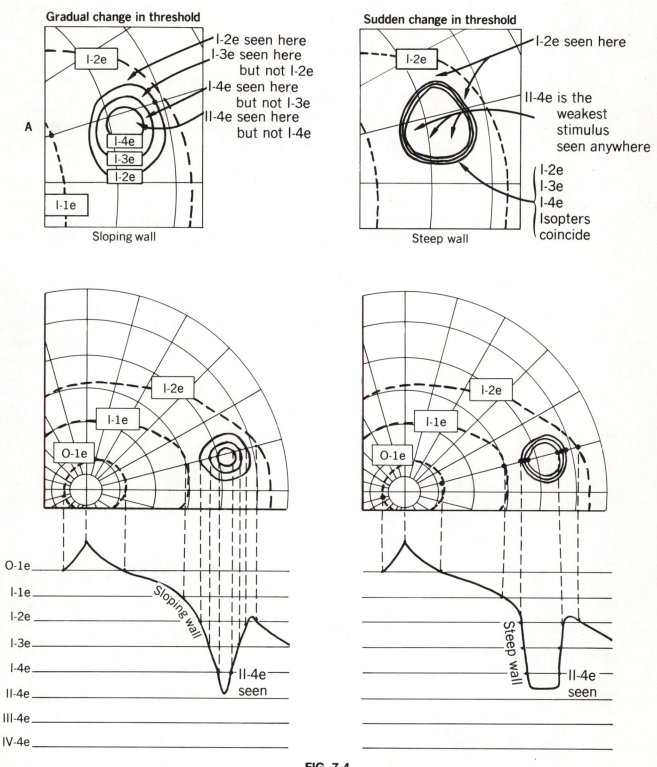

Gradual change in threshold

I-2e

I-2e seen here
I-3e seen here but not I-2e
I-4e seen here but not I-3e
II-4e seen here but not I-4e

A

I-4e
I-3e
I-2e

I-1e

Sloping wall

Sudden change in threshold

I-2e

I-2e seen here

II-4e is the weakest stimulus seen anywhere

I-2e
I-3e
I-4e
Isopters coincide

Steep wall

I-2e

I-1e

O-1e

I-2e

I-1e

O-1e

B

O-1e

I-1e

I-2e

I-3e

I-4e

II-4e

III-4e

IV-4e

Sloping wall

II-4e seen

Steep wall

II-4e seen

FIG. 7-4

HOW TO DETECT SCOTOMAS

To detect scotomas in a visual field, one must search for areas within an isopter where the stimulus should be seen but is not.

FIG. 7-5. Detecting scotomas.
A, After the isopter is drawn, the stimulus is presented at several points within the isopter and the patient is asked whether or not it is seen. The stimulus is presented at each location for about 1 second without moving it.
B, After a stronger stimulus is used to plot a larger isopter, the region between the isopters is checked for visibility of the stronger stimulus. It is not necessary to check within the smaller isopters with the stronger stimulus because if the weaker stimulus was seen it is certain that the larger one will be seen too.

In these figures the examiner asks a question and the patient responds "yes" or "no." In actual practice, the examiner simply flashes the light (in essence asking the patient if he sees it) and the patient responds with the buzzer when he sees the light, which means "yes." The lack of a response means "no." There is no actual conversation (see p. 72).

We can call this procedure for detecting scotomas STATIC SUPRATHRESHOLD SPOT-CHECKING. The procedure is "static" because the patient is asked if he can see a nonmoving object. It is not "threshold" because the threshold is not determined: the test stimulus is expected to be a "suprathreshold" stimulus. In this procedure one is "spot-checking" in areas where the object should be suprathreshold (visible) in order to detect a scotoma where, in fact, the stimulus is infrathreshold (not visible).

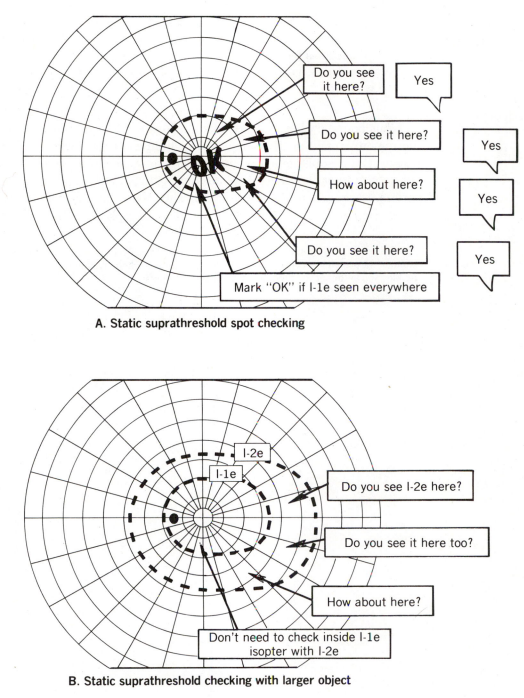

A. Static suprathreshold spot checking

B. Static suprathreshold checking with larger object

FIG. 7-5

QUANTITATING SCOTOMAS: STRATEGY

Once a scotoma is discovered in a certain location, it must be quantitated with regard to its boundary, depth, and slope.

FIG. 7-6. Step I: Outlining the boundary of a scotoma. When the stimulus is not seen, and hence a scotoma is discovered in a specific location, the stimulus is moved until it becomes visible at the boundary of the scotoma. It is then moved in the opposite direction until the opposite boundary is encountered. Subsequently the outline is determined in all directions. By this method the scotoma's boundary has been determined *kinetically.**

This boundary line is an isopter for the specific test stimulus and separates the region where the stimulus is visible from the region where it is not visible. However, the isopter of a scotoma encloses an area within which the stimulus is *not* seen, rather than enclosing an area within which it *is* seen. Note the important practical point that in either instance, the isopter is plotted by moving the target from a place where it is not seen toward a place where it is seen.

---

*One could also determine the boundary by spot checking several adjacent locations until the entire extent of the scotoma becomes evident as a cluster of spots where the stimulus is not visible. However, the kinetic plotting of the boundary is usually more efficient.

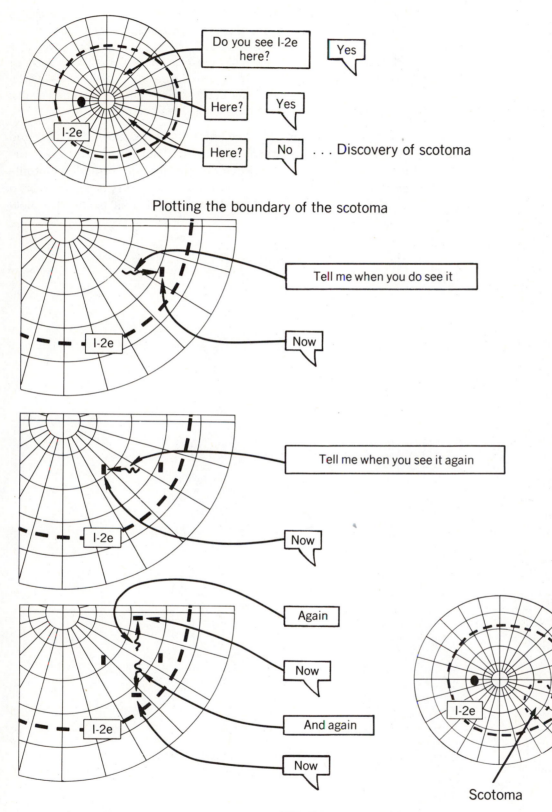

Plotting the boundary of the scotoma

FIG. 7-6

FIG. 7-7. Step II: Determining the depth of a scotoma. The next step in quantitating a scotoma is to determine its depth. At the apparent geometric center of the scotoma, which is usually but not always the deepest part, the stimulus is increased until it becomes visible. The spot is labeled with the threshold value (e.g., "II-4e is seen" or "O.K. to II-4e"). It is assumed that if a field diagram is labeled "II-4e seen," II-4e is the weakest stimulus seen—just as when visual acuity is said to be 20/70, we mean that the 20/70 letters were the smallest the patient could read correctly.

This is STATIC THRESHOLD PERIMETRY. The stimulus is not moving (static) and the threshold (weakest stimulus that is visible) is determined. However, the threshold value is simply written on an isopter chart, not represented in a profile graph. The profile graph is used when static threshold perimetry is performed at a series of points along a line (Fig. 1-6, p. 15) as "meridional static threshold perimetry."

Determine depth

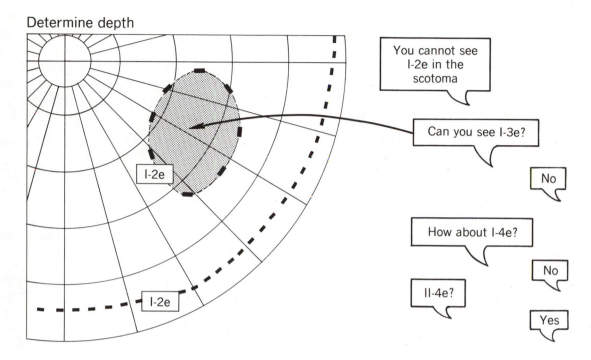

Label diagram

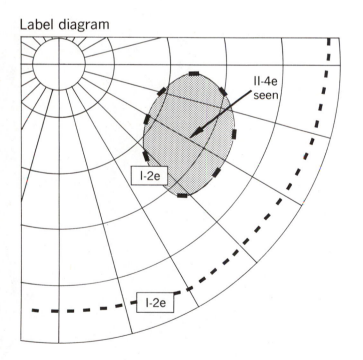

FIG. 7-7

Unless the scotoma is very shallow, the slope is determined in kinetic perimetry by plotting the boundary of the scotoma with at least two isopters—namely those representing the weakest and strongest stimuli for which the scotoma is present. Usually the weakest has already been plotted because it is the boundary of the scotoma to the test stimulus that had been used in discovering the scotoma. The second is a test stimulus just a little weaker than threshold. On occasion it is appropriate to plot additional boundary lines for complex scotomas with regions of varying depth and slopes.

FIG. 7-8. Step III: Determining the slope of the boundary. The I-2e isopter represents the boundary of the scotoma. Threshold of the center (depth) in this example is II-4e, the weakest stimulus seen. The next weakest stimulus (I-4e), which is the strongest stimulus not seen, is the second isopter plotted.
A, Sloping wall. The area enclosed by the I-4e boundary is smaller than that enclosed by I-2e.
B, Steep wall. The area enclosed by the I-4e boundary is almost as large as the area enclosed by I-2e.

To help identify the scotoma, the nonseeing area enclosed by the boundary isopters of a scotoma are shaded. In this way the isopters that form boundaries of scotomas (pp. 50 and 58) are distinguished from ordinary isopters.

Another way to quantitate the depth and slope of scotomas is by means of static threshold perimetry, either as a "static cut" through the scotoma (p. 180) or as a scatterplot (pp. 192 and 224). These more complex methods will be covered later.

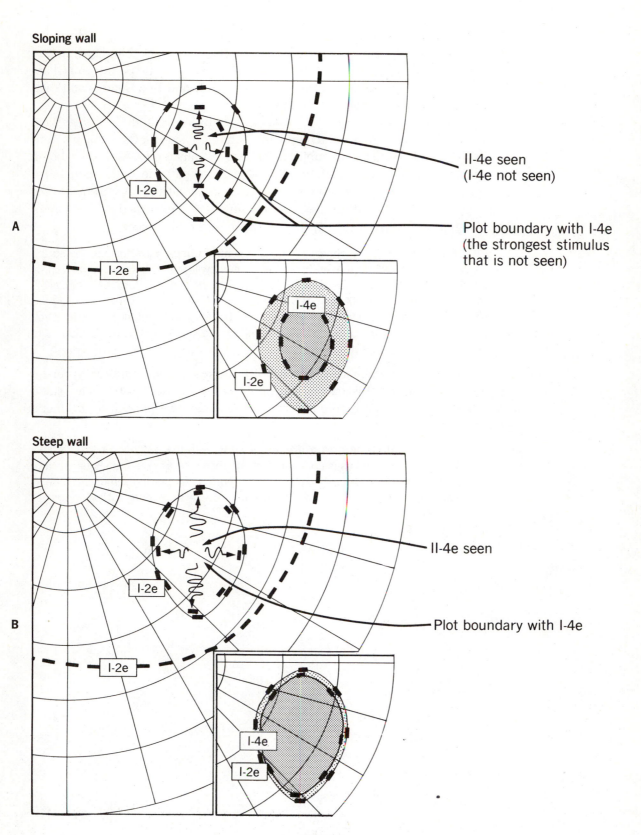

Sloping wall

A

I-2e

I-2e

II-4e seen
(I-4e not seen)

Plot boundary with I-4e
(the strongest stimulus
that is not seen)

I-4e

I-2e

Steep wall

B

I-2e

I-2e

II-4e seen

Plot boundary with I-4e

I-4e

I-2e

FIG. 7-8

PRACTICAL TECHNIQUE

The following technique is used to outline the physiologic blind spot and to look for abnormal scotomas after plotting the isopter by kinetic perimetry (Chapter 4). The beginning perimetrist should plot the I-2e and I-4e isopters and then practice the following steps on a volunteer.

The location of the physiologic blind spot is between 10 and 15 degrees from fixation just below the horizontal meridian on the right side for the subject's right eye, and on the left side for the subject's left eye. Usually the I-4e stimulus, being the smallest but most intense stimulus, is used to plot the blind spot, but a stronger stimulus is required if the I-4e isopter is too small and fails to enclose the location of the blind spot. With the stimulus set at I-4e but turned off, the pantograph handle is placed in the expected position of the blind spot.

FIG. 7-9, A. Finding the blind spot by static spot checking. After positioning the pantograph handle with the left hand, the shutter switch is depressed with the right hand to turn the I-4e stimulus on. If the subject sees the stimulus, turn the stimulus off, move to another spot but stay between 10 and 15 degrees, somewhat below the horizontal meridian, and try again. If a blind spot cannot be found, check to see if you forgot to cover the eye not being tested and if you are checking the correct side (right side for right eye, left side for left eye).

As always, the patient responds when he first sees the stimulus. After he responds, the stimulus disappears and he waits for another. In this way, static spot checking seems no different to the patient than the procedure of kinetic isopter plotting.

FIG. 7-9, B. Plotting the size of the blind spot. With the pantograph handle in a position where the stimulus is not seen, the right hand depresses the shutter switch, turning the stimulus on. After pausing for a second to be sure the stimulus is indeed not seen, the examiner moves the pantograph handle downward to find the lower boundary of the blind spot.

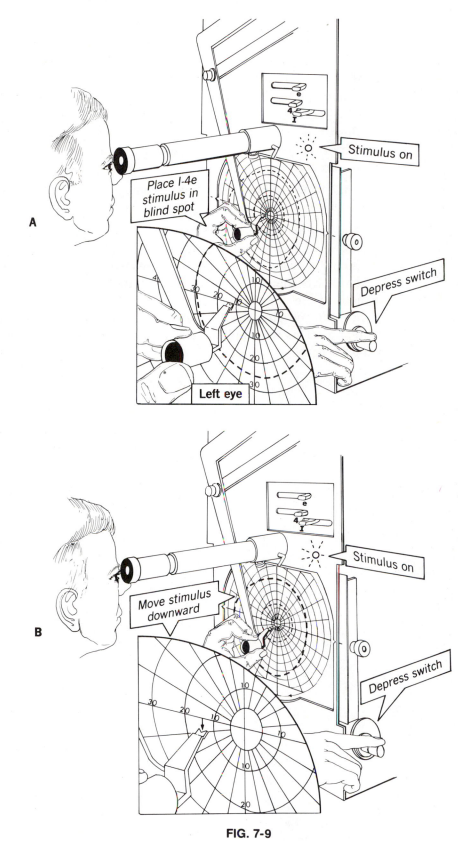

FIG. 7-9

FIG. 7-10, A. Continuing to plot the blind spot. When the subject responds by sounding the buzzer, the right hand is removed from the shutter and the position is marked with the pencil.

After the lower boundary of the blind spot is found (the stimulus is still off), the pantograph handle is moved back to the presumed center of the blind spot. Then the stimulus is turned on and, after a pause to be sure it is not seen, the stimulus is moved upward until it is seen. The process is repeated until the boundary is plotted at the top and bottom, to the right and left, and in the four oblique directions.

FIG. 7-10, B. The boundary of the physiologic blind spot is plotted. Next, the eight pencil marks should be joined and the blind spot shaded in.

From the subject's perspective the procedure continues to be exactly the same as it was during isopter plotting (pp. 38 and 40)—the stimulus is turned on without his knowing because it is in an area where he does not see. As it is moved, the stimulus becomes visible, he responds, the stimulus disappears, and he waits for the next presentation.

In plotting isopters the rule is to move the stimulus from a nonseeing area to a seeing area. This rule applies both to plotting the usual isopters and to plotting the boundary of scotomas.

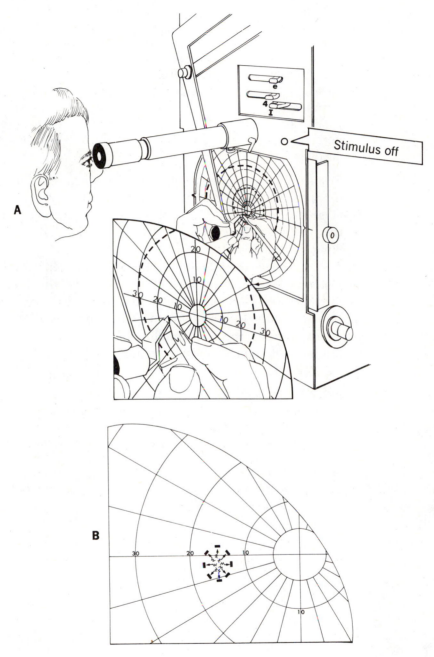

Stimulus off

A

B

FIG. 7-10

After the isopters are plotted and the blind spot is outlined, the area within the isopters is searched by static suprathreshold spot checking to find any scotomas.

FIG. 7-11. Static spot checking inside the I-2e isopter with the I-2e stimulus. The stimulus is presented at several locations within the isopter because it should be visible everywhere within the isopter. The technique here is to position the projected stimulus with the left hand and to depress the shutter switch with the right hand. When the patient responds, or after ½ to 1 second if the patient does not respond, the hand is lifted off the shutter, the stimulus is moved to a new location with the left hand, and once again the shutter is depressed in order to test a new spot. This procedure is repeated until the entire area within the isopter has been searched. In order that the patient does not know when the stimulus is presented, the examiner should learn to depress and elevate the switch gently and silently. Also an irregular rhythm should be used (see p. 122).

From the patient's perspective, the sequence remains that a new stimulus again appears, he responds, it disappears, and he waits for a new stimulus to appear in a new location. Thus, the procedure seems to him exactly the same whether you are plotting an isopter (pp. 38-41) outlining the blind spot (p. 66), or checking for scotomas.

The area inside the I-2e isopter should be checked with the I-2e test stimulus for scotomas. The region between the I-2e and the I-4e isopters should be checked with the I-4e test stimulus. It is not necessary to check with the I-4e stimulus within the I-2e isopter because this area has been checked with the I-2e test stimulus. Since the I-2e stimulus was determined to be visible everywhere, the brighter I-4e stimulus will certainly be seen also. The diagram should be labeled as shown.

FIG. 7-12. Properly labeled field diagram. This diagram indicates that the appropriate areas were spot-checked and the appropriate stimulus was seen. Either "O.K. to 1-2e" or "1-2e seen" is satisfactory. These notations are disadvantageous in that there is no indication of the number of spots checked or their precise location. In some offices and clinics, the standard practice is to mark with an *X* every spot that is tested and found to be alright. However, in other offices, the symbol *X* is used to indicate the spots where the stimulus was not seen. If *X*'s are used as symbols, it is well in addition to mark the diagram "1-2e seen" or "1-2e not seen" to clarify the meaning of the symbol.

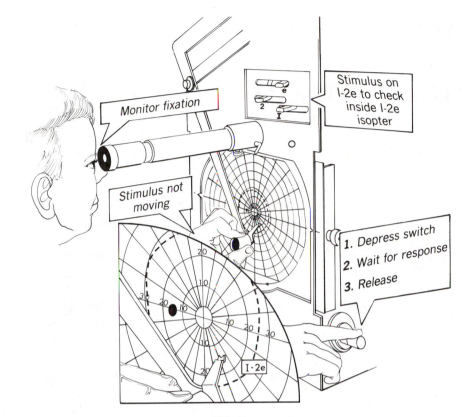

FIG. 7-11

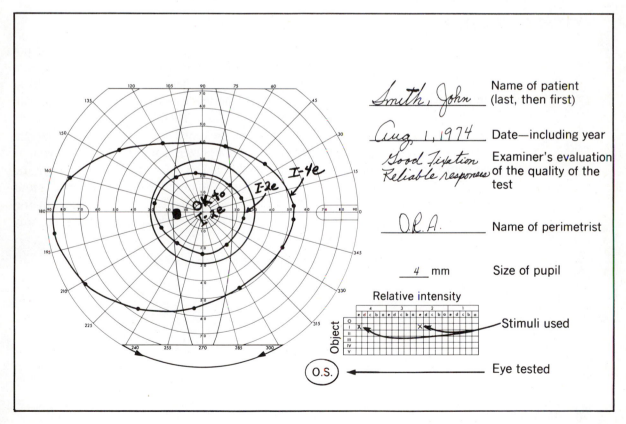

FIG. 7-12

CHAPTER **8**

Educating the patient

A very important step in performing a visual field examination is the education of the patient. The nature of the test is such that only the patient knows what he can or cannot see. Your success in quantitating a visual field will depend on your ability to get the patient to report accurately what he can see. It is up to the examiner to set him at ease, to help him achieve to the fullest his part of the test, to establish communication, and to obtain the greatest amount of information possible within the limits of the patient's ability. This is the art of visual field testing and it is just as important as knowing the switches on the instrument, the sequence in which certain areas of visual field are to be tested, and the technique of moving the stimuli.

Explanation of the test may be a good way to begin for a few patients; however, almost all patients do better if they simply learn what is required by experiencing it in a programmed manner. The nature of the test will become obvious to them as you proceed.

CONFRONTATION

To begin with, a confrontation visual field is helpful for a patient who has not experienced field testing before. For initial education of the patient, it does not matter whether he has one eye covered or not. The patient can be asked to look at your nose. Holding up your arms 1 foot to each side of the line of sight, you can ask the patient to tell you which hand is wriggling. He cannot look at both hands while waiting to see which one moves and it becomes obvious that he can look at only one point of fixation (your nose) and tell you something about what is happening to the sides without actually looking. You can then have him cover one eye if he has not done so already and ask him to count your fingers in the four quadrants (see Chapter 19, p. 230), until he seems to be able to hold fixation and report what he sees and until you would have an estimate of how severe any existing visual field defect may be.

FIG. 8-1. Educating the patient by confrontation testing.

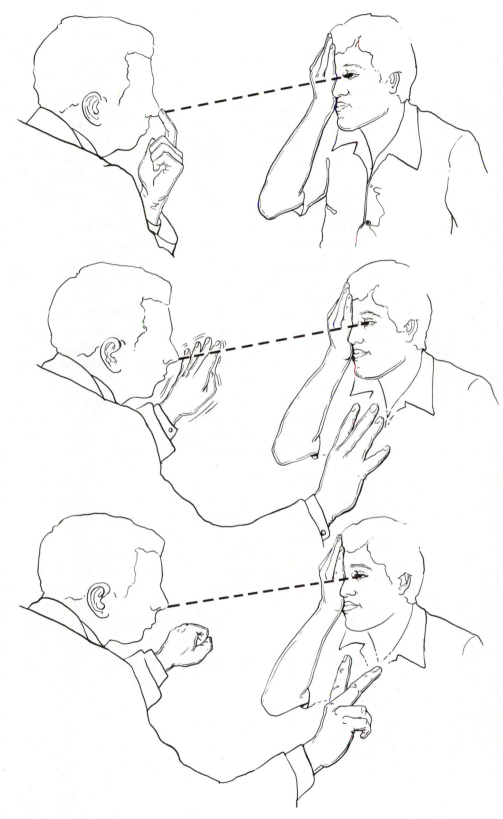

FIG. 8-1

EDUCATION AT THE PERIMETER

Then the patient can be positioned at the perimeter. If the patient has not had a field test before, the better eye should be tested first. You can learn from the patient's history, by testing his visual acuity, or from the confrontation field whether one eye is better than the other. With the eye not to be tested covered for the moment, the patient should be told to look at the fixation target.

1. The largest, brightest test object (V-4e) is then flashed for ½ second at about 5 degrees from fixation and the patient is asked if he saw it. He is then given the button to sound a buzzer when he next sees a flash of light or some other signal, e.g., tapping a coin on the table, is established, but the patient should not speak because this moves the eye away from its centered position.

2. Then a large bright object can be placed further from fixation. If the patient shifts his fixation to look at the projected spot, warn him not to do so, explaining that you want to test what he can see without looking directly at it. If necessary, repeat the presentation of a large object until the patient responds without shifting fixation.

3. Next, a small bright object (I-4e) is placed near fixation.

4. Next, a small dim light (I-2e) is placed near fixation. During this process it becomes obvious to the patient that the objects may vary in size and in location. Also, he learns that as soon as he responds the stimulus disappears, and he then awaits another.

5. Having proceeded this far, you can now begin to use some weaker stimuli further from fixation in four or five random locations in order to get an approximate idea of what the patient can or can not see in various locations, e.g., at 15, 25, and 35 degrees from fixation. This should include being sure the patient can see the I-4e at 25 to 30 degrees.

6. Finally, the physiologic blind spot is plotted with the most intense but smallest test object (I-4e) as proof that you are ready to proceed. Something is suboptimal if a known absolute scotoma (the blind spot) cannot be detected and plotted. If you cannot plot the physiologic blind spot, there may be some problems that need solving before proceeding. Have you covered the other eye? Is the patient holding fixation? Are you using stimulus size I, or is the object too big? Is the stimulus shutter switch set correctly so that the stimulus is on when the shutter switch is depressed? Is there a pathologic field defect that prevents plotting of the physiologic blind spot?

FIG. 8-2. Educational sequence at the perimeter.

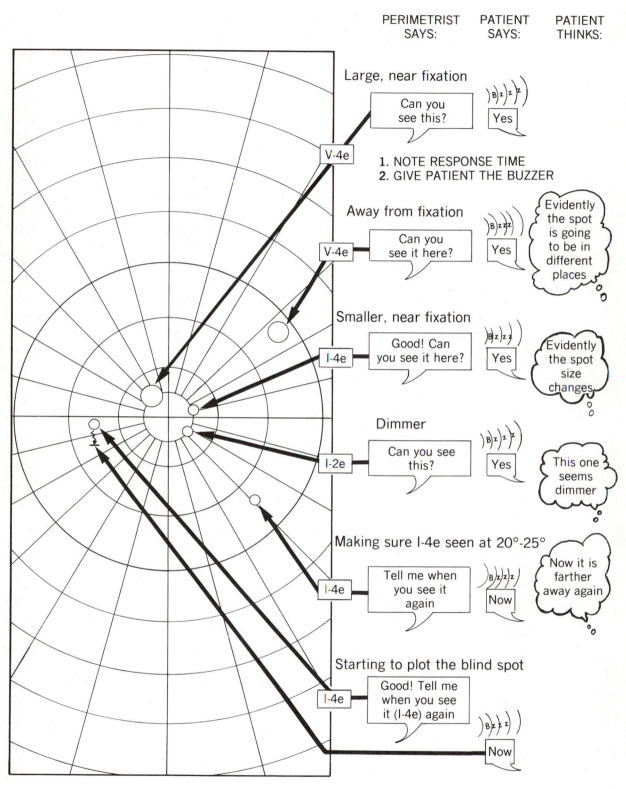

FIG. 8-2

TANGENT SCREEN

FIG. 8-3. The same basic method used at the tangent screen. A good-sized object, e.g., 5 mm, is placed on the side (not the end) of the wand covered with black felt. The wand is placed with its end near fixation but with the object hidden from view. Then the wand is rotated, exposing the object, and the patient is asked if he saw the white bead. Then he is told to respond when he sees it again. The wand is held in the same position and again rotated to get the patient's response. Immediately it is obvious to him that he is supposed to respond when he sees the white bead and not when he simply sees the end of the wand.

Several wands with different-sized objects can be held in one hand while the other hand holds one wand at the tangent screen. The wands can be interchanged easily and held in different positions until the patient realizes that the test objects may be of different sizes and in different locations. Finally, the blind spot is plotted and the next step is to proceed with plotting appropriate isopters.

The same principle can be applied with any technique for visual field examination. An obvious advantage of the projection method, e.g., the Auto-Plot, is that the patient has no prior clues as to where the test object will be projected and he may have less incentive to lose fixation. With the wand, the patient knows the object will appear on the wand and he is more apt to glance at the wand looking for the test object.

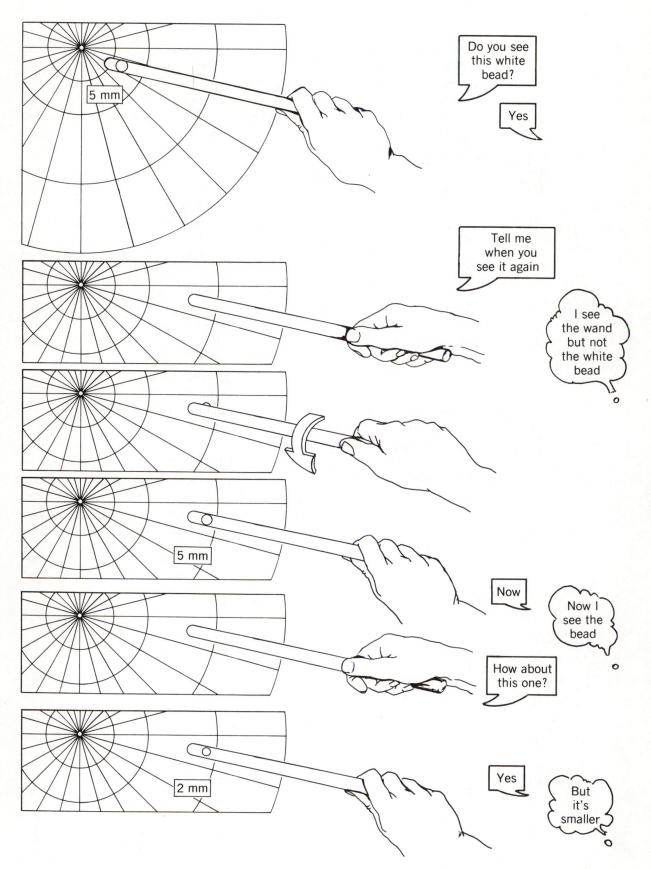

FIG. 8-3

HOMEWORK

The beginning perimetrist should at this point practice performing a visual field examination on a patient rather than a co-worker. It is helpful if your first patient has had field testing before and is experienced. However, you should also practice introducing a patient or two to field testing who has not had his field of vision tested before. Ideally, you should try to do a visual field examination of a typical late middle-aged person with no particular medical or scientific education and with almost normal eyes or at least a normal visual field. A patient who will be waiting for a while, or a person in the waiting room because he has accompanied a patient to the office, would be a very suitable volunteer subject.

There is nothing wrong with telling him that you are learning how to do visual field examinations and asking if he would mind being a "guinea pig" for 15 minutes for you to practice. Some will decline and it is their right to do so. Be sure not to coerce them. There are others in the waiting room and, if you ask pleasantly, most will be thrilled to be a subject—both because they get a good feeling from having been helpful and because it will relieve the boredom of the waiting room. Moreover, you will be less nervous yourself because you do not need to pretend. Of course, the volunteer subject, whether a patient or an accompanying person, should not be charged for the visual field test because he did not need it in the first place.

If you find yourself fumbling, be sure to let the patient go after 15 minutes, even if you did not complete everything you intended. That way you will not impose on any one person too much and you will feel better after a fresh start on a new subject. Be sure to thank the person for helping you.

If your volunteer subject asks if the test results were normal, you can say that you really did not find anything wrong but (be honest with yourself!) that you are really not too good at this yet so you cannot say for sure. If you do find something wrong, obviously someone more experienced will have to check it out. If it turns out to be a false alarm, you will benefit by learning about some mistake you are making. If the defect is a true one, you can be proud to have discovered an unsuspected problem in a patient so early in your career as a perimetrist.

If your situation is such that you cannot spend time practicing on normal subjects, you can start with patients believed to have a field defect and therefore needing to have their visual field tested. In this case you can acquaint the patient with the test, plot the blind spot, and plot one or two isopters—but with an experienced person standing quietly behind you to be sure you are doing it correctly and to take over if there is a problem. Then you can watch as a real expert completes the job. With this arrangement, you become experienced in the steps you can already handle and you have an opportunity to watch an expert's technique as a preview of the more difficult steps ahead. Most important, the patient gets the skilled visual field test that he deserves.

CHAPTER 9

Localized depressions

SCOTOMAS: REVIEW

A scotoma is a region in which sensitivity to light is less than in the area immediately surrounding it. In an isopter plot, a scotoma is represented as an area within an isopter where the test stimulus is not seen.

A scotoma is discovered by finding an area within an isopter where the stimulus for that isopter is not seen. When a scotoma is found, its boundary is plotted. Then the depth and slope or steepness are measured, or quantitated.

DEPTH—Determine the threshold or determine that the strongest available stimulus is invisible.

SLOPE OR STEEPNESS OF THE BOUNDARY—Plot the boundary with several stimuli or at least with both the weakest and the strongest stimuli for which the scotoma is present.

FIG. 9-1. Comparison of isopter and profile plots of shallow and deep scotomas with sloping and steep margins.

A, A shallow scotoma within the I-2e isopter. The I-2e stimulus is not seen but the I-3e stimulus is seen. This is compared to the physiologic blind spot, an absolute scotoma within which the strongest available stimulus (V-4e) is not seen.

B, A moderately deep scotoma with sloping margins. The size of the scotoma is smaller for stronger stimuli (I-4e) than for weaker stimuli (I-2e). On the right is the physiologic blind spot, a steep-walled scotoma that is essentially the same size for all stimuli.

A scotoma is said to be a *shallow* scotoma if a slightly stronger stimulus is visible, a *deep* scotoma if only a very strong stimulus is visible, a *maximal luminosity* scotoma if the strongest stimulus on the testing apparatus is not visible, and an *absolute* scotoma if no stimulus is visible.

If the scotoma is the same size for all test stimuli, it is said to have a *steep margin*. If the scotoma is larger for weaker stimuli, it is said to have a *sloping margin*.

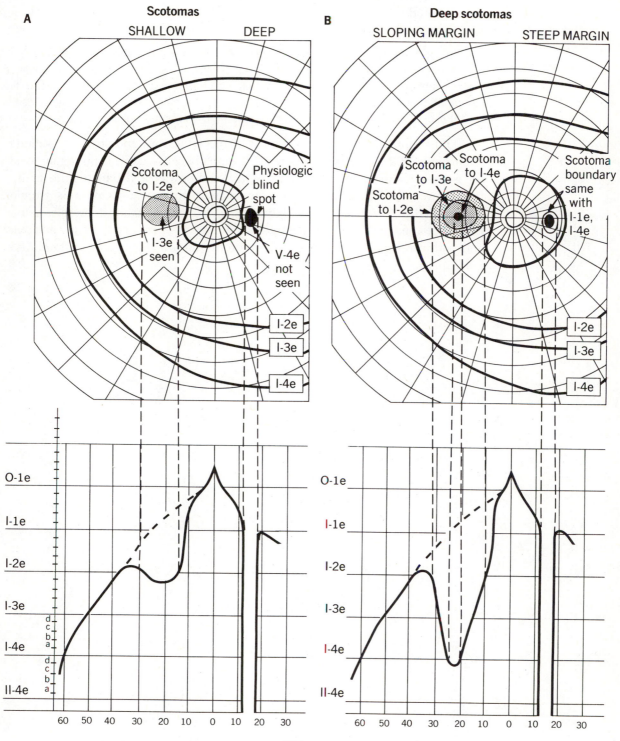

FIG. 9-1

CHARACTERISTICS OF LOCALIZED DEPRESSIONS: THEORY

Visual sensitivity may be reduced in a localized region of the visual field without producing scotomas. Such an area of reduced visual sensitivity is a "localized depression."

FIG. 9-2. Plot of a localized depression, A, compared to that of a scotoma, B. In *A*, point *K* is in a region of reduced visual sensation. The isopter for I-2e should continue in a smooth contour enclosing *K*, in which case I-2e would be visible at *K*. Instead, the isopter dips inward so that *K* is outside the isopter, which means that I-2e is not visible at *K* and visual sensation is reduced. I-2e should be seen but is not.

Thus, in a depression the isopter is displaced inward and visual sensation is abnormal, but the abnormality is not a scotoma because there is no region inside the isopter where the stimulus is not seen. Another way of visualizing the distinction between a depression and a scotoma is to think of a scotoma as a region surrounded by a zone where the stimulus is visible, whereas a depression is not. Both scotomas and localized depressions are areas of reduced visual sensitivity and both are localized, but they are different and are represented differently in field charts.

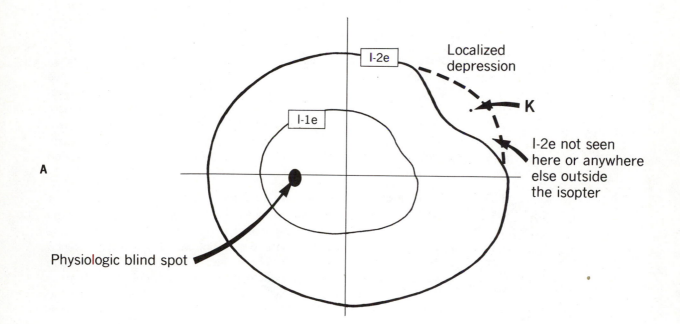

A

I-2e

Localized
depression

← K

I-2e not seen
here or anywhere
else outside
the isopter

I-1e

Physiologic blind spot

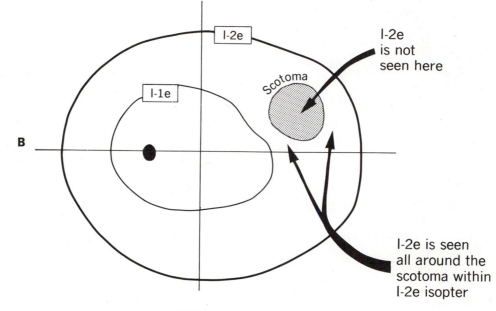

B

I-2e

I-1e

Scotoma

I-2e
is not
seen here

I-2e is seen
all around the
scotoma within
I-2e isopter

FIG. 9-2

81

The distinction between scotomas and localized depressions is important because they are differently represented on the field chart and may be approached differently for detection and quantitation. However, it is equally important to recognize that they have the same underlying basis (reduced visual sensation) and that they are therefore closely related.

FIG. 9-3. Close relationship of scotomas and localized depressions. Scotomas may become depressions if the zone between the scotoma and the isopter becomes abnormal. When this occurs, it is sometimes said that the scotoma has "broken through to the periphery." The abnormal area at one time surrounded by an area of sight is no longer surrounded by such an area and hence is no longer a scotoma. Visual sensation in the area that was formerly a scotoma is not changed at all; however, it is no longer a scotoma—not because the scotoma changed but because an *adjacent area* changed.

FIG. 9-4. Deviation of an isopter around a scotoma. A region that seems to be a depression because an isopter is deviated inward locally may actually be a scotoma with the isopter by necessity simply skirting around the scotoma. In this example, if the I-2c isopter alone had been plotted, the inward deviation would seem to represent a depression, but in fact it results from a scotoma. Indeed, every scotoma can be made to have an isopter deviate around it if one plots the isopter that would normally pass through the center of the scotoma. Obviously, if the I-2e test object is not seen in the area of the scotoma, a weaker stimulus I-2c (with its isopter closer to fixation than the strong object I-2e) will not be seen within the scotoma either, and hence the scotoma must lie outside the isopter for I-2c.

Scotoma becoming a depression

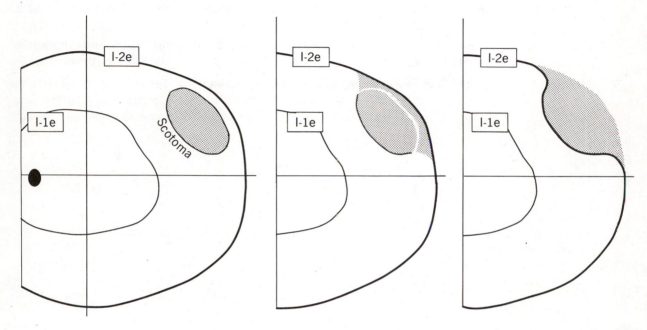

FIG. 9-3

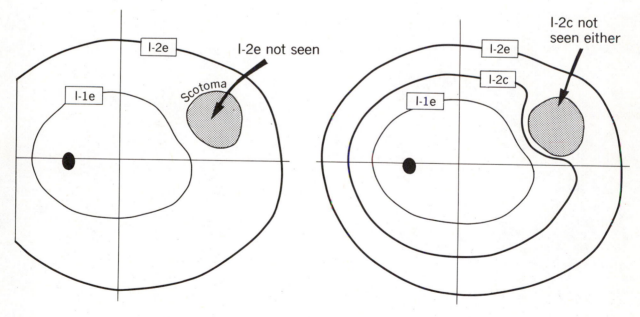

FIG. 9-4

QUANTITATING DEPRESSIONS: STRATEGY

If, while an isopter is being plotted, a localized depression is discovered, it must be measured quantitatively. As with scotomas, the basic rule is to measure the depth of depressed visual sensation in this location. To be specific, in discovering a depression along the isopter for I-2e, for example, one has determined that I-2e is not seen in a certain location where it should be seen—but now it must be determined what *is* seen.

In any abnormal region, whether a scotoma or a depression, the question is not what is not seen, but rather what *is* seen or what the visual threshold is.

FIG. 9-5. The first step in quantitating depressions. The first step in determining what *is* seen is to plot the isopter for a stronger stimulus, in this case I-3e. This new isopter may be **A,** normal, **B,** slightly depressed, or **C,** markedly depressed inward.

Depression discovered

Plot second isopter

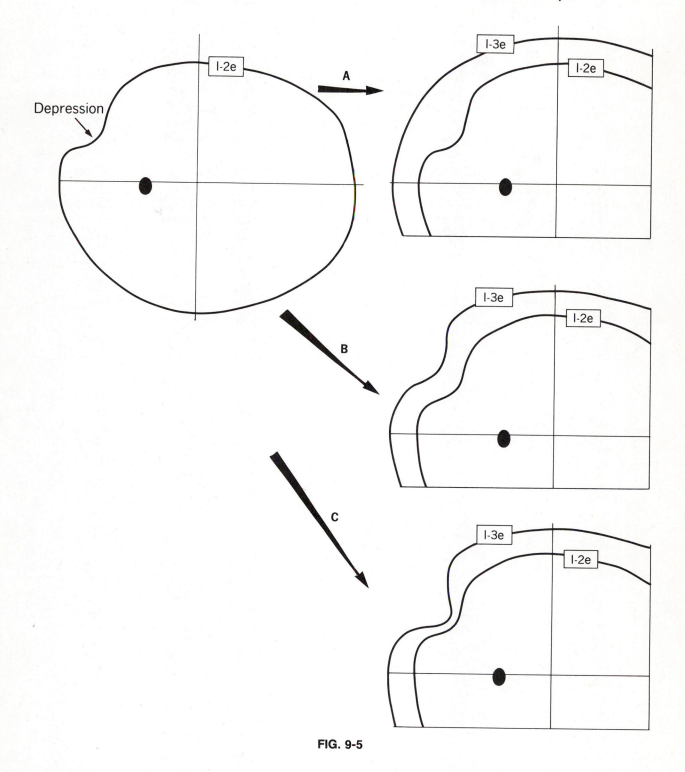

FIG. 9-5

FIG. 9-6. Subsequent steps in quantitating depressions.

A, If the newly plotted isopter for a stronger stimulus does not have an inward deviation, there is evidence of reduced visual sensation between the two isopters, specifically in the concavity of the inward deviation of the weaker isopter. With static spot checking, this area needs to be searched for scotomas with a stronger stimulus (I-3e). One may or may not find a scotoma. If a scotoma is found, its depth and slope must, of course, be quantitated in the same manner described in Chapter 7.

B, If the second isopter (I-3e) shows an inward deviation of approximately the same degree as the initial isopter, one has discovered an area of reduced visual sensation in relationship to the I-3e isopter. Therefore, one must plot an even stronger isopter (I-4e), continuing to plot stronger isopters until (1) the isopter does not show evidence of depressed visual sensation, (2) the extreme periphery of the visual field is reached, or (3) there are no longer stronger stimuli available. Then the spaces between each isopter need to be explored for scotomas. If scotomas are found, they need to be quantitated.

C, If the newly plotted isopter is steeply deviated inward, it is necessary in the same way to plot the isopters for consecutively stronger stimuli. Spaces betweeen isopters are searched for scotomas with the appropriate stimulus.

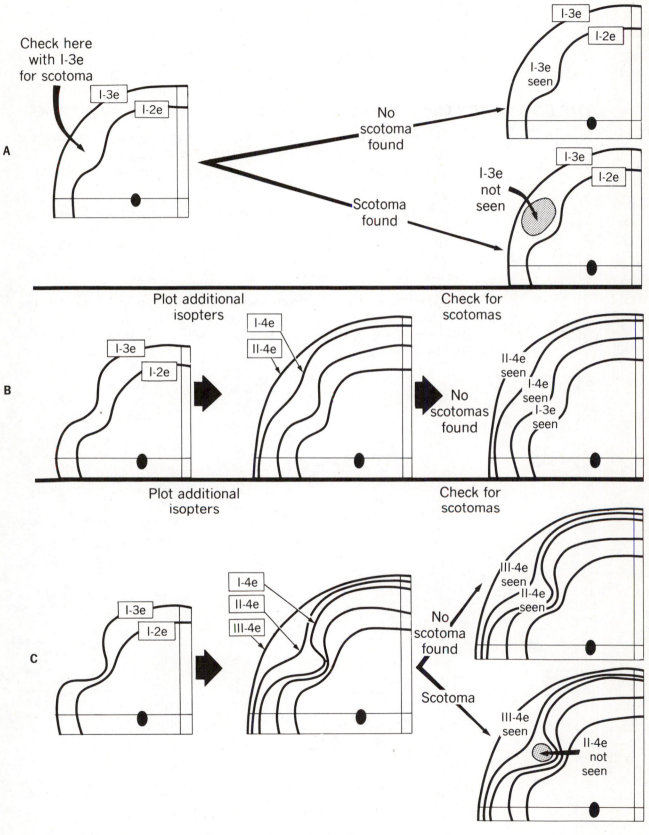

FIG. 9-6

FIG. 9-7. The final step in quantitation. It is also necessary to plot isopters for weaker stimuli inside the depressed area until (1) one with a normal contour is found or (2) the center of the visual field is reached. In this example, I-1e and 0-1e are plotted within the abnormal I-2e. Thus, when a depression is discovered, it is necessary to plot isopters for both stronger and weaker stimuli.

THE BOUNDARY OF A LOCALIZED DEPRESSION: INTERPRETATION

After all the isopters are plotted, the examiner can recognize the extent of the depression—that is, the extent of the region affected with reduced visual sensation. Visual sensation is reduced in every place where the isopter is deviated inward.

FIG. 9-8. The extent of a localized depression. Visual field charts are never actually marked to show the boundary of a depression, but the extent of the depressed region (emphasized in this illustration) is simply visualized mentally. With attention to all the locally deviated isopters, it is easy to recognize the extent of the area within which there is reduced visual sensation.

Now a distinction between depression and scotoma becomes apparent. The boundary of a scotoma is marked by an isopter separating the region where a particular stimulus is not seen from the region where it is seen. However, the boundary of a depression is not an isopter.

Plot additional isopters

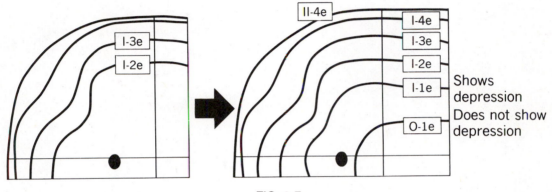

FIG. 9-7

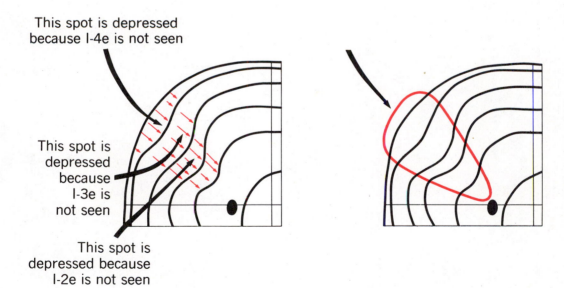

FIG. 9-8

FIG. 9-9. Examples of localized depressions contrasted with a scotoma. The abnormal region is shaded in red. A depression can contain a scotoma, with the extent of the depression being greater than the boundary of the scotoma. This differs from a pure scotoma, which may show isopters deviating around it but will not show a depression of visual sensation outside the boundary of the scotoma.

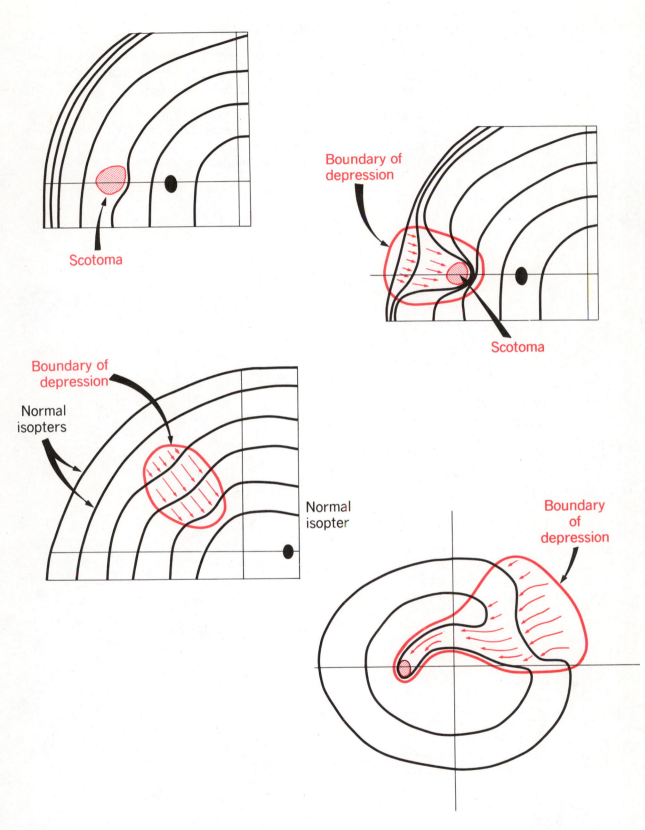

FIG. 9-9

"DEPTH" OF A DEPRESSION: INTERPRETATION

In plotting multiple isopters and looking between isopters for scotomas, the examiner not only determines the boundary of a depression but also quantitates the depth and the slope of the margin of the depressed region.

FIG. 9-10. Shallow depression. In the isopter plot of the depression the isopters are locally displaced inward only slightly compared to the normal field. At every point within the depression, visual sensation is reduced. For example, at point *R*, I-2e would be seen in the normal field but I-3e is the weakest stimulus seen in the depression.

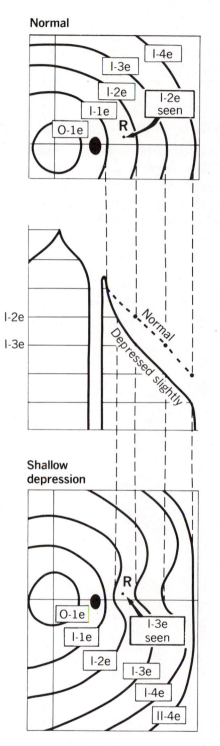

FIG. 9-10

FIG. 9-11. Examples of localized depression—one with a scotoma to show how visual threshold at points within the depression is represented. In the three depressions illustrated here, one can select any location on the isopter plot, e.g., *R*, and know the visual threshold, i.e., know the weakest test stimulus visible at that location. *Top,* At point *R* in the normal field I-2e is seen. *Bottom left,* In a shallow depression I-3e is the weakest stimulus seen. *Bottom center,* In the deeper depression II-4e is the visual threshold. *Bottom right,* In the depression containing a scotoma III-4e is the threshold.

SLOPE OF THE WALL OF A DEPRESSION: INTERPRETATION

The slope of the wall is also apparent in the isopter plot of depressions. In the shallow depression illustrated in Fig. 9-11, for example, the isopters remain separated and there is a sloping wall to the region of depressed visual sensitivity. In the deeper depression, the wall toward fixation has a steep slope with the isopters crowded together in that location.

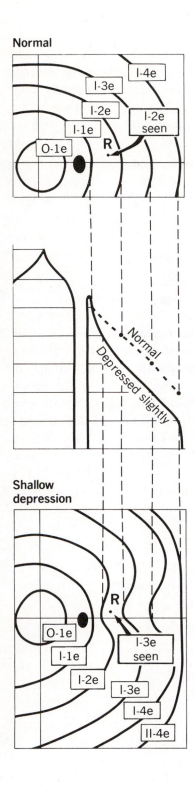
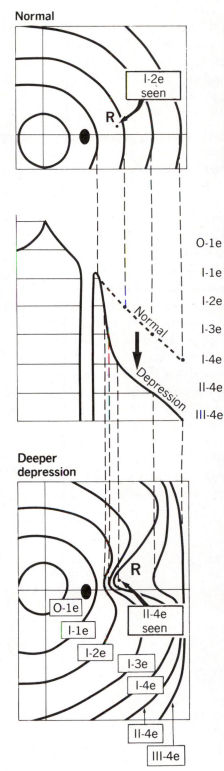
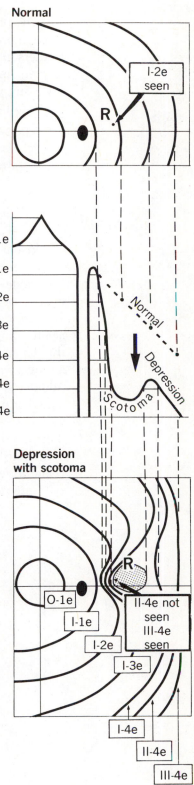

FIG. 9-11

PRACTICAL TECHNIQUE

The practical technique of plotting isopters is obvious from the strategy outlined in previous pages. The principle of quantitative perimetry is to plot multiple isopters in the abnormal region to be quantitated, checking for scotomas between isopters and quantitating any scotomas found. If no scotoma is found when spot checking with a certain stimulus, e.g., I-4e, the region is labeled "I-4e seen" or "O.K. to I-4e" (see also Fig. 7-12, p. 69).

FIG. 9-12. Correctly labeled isopter plot of a localized depression. Within the depression, visual threshold is obvious at every location. Some of the isopters are plotted only in the depressed area, illustrating the principle that abnormal regions need to be quantitated more carefully than normal regions.

SUMMARY

Visual sensation can be reduced in a region without producing a scotoma. This reduction of visual sensation is called a depression and is represented by inward deviation of the isopters. In contrast to that of scotomas, the boundary of a depression is not outlined by an isopter enclosing the region of reduced sensation.

In order to quantitate either a localized or a generalized depression additional isopters are plotted toward the periphery of the field until the outside boundary of the depression is reached, the extreme periphery of the field is reached, or the strongest available stimulus has been plotted without reaching the periphery. Additional isopters are also plotted toward fixation until a normal isopter is obtained or until the center of the field is reached. As the isopters are being plotted, spaces between isopters are spot-checked for scotomas. If scotomas are found, their depth and slope are quantitated. If scotomas are not found, the spot is marked to show that the stimulus was seen, thereby indicating the approximate visual threshold in that region.

Generalized depressions are discussed in Chapter 13.

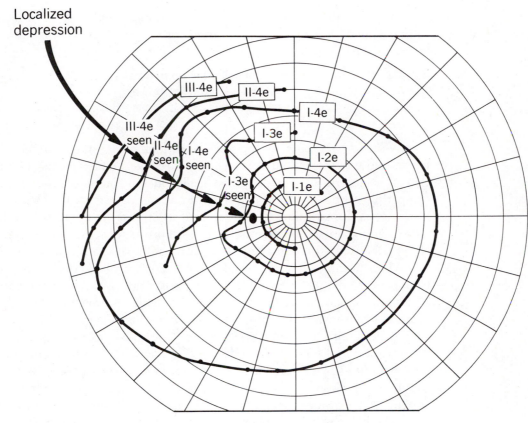

FIG. 9-12

CHAPTER 10

Corrective lenses

GENERAL PRINCIPLES

For optimum visualization of the test stimuli, they must be in focus on the retina. Therefore, the patient may need corrective lenses to obtain an optimum visual field examination with consistent responses.

FIG. 10-1. Lens holder for the Goldmann perimeter.
A, Post for storing the lens holder when not in use.
B, Placing the lens holder in position for use. When placing the lens holder in position be sure not to have a pencil in your hand that will scratch the inside of the bowl.

By turning the knob on the base of the lens holder, the examiner places the lens as close to the patient's eyelashes as possible. The lens is used for examination of the central 30 degrees of the visual field, but is removed for examination of the peripheral field. Optical correction for the entire visual field would be ideal; however, as a practical matter, the rim of the lens gets in the way, and therefore a lens cannot be used outside 30 degrees. Fortunately, there is less need for a sharply focused retinal image in the peripheral field than in the central field.

When placing the lenses in the lens holder, the spherical lens goes in the back (toward the patient) and the cylinder in front (away from the patient).

It is important to use full aperture lenses with a narrow metal rim around the glass, not those with a broad metal rim around a smaller lens.

To determine the appropriate lenses one must take into account (1) the refractive error of the patient at distance; (2) an added adjustment that must be provided either by accommodation or by a lens in order to see the test stimuli, which are up close (30 cm in the case of the Goldmann perimeter); and (3) the amount of the required near add that can be provided comfortably by the patient's accommodative ability, which reduces the amount to be provided by lenses. The patient's accommodative ability is determined by his age, but the accommodative ability is zero no matter what the age if the eye is aphakic or under the influence of a cycloplegic drug.

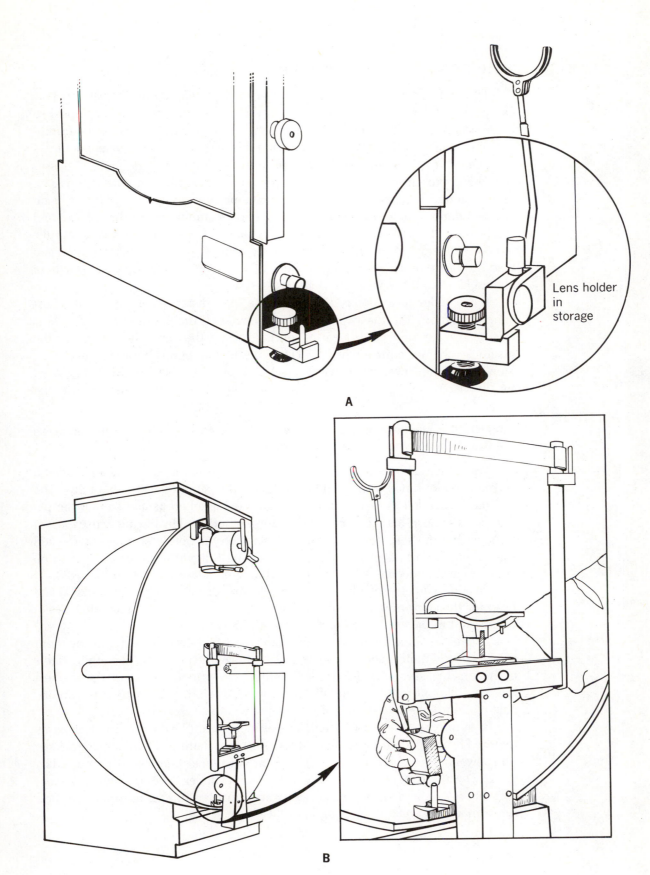

Lens holder
in
storage

A

B

FIG. 10-1

CHOOSING THE CORRECT LENS POWER

The first step is to determine the *best distance correction* for the patient. This can be done by means of a complete refraction, but more often it is accomplished by determining the power of the patient's present distance glasses and determining the visual acuity at distance with the present glasses. If the visual acuity is 20/20, or if it is less but cannot be improved with a pinhole, the present glasses probably represent the best distance correction. If a pinhole improves the vision, plus or minus spheres can be placed over the present glasses to see if the vision can be improved to a satisfactory level. If so, the combination of the spheres and the present glasses is considered the best distance correction. As a general rule, +0.50 D sphere and −0.50 D spheres should be tried over the glasses if the vision is in the range of 20/50. Similarly, the +1.00 D sphere and the −1.00 D sphere should be tried if the vision is 20/100.

If a cylinder correction is included in the "best distance correction," it is best simply to ignore it if it is a 0.25 D cylinder or less. If the power of the cylinder is 0.50 to 0.75 D, no cylindric correction is used for the visual field test, but the distance sphere is adjusted by 0.25 D in order to maintain spherical equivalence. However, if the power of the cylinder is 1.00 D or more, the cylindric lens is used for the visual field test. Be sure that the lens is placed in the lens holder at the correct axis.

FIG. 10-2. Markings on the lens holder to indicate the axis of the cylinder. In this example the cylinder axis is at 45 degrees.

The spherical lens used for visual field testing is the "best distance sphere correction" combined with an add according to the patient's age. Table 1 gives the add recommended by Goldmann and represents a generous add so that the patient uses some of his accommodation but is not fatigued by having to use most of it. Note that the selection of the add for perimetry is not determined by the add the patient has in his own reading glasses. The full add used for those with no ability to accommodate is +3.25 D, which is quite close enough to the +3.33 D sphere add that corresponds to the 30 cm testing distance. The full +3.25 D add used for those over 60 years old is also used at any age in aphakia, after cycloplegia, and in patients who are more than 3.25 D myopic.

The reason for not using the full +3.25 D add on everyone and requiring them to use some of their accommodation is to minimize the prismatic and other effects of the lens by using the weakest lens possible. The principle is to use the weakest lens possible but to provide an add generous enough that the patient is comfortable without having to use all of his accommodative reserve.

In summary, the lenses used for perimetry are (1) the cyclindric lens as required by the patient for distance if it is 1.00 D or more and (2) a spherical lens. The power of the spherical lens is the patient's distance spherical lens adjusted by +0.25 D if the patient has a +0.50 or +0.75 D cylinder in their distance correction that is not being used for perimetry and adjusted further according to their accommodative ability—age and other factors.

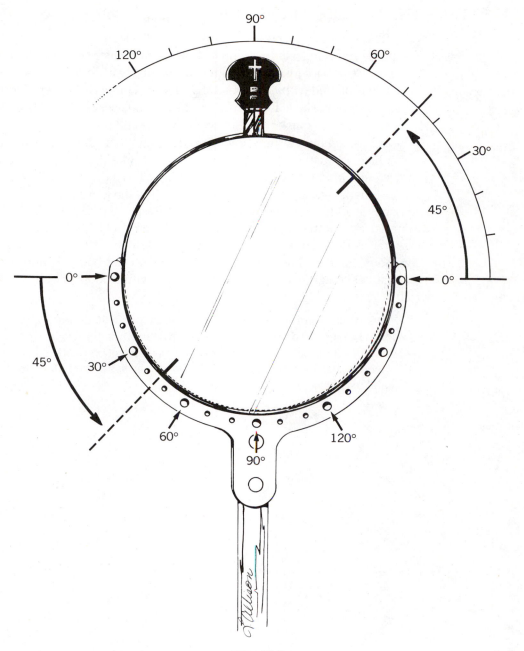

FIG. 10-2

Table 1. Add for age according to Goldmann

Age (Years)	Add for perimetry (Diopters)
30-40	+1.00
40-45	+1.50
45-50	+2.00
50-55	+2.50
55-60	+3.00
Over 60	+3.25

ISOPTERS THAT CROSS FROM CENTRAL TO PERIPHERAL

The need for a corrective lens inside 30 degrees does not relate to which isopters are being plotted. Thus, if an isopter has part of its course inside 30 degrees, the part inside 30 degrees is plotted with a lens in use and the part outside is plotted without the use of a lens. It is more convenient for the examiner and more comfortable for the patient if each and every isopter inside 30 degrees is plotted until it begins to leave the central zone and then, after the lens is removed, the remainders of all the isopters are plotted. When the lenses are removed, the lens holder must also be removed because it, like the rim of the lens itself, can interfere with visibility of the stimulus outside 30 degrees inferiorly (p. 281).

Sometimes the isopter shifts slightly when the lens is removed because of the prismatic effect of the edge of the lens and because the visibility of the stimulus is altered by whether or not it is in focus. When this happens, the segment of the isopter plotted with the lens in use does not join exactly with the segment plotted without the lens. The break in continuity does not hamper interpretation of the visual field diagram and is simply indicated with a double slash, as shown in Fig. 10-3.

FIG. 10-3. Isopters plotted with correction inside 30 degrees and without correction outside 30 degrees. The portions plotted while the lens is in place are in red for illustrative purposes in this diagram. Ordinarily, only a double slash-mark, not color coding, is used to indicate that part of an isopter was plotted with a corrective lens and part was plotted without a lens.

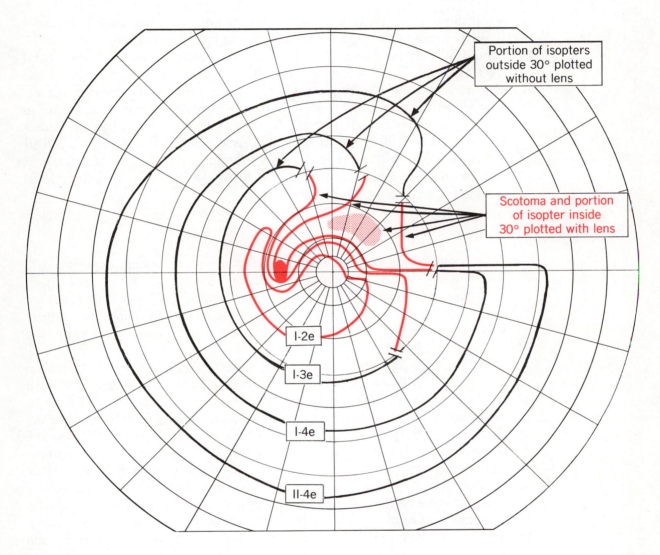

Portion of isopters
outside 30° plotted
without lens

Scotoma and portion
of isopter inside
30° plotted with lens

I-2e

I-3e

I-4e

II-4e

FIG. 10-3

CYCLOPLEGIA

If a patient has had cycloplegic drops to dilate the pupil or for a refraction, the full +3.25 D add is required for any age because the cycloplegic drug will have eliminated all accommodative ability.

CONTACT LENSES

If the patient wears contact lenses representing his proper distance correction, the contact lenses are left in for the entire field examination for both the central and peripheral visual field. Only the contact lens is used for the peripheral field. However, when testing the central 30 degrees of the field, the required add for perimetry is provided by using a loose trial lens in addition to the contact lens. In essence, the patient who wears only a contact lens for distance is considered to be a person without any refractive error at distance, requiring an add for perimetry in the central 30 degrees according to his accommodative ability. If a patient wears glasses over the contact lenses for distance, the spectacle correction is considered the distance refractive error to be used as the starting point in determining the near correction for perimetry.

APHAKIA

If a patient has had a cataract extraction, he has no accommodation and will require a +3.25 D add no matter what his age.

If the patient wears contact lenses, a +3.25 D add combined with a *distance* overcorrection in the spectacles is used in addition to the patient's own contact lens for the central 30 degrees. The contact lens alone is used for the peripheral field outside 30 degrees.

If a patient does not wear a contact lens, the distance spectacle correction plus the +3.25 D add for perimetry is needed. There are problems with such strong lenses. First, the prismatic effects of the lens cause the central field to be miniaturized on the field diagram: the blind spot migrates toward fixation and the apparent limit of the field produced by the lens edge moves inside 30 degrees. A second problem is that the vertex distance (distance from the lens to the cornea) is very critical with strong lenses, and it is difficult to maintain the proper vertex distance during the entire field examination, especially for elderly patients.

To overcome these problems, we have found it good to use a contact lens for the visual field examination in patients with aphakia, even if they usually do not wear contact lenses. Contact lenses that provide both the distance correction and the +3.25 D add for perimetry are used for both the central and the peripheral field examination. Using the contact lens for testing the peripheral field provides the additional theoretical advantage of allowing stimuli adequately focused on the retina. This seems to allow a better examination of the peripheral visual field when there is a strong refractive error (as in aphakia), even though the use of a corrective lens is not extremely important for testing the peripheral field in the presence of the usual refractive error.

A hard contact lens of 10-mm diameter and a steep base curve (7.60 mm) is used to reduce lens movement that would be disturbing to a patient not accustomed to wearing contact lenses. A steep immobile lens is tolerated by the cornea for the duration of the field examination, even though it would not be suitable for regular wear. Additional comfort is provided by instilling topical anesthetic before putting the lens in place.

A selection of four lenses is kept for use in perimetry (+13.00 D, +16.50 D, +19.00 D, and +21.00 D). To select the proper lens, the spectacle correction is determined, adding together the power of the sphere and the cylinder expressed in the plus cylinder form (cylinder expressed in the minus cylinder form is ignored), and the +3.25 D add for perimetry is added also. The vertex distance of the spectacle is determined and the total required correction (sphere, plus the + cylinder, plus the +3.25 D add for perimetry) is converted to a vertex distance of zero, and the lens strength closest to this result is selected from the four standard lenses. Often this will be the +16.50 D lens.

Of course because the corneal curvature was not considered, the correction of the refractive error will rarely be perfect. Plus and minus spheres can be used over the contact lens, asking the patient which lens brings the fixation spot into best focus. Any additional lenses required can be used in addition to the contact lens for the central 30 degrees, but the contact lens alone is used for the peripheral field.

It is not always practical to spend the time to achieve a perfect optimal correction. Most of the time a +16.50 D contact lens will do an adequate job. When a little extra care is needed, calculation of the lens strength from the spectacle correction and vertex distance may be warranted. For those patients in whom it is expected that visual field examinations will be required often, e.g., a patient who has glaucoma, it may be worth the effort to perform an overrefraction with spheres over the contact lenses selected to determine which contact lenses and which loose trial lenses will be required. The same lenses can be used for all subsequent field examinations without having to go through the effort of determining the best lens each time.

REFINEMENTS

It is ideal to minimize the lens thickness as much as possible to avoid distortions and prismatic effects. We already noted that for this purpose we do not routinely use the full +3.25 D add on all patients.

To reduce even further the use of strong lenses unnecessarily, we can apply two additional principles:

1. To reduce the strength of minus spheres as long as the patient is using any accommodation. There is the double advantage of reducing the strength of the minus sphere while simultaneously reducing the need for the patient to accommodate.

2. To avoid using a cylinder of sign opposite from the sphere. When the sphere and cylinder are of like sign, the cylinder augments one meridian of the sphere, and the strength of the spherical lens is less than it would be with the opposite cylindric form. When the sphere and cylinder are of opposite sign, the cylinder weakens one meridian of the sphere.

To implement these principles, start with the distance spectacle refraction of the patient expressed in the plus cylinder form and apply the following rules:

1. If the sphere component is a plus lens, use the spherocylinder lens combination calculated by providing the usual add for age from Table 1 (p. 101).

2. If the sphere component is between −3.25 D and plano, use the age correction to calculate the required near correction for perimetry. If the calculated required sphere is plus, use it and any plus cylinder that is needed. If the calculated sphere needed for perimetry is minus, then use no sphere but use only the plus cylinder that is needed.

3. If the sphere component of the distance correction represents myopia greater than 3.25 D, calculate the near correction for perimetry by using the full +3.25 D add. Convert the result to the minus cylinder form and use it. Exception: do not convert to the minus cylinder form if it happens that the plus cylinder power is more than twice the minus sphere in the spherocylinder lens needed for perimetry. Use the lenses in the plus cylinder form.

TANGENT SCREEN

The distance to the tangent screen is 1 meter and the +1.00 D add can usually be ignored. Therefore, the patient's own glasses can be used. This is especially helpful for patients with aphakia because there need be no concern about the vertex distance if properly fitting glasses are used. However, one must beware of the reading segment if bifocals, which can interfere with testing of the inferior arcuate region. To test the inferior portion of the field, it may be necessary to have the patient tilt his head down while looking straight ahead, thereby moving the reading segment downward and out of the way.

CHAPTER 11

Visual field loss in glaucoma

ANATOMICAL BASIS OF GLAUCOMATOUS FIELD DEFECTS

As discussed in Chapter 2, each location in the retina corresponds with a certain direction in the visual field, e.g., a specific location on the inferior retina corresponds with a location in the superior visual field. The nasal retina represents the temporal visual field. The fovea corresponds to the point of fixation and thus is the point separating the nasal and temporal sides.

The optic nerve exits from the nasal side of the fovea. Therefore, the physiologic blind spot is in the temporal visual field. Because the visual field diagrams show the visual field "as the patient sees it," the blind spot is to the right of fixation for the right eye and to the left of fixation for the left eye.

Nerve fibers pass from every point in the retina to the optic nerve head, or optic disc. The pathway of the nerve fibers is important. From the retina nasal to the optic disc the fibers take a straight course to the optic disc. Fibers from the nasal side of the macula also pass rather directly toward the temporal margin of the disc, but with an increasingly curved course as one goes farther above or below the horizontal meridian. However, the fibers from the retina temporal to the fovea pass in an arcuate pathway around the fovea to pass into the upper and lower poles of the optic disc. The arrangement is quite orderly so that if the retina is divided by an imaginary horizontal line on the temporal side of the fovea, fibers from above the line are around the fovea superiorly and enter the upper pole of the disc. Similarly, from points below the line, the fibers arc inferiorly around the fovea to enter the inferior pole of the disc.

FIG. 11-1. Relationship of the retina to the visual field.

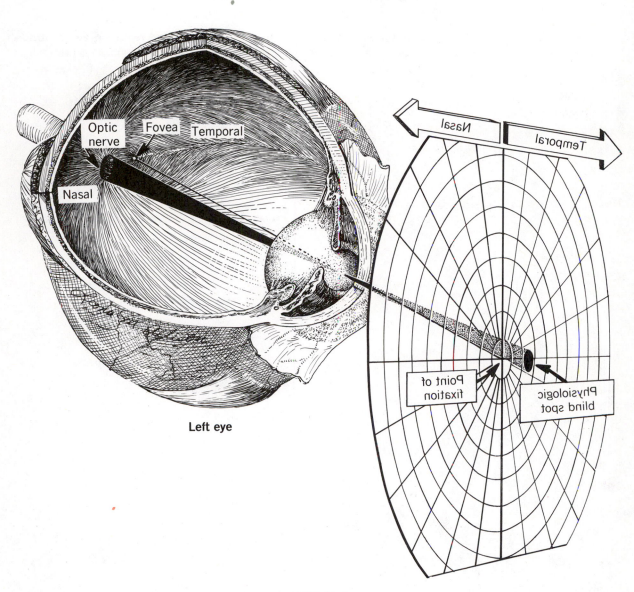

Optic
nerve

Fovea

Temporal

Nasal

Left eye

Nasal

Temporal

Point of
fixation

Physiologic
blind spot

FIG. 11-1

109

In glaucoma bundles of nerve fibers are damaged at the optic disc. As each bundle is damaged, the visual field supplied by that bundle loses sensitivity, resulting in a scotoma or a localized depression.

Typically, the first nerve fibers affected as bundles in glaucoma are those entering the upper or lower pole of the optic disc. Because of this, paracentral scotomas appear within an arcuate region around fixation, the "Bjerrum region," or there is a depression in the nasal field of vision, or both.

FIG. 11-2. Glaucomatous damage to nerve bundles and resulting visual abnormalities. Damage at the lower pole of the optic disc causes abnormalities in the visual field as shown (left eye).

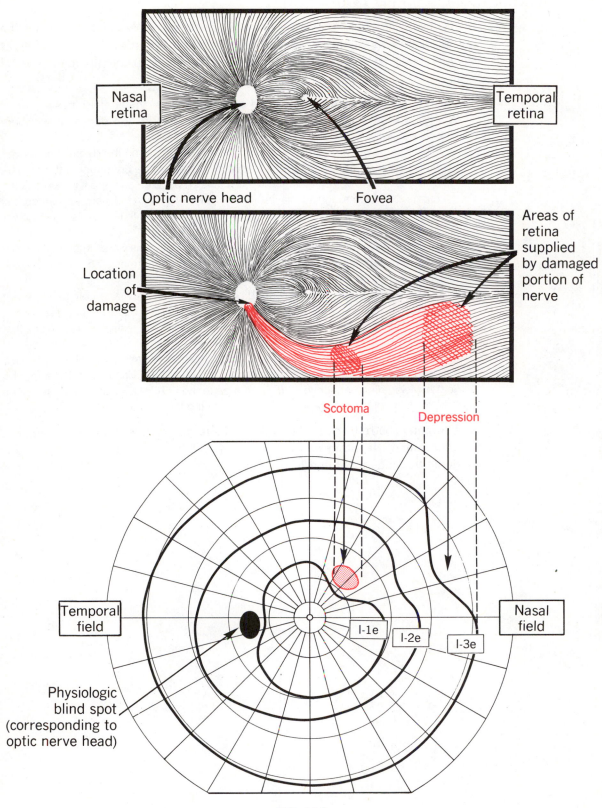

Nasal retina

Temporal retina

Optic nerve head

Fovea

Location of damage

Areas of retina supplied by damaged portion of nerve

Scotoma

Depression

Temporal field

Nasal field

I-1e

I-2e

I-3e

Physiologic blind spot (corresponding to optic nerve head)

FIG. 11-2

111

PROGRESSION OF FIELD LOSS

Typically, either a paracentral scotoma or a peripheral nasal depression is the first localized abnormality to appear. As the disease progresses, additional areas become abnormal and visual sensation becomes worse in the already abnormal areas.

FIG. 11-3. Stages in the progression of glaucomatous visual field loss.

A, An arcuate Bjerrum scotoma to I-3e superiorly contains two dense nuclei where V-4e is not seen. A peripheral nasal depression is also seen.

B, In a more advanced stage of glaucoma, the I-3e isopter in the depression moves inward to meet and unite with the I-3e isopter that formed a boundary of the arcuate Bjerrum scotoma. The scotoma and the depression become one and it is said that the "scotoma breaks through to the periphery." The two nuclei remain as paracentral scotomas within the arcuate depression. A shallow scotoma to I-3e is also in the lower Bjerrum region.

C, At a more advanced stage of glaucoma, visual sensitivity is worse in both the upper and the lower arcuate regions, with a dense arcuate abnormality above and a shallower arcuate defect below.

D, After arcuate scotomas have formed both above and below and both have broken through the periphery, there remains a central island of vision and a temporal crescent of vision. At this stage, by imagining a line vertically through fixation, one can see that nearly all of the nasal field of vision is gone. However, the temporal half of the field of each eye is present and each compensates for the absent nasal field of the other such that with both eyes open the patient is often unaware of the visual loss. The temporal field of vision of the right eye covers the area to the right of fixation and the temporal field of vision of the left eye covers the area to the left of fixation.

Ultimately both the central island and the temporal crescent become smaller, and then one or the other is lost completely. When sight is later lost from both locations, the patient is blind in that eye.

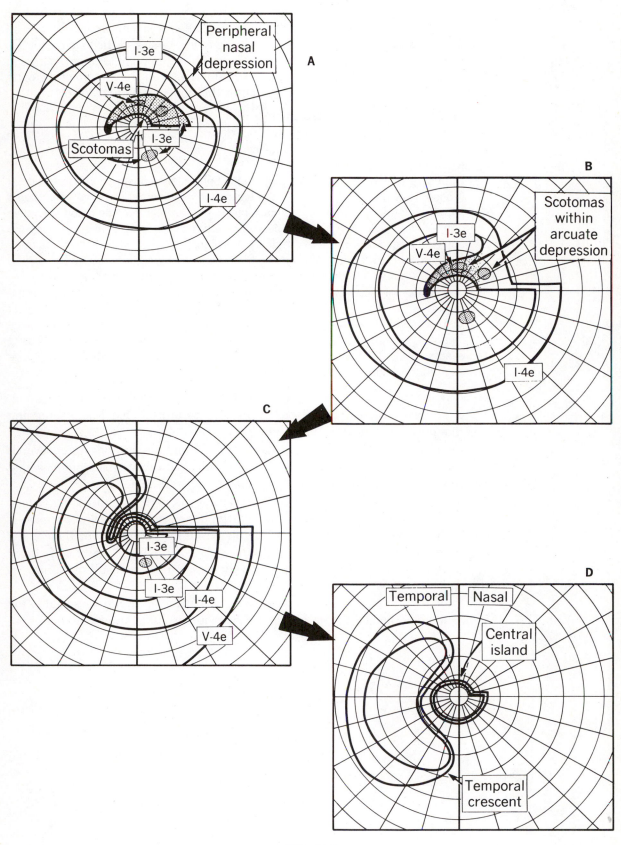

FIG. 11-3

NASAL STEPS

The arcuate route of the nerve fibers around the fovea causes the retina to be divided into an upper and lower portion on the temporal side of the fovea, which is represented nasal to fixation in the visual field. Thus, temporal to the fovea, nerve fibers originating below an imaginary horizontal line enter the bottom of the optic nerve disc, while those above the line enter the upper pole of the disc.

FIG. 11-4. Basis of the nasal step.

A, When a bundle of nerve fibers that enters the bottom of the optic disc is damaged in glaucoma—or in other diseases affecting the optic nerve head—a scotoma may result in the upper nasal visual field.

B, Such a scotoma may be very close to the horizontal meridian on the nasal side of fixation. However, it will not cross the horizontal meridian because the nerve fibers supplying the area just below the horizontal meridian enter the side of the optic disc opposite to the location of the damage. The scotoma will have a flat edge along the horizontal meridian and the isopter that skirts around the scotoma will have a "step."

C, This sharp demarcation along the horizontal nasal meridian applies not only to scotomas but also to peripheral depression. If there is upper nasal depression, the depression will end abruptly at the horizontal meridian, producing a "step" in the isopter.

D, The arcuate Bjerrum scotoma typically ends with a steep edge at the horizontal meridian. If there are Bjerrum scotomas both above and below, they will not meet exactly and, thus, they will not likely form a perfect ring-shaped scotoma but will have an abrupt horizontal step on the nasal side.

A nasal step may result either from a scotoma or from a nasal depression. There are two reasons why the nasal step is important in visual field screening and diagnosis of glaucoma.

First, it is very easy to look for a nasal step. When there is a nasal step, even if the result of a peripheral depression, there is almost always also a scotoma somewhere in the paracentral region, but it may have escaped detection.

Second, isopters may seem constricted as a result of many causes, e.g., age or cataract (pp. 150 and 280). Such generalized depression or nasal depression is common and would be difficult to distinguish from the depression of glaucoma if it were not for the fact that age and cataract will *not* produce a nasal step. If the constricted isopters have a nasal step, the depression is the result of damage to the optic nerve.

Therefore, in glaucoma visual field testing, particular attention is paid to the horizontal meridian on the nasal side. It is very important to know whether or not

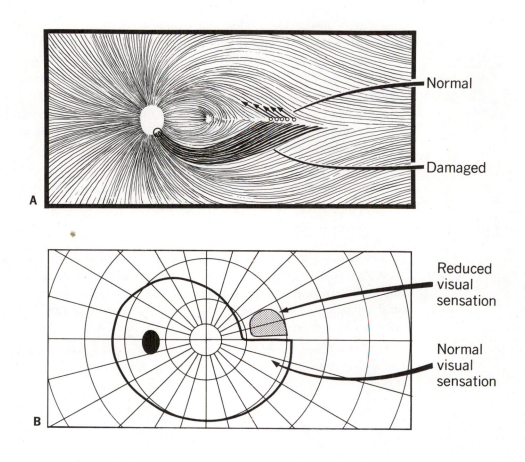

A

Normal

Damaged

B

Reduced
visual
sensation

Normal
visual
sensation

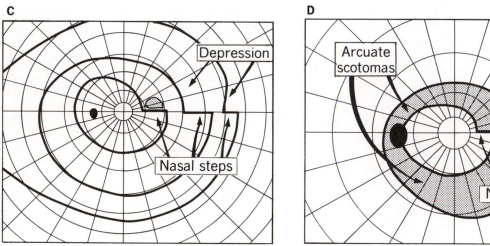

C

Depression

Nasal steps

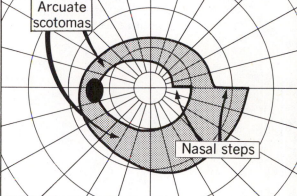

D

Arcuate
scotomas

Nasal steps

FIG. 11-4

the isopters have a nasal step. While glaucoma is the most common cause of field defects with nasal steps, other less common diseases affecting the optic nerve head may cause an identical field defect.

In summary, the visual field loss in glaucoma typically consists of paracentral scotomas that may enlarge and join together to become an arcuate or Bjerrum scotoma. There is also depression on the nasal side that may merge with the reduced visual sensation of the arcuate scotoma. Nasal steps are produced because the depression and the scotomas are of unequal severity above and below the horizontal meridian.

FIG. 11-5. Typical glaucomatous defects. This composite of glaucomatous visual field defects might occur in moderately advanced glaucoma.

LESS FREQUENT DEFECTS

Not all cases of glaucoma are typical. For example, there may be depression in a wedge on the temporal side, with the apex of the wedge pointed at the blind spot. A scotoma may appear on the nasal side outside 30 degrees. Or, the reduced visual sensation in the arcuate region may be represented by depressed isopters instead of by a scotoma.

FIG. 11-6. Less common defects. Shown here are a wedge-shaped temporal depression pointing to the blind spot and a midperipheral nasal scotoma with a nasal step.

There is more about glaucoma in Chapter 18 (p. 209), and further details are in the references given on pp. 218, 226, and in Appendix B.

ADDITIONAL READINGS

To become better acquainted with the basic visual field defects in glaucoma look at the examples in the following articles by Dr. Stephen M. Drance:

Drance, S.M.: The glaucomatous visual field, Br. J. Ophthalmol. **56:**186-200, 1972.
Drance, S.M.: Glaucoma. In Reed, H., and Drance, S.M.: The essentials of perimetry: static and kinetic, ed. 2, New York, 1972, Oxford University Press, pp. 66-89.

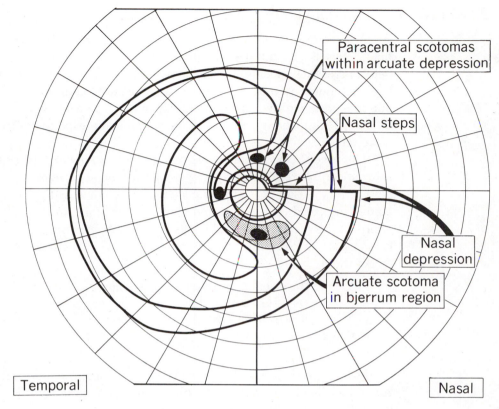

FIG. 11-5

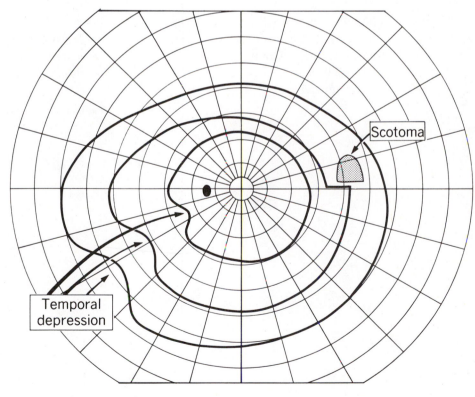

FIG. 11-6

SCREENING EXAMINATION: INTRODUCTION

A screening examination is intended to determine whether or not a visual field defect is present. The technique must be sensitive (detecting most of the defects present), specific (not too many false positives), and not too time-consuming. In general, 10 minutes per eye should be the maximum time spent in ruling out the presence of a defect. The 10-minute time limit *for screening* avoids fatigue to the patient and makes the test results, especially of the second eye, more reliable.

The trick to saving time while retaining sensitivity in detecting abnormalities is to concentrate efforts on the regions where the abnormalities are most likely to be. For this reason, it is always necessary to know why the field examination is being performed (e.g., suspected glaucoma or brain tumor) and to concentrate efforts in the region where field defects first appear in the condition suspected. It is necessary to know both where the defects are likely to occur and how best to detect them.

FIG. 11-7. The visual field defects in glaucoma. The earliest visual field defects will almost always be found in the central region (paracentral scotoma, arcuate scotoma, and nasal steps) or in the nasal periphery (depression producing nasal steps). If there are no abnormalities in these regions (outlined in red), it is not likely that there are defects elsewhere.

For glaucoma, we can examine carefully the central area and the nasal horizontal meridian. If no abnormalities are found it is unlikely that there are any in the broad crescent above, below, and temporal to the central 30 degrees. The area needing special attention is only about one-fourth of the total area of the visual field.

There are several excellent strategies for exploring the visual field for glaucomatous abnormalities. The next several pages will show one of these techniques that should be mastered completely before learning several others, which are discussed in Chapter 18. In the method to be described here the central field is tested first and the peripheral field last. In some clinics the sequence is arbitrarily the reverse.

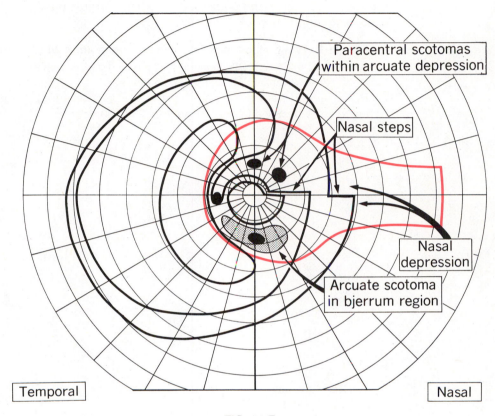

Paracentral scotomas
within arcuate depression

Nasal steps

Nasal
depression

Arcuate scotoma
in bjerrum region

Temporal

Nasal

FIG. 11-7

SCREENING EXAMINATION: THE CENTRAL FIELD

After selecting the appropriate corrective lenses (Chapter 10), the usual preliminaries consist of educating the patient (Chapter 8) and plotting the physiologic blind spot with the I-4e stimulus. At the same time, it is determined which test stimulus will form an isopter that encloses most of the central 20 to 30 degrees of the field, including the physiologic blind spot. If the choice of stimulus is not obvious, threshold is determined at 20 to 25 degrees temporal to fixation, just above and below the horizontal meridian and just outside the location of the physiologic blind spot.

FIG. 11-8. Two methods for determining threshold at 20 to 25 degrees.
A, The first method (static perimetry) is to position the stimulus in this location and increase the stimulus until it first becomes visible.
B, The second method (kinetic perimetry) is to bring several stimuli in from the periphery to see which one forms an isopter at 25 to 30 degrees.

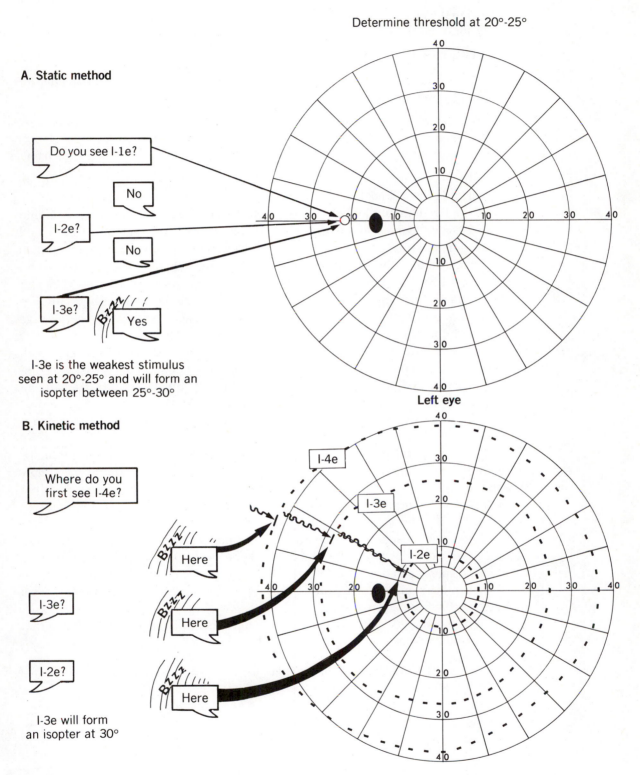

FIG. 11-8

An isopter is plotted with the selected stimulus and particular attention is given to the area just above and below the horizontal meridian on the nasal side to look for a nasal step.

FIG. 11-9. Plotting the isopter with the selected stimulus.

With that same stimulus, the entire area within the isopter is explored for scotomas by presenting the test stimulus at 75 to 100 locations.

FIG. 11-10. Exploring for scotomas. This exploration for scotomas by supra-threshold static spot checking concentrates on the two arcuate regions (Bjerrum regions) indicated in red. It is the single most important step in glaucoma defect detection.

Testing of many points is necessary because early scotomas may be quite small and they will not be found if the spots tested are too widely distributed.* The area explored should include the entire inner 20 degrees of the visual field and also 20 to 30 degrees on the nasal side. Be sure to test in the region just above and below the physiologic blind spot. Some offices and clinics use a regimented plan in which there are four spots tested inside 5 degrees, then 72 spots where the 5-, 10-, and 15-degree circles cross the 24 meridians, for a total of 76 spots (Chapter 18, p. 212). It is wise also to test at 20 degrees and 25 degrees nasally. Thus, 76 spots are an absolute minimum and perhaps 100 spots should be the average number checked.

It is important that the stimulus appear and disappear in each location, with the patient responding each time that the stimulus appears. This is easily accomplished with the projection perimeter but can also be performed at the tangent screen. Scotomas will be missed if you make the mistake of leaving the stimulus on continuously, moving it around, and asking the patient to tell you when it disappears.

The stimulus should be presented in a somewhat irregular rhythm to make sure that the patient is actually responding to the visual stimuli and not simply sounding the buzzer rhythmically at 1-second intervals. If the patient does not respond to a stimulus in a certain location, that location should be retested (pp. 212 and 266) because occasionally a stimulus will be missed even by a person with a normal visual field. However, areas where the patient responds inconsistently or more slowly than elsewhere must be explored with extra care because these responses may indicate an area with a shallow scotoma. Further details will be given later on the technique of static spot checking (p. 160) and how to deal with inconsistent responses (p. 170).

After completing this step, the field chart should be labeled to indicate that this stimulus was seen everywhere inside the isopter.

---

*Fankhauser, F., and Bebie, H.: Threshold fluctuations, interpolations, and spacial resolution in perimetry, Doc. Ophthalmol. Proc. Series **19:**295-309, 1970.

Plot the isopter

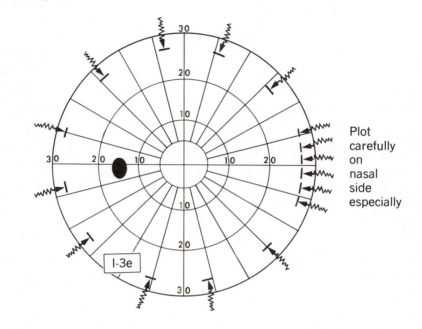

30
20
10
30
20
10
10
20
10
20
I-3e
30
Plot
carefully
on
nasal
side
especially

FIG. 11-9

Check for scotomas

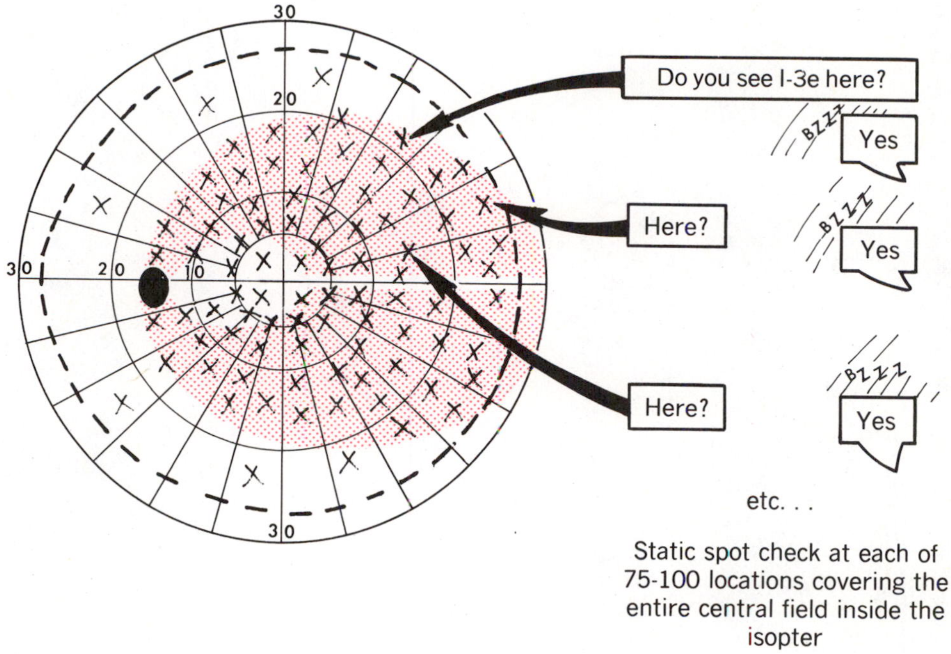

30
20
30
20
10
30
Do you see I-3e here?
BZZZ
Yes
Here?
BZZZ
Yes
Here?
BZZZ
Yes
etc. . .
Static spot check at each of 75-100 locations covering the entire central field inside the isopter

FIG. 11-10

It may happen that a single stimulus is not sufficient for exploring the area inside 30 degrees. Suppose there is a significant area inside 30 degrees that does not lie within the isopter plotted in the previous step, e.g., if the isopter extended to 25 degrees temporally and surrounded the blind spot but only to 10 to 15 degrees superiorly and nasally. In that case, the area outside 15 degrees superiorly and nasally cannot be explored for scotomas with this test stimulus because only the area inside the isopter can be tested. Therefore, the next larger isopter must also be plotted to surround the area within 30 degrees that has not been explored for scotomas, but this isopter is used only in those sectors where the weaker stimulus was not usable. The idea is to explore the entire central 25 degrees for scotomas and not to leave any regions unexplored.

FIG. 11-11. Use of two stimuli to test the central 25 degrees.

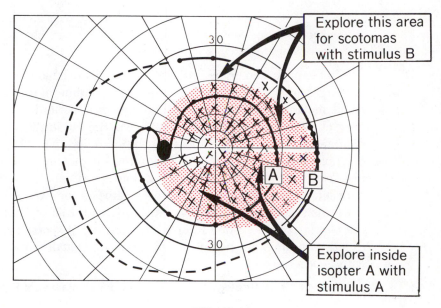

Explore this area for scotomas with stimulus B

Explore inside isopter A with stimulus A

FIG. 11-11

The examiner must realize that testing for paracentral scotomas is the single most important component of screening for glaucomatous defects. The two important principles in screening the central visual field are (1) to select the correct test stimulus and (2) to explore the entire central area that might be involved in glaucoma with a sufficient number of test points.

FIG. 11-12. Example of a scotoma for the I-3e isopter, which encloses the inner 35 degrees. This scotoma would not be detected if the examiner incorrectly chose the I-4e test stimulus, whose isopter is at about 45 degrees), to look for scotomas.

It is possible that some scotomas will be missed even by using the correct stimulus.

FIG. 11-13, A. Example of a shallow scotoma near fixation. The I-2e isopter encloses 15 degrees, while the I-3e isopter encloses 25 degrees. There may be a scotoma at 5 degrees where the I-2e isopter is not seen but the I-3e isopter is still visible. Such an early scotoma would be missed with the method described, in which the I-3e stimulus is used because it is the threshold at 25 degrees. However, by this method the examiner would miss only the early, very shallow scotomas, not established deeper scotomas.

In the usual screening setting, some small or shallow scotomas will be missed but larger deeper ones will not be missed. Sometimes it may be acceptable to miss small shallow scotomas, as long as the more important ones are detected. However, at other times, e.g., considerable elevation of intraocular pressure or rather definite optic disc damage, there may be extra reason to test more thoroughly. For example, it is possible to select a stimulus and plot an isopter at 10 to 20 degrees to explore within this isopter for scotomas, and then to plot a second isopter between 20 and 30 degrees. The space between the two isopters is then explored with this second stimulus. The extra time with this additional step is related to the plotting of the second isopter. The number of spots checked for scotomas is exactly the same but half of the locations are tested with one stimulus and half with another.

FIG. 11-13, B. Strategy to avoid missing a shallow scotoma.

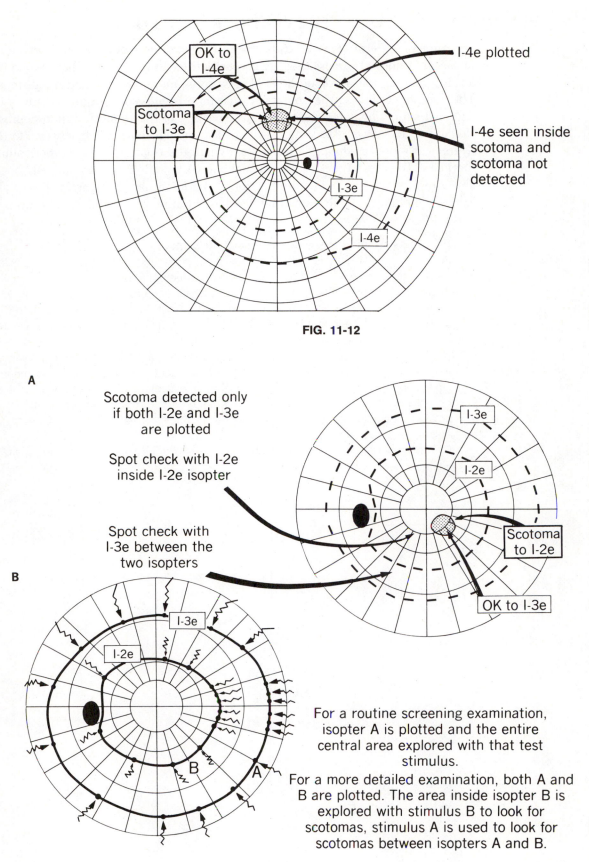

OK to I-4e

Scotoma to I-3e

I-4e plotted

I-4e seen inside scotoma and scotoma not detected

I-3e

I-4e

FIG. 11-12

A

Scotoma detected only if both I-2e and I-3e are plotted

Spot check with I-2e inside I-2e isopter

Spot check with I-3e between the two isopters

I-3e

I-2e

Scotoma to I-2e

OK to I-3e

B

I-3e

I-2e

B

A

For a routine screening examination, isopter A is plotted and the entire central area explored with that test stimulus.

For a more detailed examination, both A and B are plotted. The area inside isopter B is explored with stimulus B to look for scotomas, stimulus A is used to look for scotomas between isopters A and B.

FIG. 11-13

SCREENING EXAMINATION: THE PERIPHERAL FIELD

After the central 25 degrees has been explored for scotomas, the corrective lenses are removed (unless they are contact lenses, in which case they should be left in), and the nasal side of the field is explored for depression and nasal steps. The manner of plotting the isopters is important. Depression of light sensitivity is detected simply by determining inward deviation of the isopters. When depression occurs nasally in glaucoma, it is typically unequal above and below by 5 to 10 degrees or more, producing a nasal step where the isopters cross the horizontal meridian. To detect a nasal step, the plot should include 3 to 4 points just above and 3 to 4 points just below the horizontal meridian nasally. This applies to all isopters, including the first one that was plotted in preparation for exploring the central field for scotomas.

FIG. 11-14. Testing for nasal depression or steps.

A, An additional isopter is plotted with a stimulus stronger than the one used to look for paracentral scotomas. It is not necessary to plot the entire isopter because the main interest is in the nasal field. Instead, the isopter for each stimulus is plotted only just above and just below the horizontal meridian nasally to look for nasal steps. It is important that three to four points be plotted close together just above the horizontal meridian and 3 to 4 points just below the meridian.

B, In this manner, successively stronger stimuli at intervals of 0.5 log unit or equivalent (e.g., I-3e, I-4e, II-4e or I-2b, I-3b, I-4b) are plotted across the horizontal nasal meridian at about 10-degree intervals, beginning with the isopter used to explore the central field. As progressively stronger stimuli are used, each isopter is farther out than the previous one until the absolute nasal periphery of the visual field is reached—i.e., until a stronger stimulus does not increase the size of the field.

C, The keyhole-shaped area in which most glaucomatous defects are found (p. 118) has now been explored.

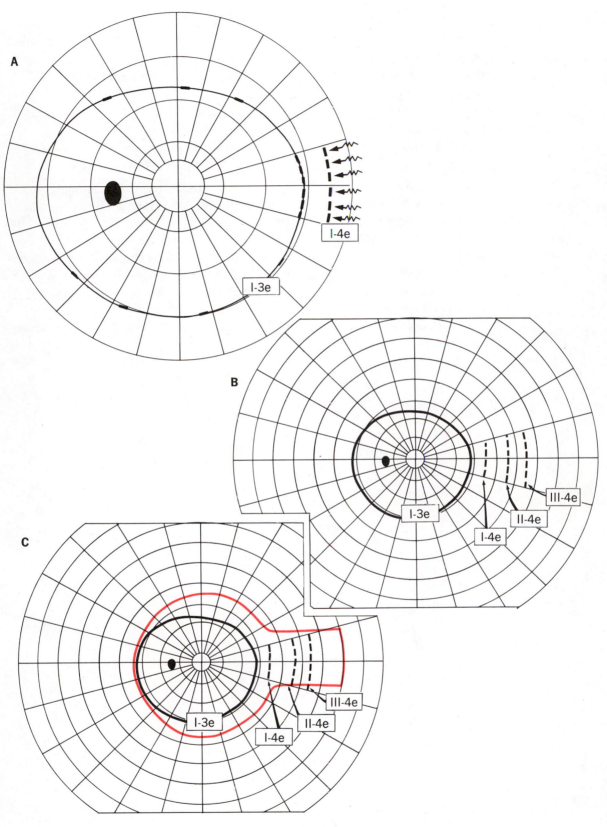

FIG. 11-14

When the periphery is reached, the *weakest* stimulus that is visible at or just within the absolute periphery is plotted all the way around. When mapping this isopter, the examiner should plot a sufficient number of points to pick up a wedge-shaped depression that sometimes occurs in the temporal field.

FIG. 11-15. The peripheral isopter.

A, In plots of progressively stronger stimuli, the IV-4e coincides with the previously plotted III-4e.

B, Therefore the III-4e is chosen to plot the peripheral isopter because the III-4e is the weakest stimulus at or just inside the absolute nasal periphery.

If the existence of a scotoma is strongly suspected, the examiner might explore inside each isopter for scotomas, although this is not part of the standard screening procedure. In addition, the temporal field can be explored by plotting the isopters all the way around, checking for scotomas, or both. Naturally, one would always be very suspicious of any irregularity in the contour of the isopters, or be suspicious in areas where the patient's responses were somewhat slow or inconsistent. Such areas could be explored with careful plotting of additional isopters and careful searches for scotomas.

The reason for plotting the *weakest* stimulus at the periphery will be given later (p. 146).

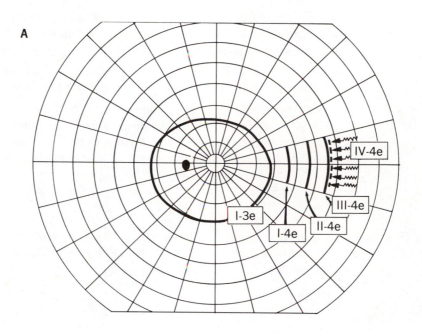

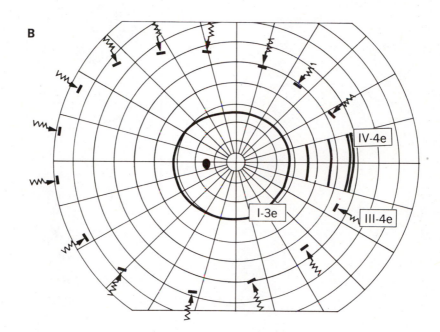

FIG. 11-15

SCREENING EXAMINATION: QUANTITATING AN ABNORMAL FIELD

If abnormalities are discovered, they must be quantitated. The 10-minute limit for screening is lifted. On encountering an abnormality during a screening examination, an experienced perimetrist will immediately plot its boundary and quantitate its depth and slope before proceeding to screen the remaining regions for other defects. Thus, the technique becomes a combination of screening for defects and assessment of any defects that are found.

FIG. 11-16. Quantitating a scotoma.

A, When a scotoma is discovered, its extent and depth must be determined.

B, First, the boundary of the scotoma is plotted kinetically with the stimulus used to discover the scotoma by moving the stimulus from the center of the scotoma outward, with the patient reporting when it becomes visible.

C, Next the examiner quantitates the depth. The threshold is determined at the center by testing with progressively stronger stimuli until one becomes visible.

D, With the strongest test stimulus that is still invisible, the boundary of the scotoma is again plotted to determine the slope of the boundary. The boundary with this stimulus may be the same as it was with the weaker stimulus or it may be smaller.

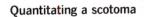

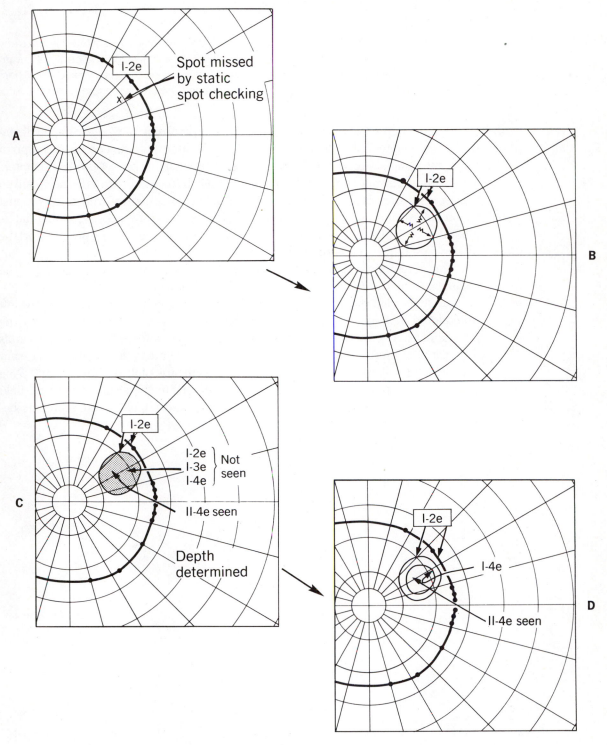

FIG. 11-16

133

FIG. 11-17. Quantitating a nasal step. When a nasal step is discovered, its presence can be confirmed by moving the stimulus across the horizontal meridian to establish that it becomes visible at the horizontal meridian as it passes from a position that is outside the isopter to a position that is within the isopter. (The step may not be *exactly* at the horizontal meridian.)

Then, because a nasal step represents a depression, it is quantitated just like any depression (p. 84). Additional isopters are plotted toward fixation and outward toward the periphery to see how far inward and outward the abnormal region extends. Where isopters separate because only one of them has a nasal step, there may be a scotoma.

When a depression is discovered on the temporal side (a wedge-shaped deviation of the isopter), this depression must also be quantitated. The quantitation of temporal wedge defects has been illustrated previously (pp. 84-89, 96). Isopters for stronger stimuli in 0.5 log unit steps must be plotted through the involved region until the absolute boundary of the field is reached or until the strongest acceptable stimulus has been plotted. Also, the isopters for weaker stimuli must be plotted in 0.5 log unit steps until the inner boundary of the depression or the physiologic blind spot is reached.

The screening examination concentrates on the most likely areas for the occurrence of the *first,* or earliest, visual field defect in glaucoma (e.g., paracentral scotomas, nasal steps, or peripheral depression). Other regions are left unexplored in a screening examination because they are unlikely places for the first defect to occur. However, these areas can have defects later and as soon as the examination discloses defects in the most likely areas, it becomes necessary also to look in all other regions of the field. This means plotting isopters in 0.5 log unit steps, or approximately every 15 to 20 degrees in the entire peripheral field and every 10 to 15 degrees in the central field, and checking for scotomas between the isopters.

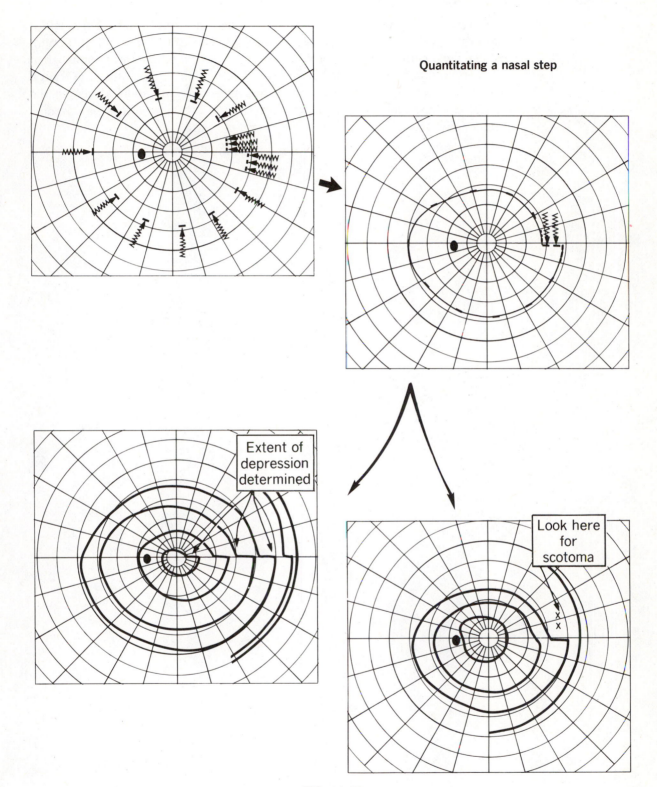

Quantitating a nasal step

Extent of
depression
determined

Look here
for
scotoma

FIG. 11-17

TANGENT SCREENS

The tangent screen can only be used to test the central field. Fortunately, fewer than 10% of patients with field defects will have defects *only* in the periphery. So if the central field is absolutely normal, the examiner can be more than 90% certain that there is no defect in the peripheral field either. Thus, the central field is the most important part of the glaucoma field examination. Moreover, the central field certainly will be involved by the time the visual loss has become functionally significant.

No one who is comfortable with the Goldmann perimeter would voluntarily go back to using the tangent screen, which does not allow examination of the peripheral field. However, if a perimeter is not available, a careful tangent screen examination can certainly be more than adequate for most clinical purposes, provided the basic principles of target selection and spot checking many spots are followed. The isopter for the smallest test object visible at 25 to 30 degrees must be plotted and many places spot-checked statically. The static spot checking is done by turning the wand as illustrated before (p. 75). Scotomas are quantitated by plotting the boundary of scotomas and by determining their depth (how large the object must be to become visible) and slope. Frequently overlooked with the tangent screen is the need to plot several isopters in abnormal regions to fully quantitate the depressions, whether localized (nasal steps) or generalized. For example, if isopters become constricted on one examination compared to a previous examination, it is necessary to plot isopters with progressively larger stimuli until the edge of the tangent screen is reached.

CHAPTER 12

Calibration of Goldmann perimeter

CALIBRATION METHOD

The perimeter should be calibrated often—perhaps at the beginning of each day or whenever you are not certain whether someone else may have turned the knobs while dusting or while looking for the on-off switch. Calibration is fast and easy. If you have to look up how to do it, you are not doing it often enough!

For the perimeter to be calibrated, it is necessary to calibrate both the intensity of the projected stimulus and the intensity of the background.

The first step is to make certain the room lights are off and the door to the room is closed so that there is no stray light inside the perimeter bowl. The stimulus switch should be turned such that the stimulus is on without the knob being depressed, the opposite of the position when the perimeter is being used for visual field testing.

FIG. 12-1. Setting the perimeter for calibration. The pantograph handle is moved to a position at 70 degrees on the right side and locked in position. The stimulus control is set at the largest and brightest (V-4e), with all the levers to the right. The stimulus switch is turned such that the projected stimulus is on without the switch being depressed. After the calibration is complete, be sure to reset the knob to the proper position for field testing.

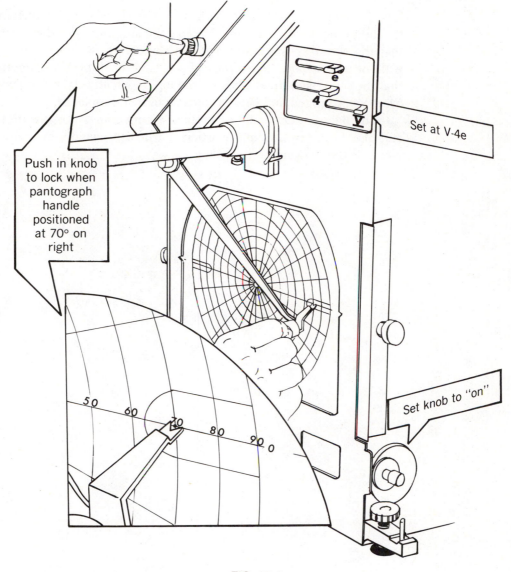

Push in knob to lock when pantograph handle positioned at 70° on right

Set at V-4e

Set knob to "on"

50   60   70   80   90   0

FIG. 12-1

Calibration of the stimulus

FIG. 12-2. Calibrating the stimulus. The light meter is inserted into position. Then the flaglike photometer screen is raised out of the way so that the projected stimulus shines into the light meter. With the stimulus control on the largest and brightest, V-4e, the rheostat is adjusted until the light meter registers 1000 apostilb (asb). There is a special light operated by a push button just below it to help you see the light meter in the darkened room.

If the intensity will not go high enough to show a reading of 1000 asb, replace the light bulb of the perimeter after making sure that the stimulus is set for V-4e, that the stimulus is on, and that the stimulus is shining onto the light meter without obstruction. Sometimes, the reason for diminished intensity is simply that the bulb has turned black on the top, in which case it can simply be turned over (inverting top and bottom) instead of being replaced.

The light meter should be protected from constant exposure to bright light and also from physical abuse when not in use, usually by simply putting the meter in the drawer carefully.

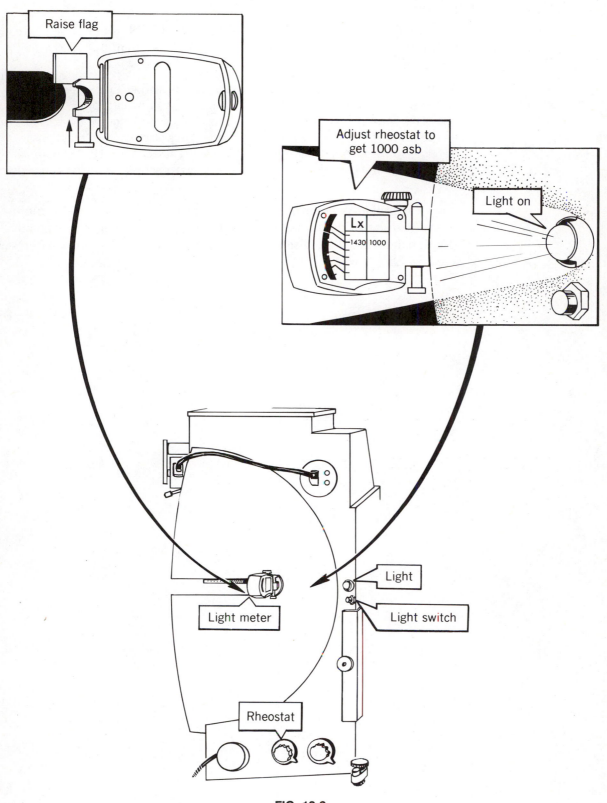

FIG. 12-2

Calibration of the background

To calibrate the background, the stimulus should be dim but large (V-1e), which reduces the stimulus to 32.5 asb, 1.5 log units less than the 1000 asb of a V-4e stimulus.

FIG. 12-3. Adjusting the background to 32.5 asb. The flaglike photometer screen is lowered so that it intercepts the projected stimulus. By looking through one slot at the edge of the hemisphere and through the hole of a ring at the other slot the perimetrist can see the projected stimulus. The lamp shade is adjusted until the light intensity of the ring (representing the background illumination) is equal to the 32.5 asb light intensity of the stimulus projected onto the photometer screen, as seen through the hole.

When calibration is complete, the light meter is put away, the stimulus switch is turned so that the stimulus is off with the switch not depressed, and the pantograph handle is unlocked so that the arm will swing into its position of rest and be out of harm's way.

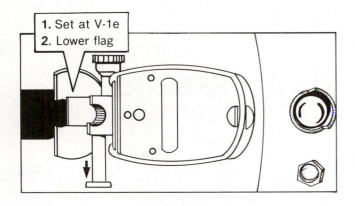

1. Set at V-1e
2. Lower flag

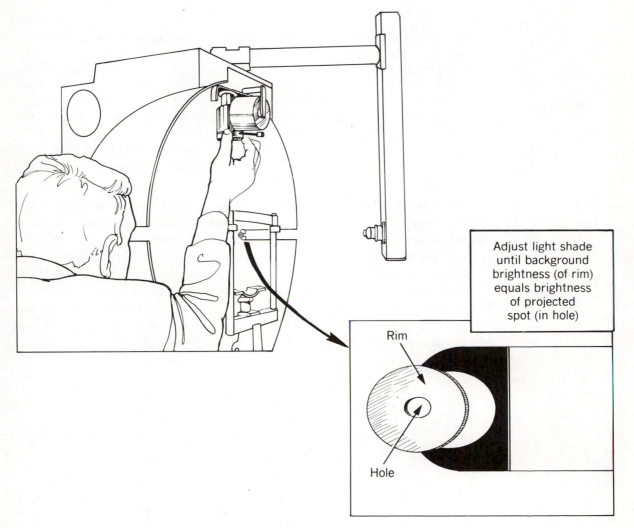

Adjust light shade until background brightness (of rim) equals brightness of projected spot (in hole)

Rim

Hole

FIG. 12-3

CHAPTER 13

Generalized depressions

CHARACTERISTICS OF GENERALIZED DEPRESSIONS

There is a "generalized depression" of the visual field when there is depressed (reduced) sensitivity to light *everywhere* in the visual field. When light sensitivity is less than usual throughout the entire visual field, all test stimuli are generally less visible and the visual threshold has become abnormal at every spot in the visual field.

FIG. 13-1. Isopter plot of generalized depression compared to that of the normal eye. I-3e is visible at location *N* inside the I-3e isopter of the normal field, *above,* but in the depressed field, *below,* I-3e is not visible at location *N*. On an isopter plot, this means that the I-3e isopter has moved inward so that it no longer encloses location *N*.

Indeed, since visual sensation is reduced everywhere, all isopters move inward from all sides. Each isopter encloses a smaller area than before; this signifies that each stimulus is visible in a smaller region than before.

Location *N* is still within the I-4e isopter, which means that I-4e has remained visible at *N*, even though I-3e is not visible. Now the threshold at *N* is between I-3e and I-4e, whereas before it was between I-2e and I-3e.

In a localized depression (Chapter 9) the isopters move inward, but only within a localized region. In a generalized depression the same inward movement occurs but the entire field is involved, so that each isopter is moved inward along its entire length. In addition, the diagnostic implications are very different.

At the center of the normal field in Fig. 13-1 the I-1e and 0-1e are visible and there are isopters enclosing the regions within which these stimuli are visible. With the generalized depression, these stimuli are no longer visible at all. Therefore, in the plot of the depressed field there are no longer any isopters for I-1e and 0-1e because there is no region within which these stimuli are visible.

144

Normal

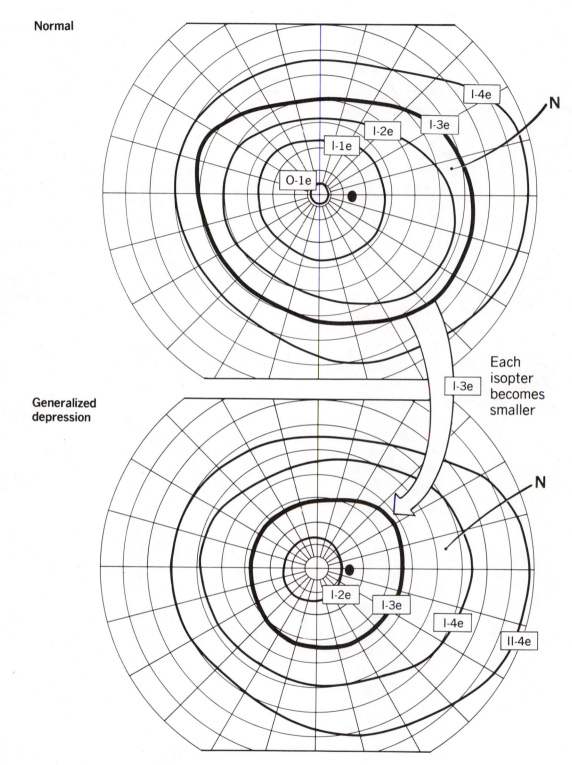

Generalized depression

Each isopter becomes smaller

FIG. 13-1

FIG. 13-2. Plot of normal field compared to that of a depressed field.

A, Normal field. In a normal field of vision, if I-4e forms an isopter at the extreme border of the field, then all stronger stimuli will also form isopters at the same place when plotted kinetically, i.e., those stronger stimuli, when brought in from the periphery, will first become visible at the extreme boundary and their isopters will be superimposed on one another. The "isopters" so plotted do not really represent the visual threshold because they are not the *weakest* stimulus visible at the boundary. However, they do enclose the area within which the stimulus is visible. Several isopters superimposed on one another represent a very steep cliff at the extreme border of the hill of vision.

B, Generalized depression. When the visual field becomes generally depressed, visual sensation will become reduced at all locations, including location *M* near the periphery, where neither I-4e nor II-4e is visible any longer but the stronger test stimuli may still be visible. Thus, the I-4e and II-4e isopters move inward and separate from each other such that *M* is no longer enclosed by the I-4e and II-4e isopters. Isopters of III-4e and stronger stimuli remain at the extreme boundary and do enclose *M*.

With a generalized depression the extreme periphery of the visual field does not move inward. This has two practical implications:

1. If the outer limit of the field is routinely plotted only with very strong suprathreshold stimuli, such as II-4e, or even V-4e, the extreme boundary of the field will be determined, but a depression of the visual field will not be detected. A depression will be detected only if the isopter for the weakest stimulus that should be at the periphery (I-4e) is plotted and it is discovered that the isopter is moved inward. This principle was applied when looking for localized depressions in glaucoma (p. 130).

2. In the presence of a generalized depression it should be possible to increase the stimulus to a sufficient strength that it becomes visible in the periphery of the visual field. For example, if the I-4e isopter is plotted and found to be constricted, suggesting a depression, it should nonetheless be possible to plot the isopter for a stronger stimulus that will enclose the peripheral field—unless the field is so depressed that it would require a stimulus stronger than the strongest available on the perimeter.

Normal

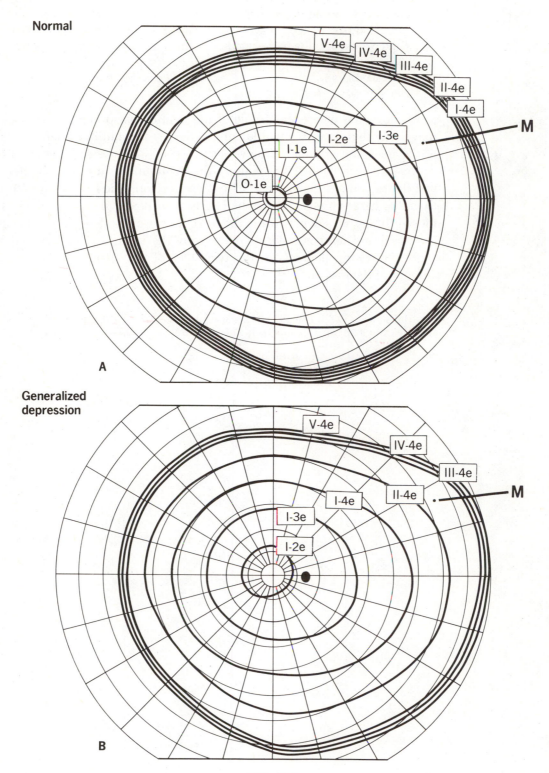

A

Generalized
depression

B

FIG. 13-2

147

FIG. 13-3. Comparison of isopter plots of a normal field and a generalized depression to profile plots. In this illustration visual sensation in the depressed field is reduced by 0.5 log unit* at every point in the visual field. Thus, where I-2e is threshold in the normal field (namely at the I-2e isopter), the threshold becomes I-3e. Thus, the I-3e isopter in the depressed field is in the same place where the I-2e isopter is normally. Moreover, in the profile plot the hill of vision has the same shape but has simply moved downward 0.5 log unit.

In a region where the profile of the field of vision is steep, the isopter will move only slightly with a half-log unit of depression, but in a relatively flat region of the field, the isopter will move more. Thus, with the same amount of visual depression everywhere (0.5 log unit), the isopter moves inward a greater distance in a flat region of the field than in a steeper region. The I-2e isopter moved more than 20 degrees inward, while the I-3e isopter moved in only 10 degrees, having moved through a steeper part of the field. Because the slope of the visual field on the nasal and temporal side is not exactly the same, the isopter may move to slightly differing degrees on the two sides of the visual field with a specific amount of depression.

---

*The difference between I-4e and I-3e is 0.5 log unit intensity as is that between I-3e and I-2e, I-2e and I-1e. Also, I-3c is 0.5 log unit more intense than I-2c (see pp. 46-47).

Normal

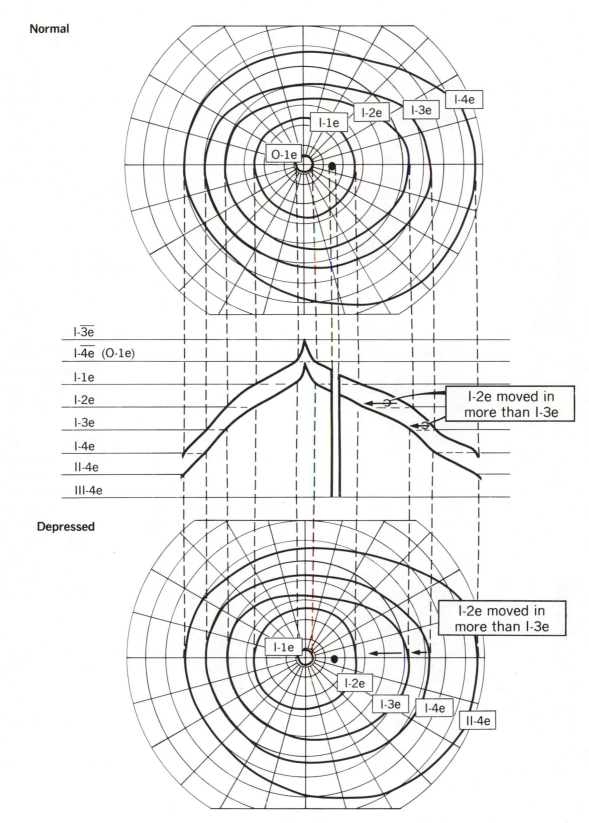

I-3e
I-4e (O-1e)
I-1e
I-2e
I-3e
I-4e
II-4e
III-4e

I-2e moved in
more than I-3e

Depressed

I-2e moved in
more than I-3e

FIG. 13-3

The amount of depression is not always the same everywhere in the visual field, e.g., with the development of cataract the defocused image may have more effect on the central visual field than on the periphery.

FIG. 13-4. Example of unequal generalized depression. Visual sensation is reduced by 0.5 log unit in the periphery and by 1 log unit in the center; however, this is still a *generalized* depression, which means that visual sensation is reduced *everywhere*, even though not to an equal degree in all places.

Location *R* in the normal field is within the I-1e isopter but in the depressed field is no longer enclosed by either the I-1e or the I-2e. Thus, two isopters, each *representing* 0.5 log unit of intensity, no longer enclose point *R* and this represents 1 log unit of depression. In contrast, point *S* was in the normal field enclosed by the I-4e isopter. In the depressed field, *S* is no longer enclosed by the I-4e isopter but is within the next stronger isopter, II-4e,* and therefore has only 0.5 log unit of depression.

We will see later (pp. 280-285) how important it is to understand thoroughly generalized depression, and especially the relationship between isopter movement and threshold change.

SIGNIFICANCE OF GENERALIZED DEPRESSION

There is a certain variability of visual sensation from one person to another— so that the location of the isopters is variable. Thus, the I-2e isopter may be at 30 degrees in one person but at 15 degrees for another person. Because of this, if the I-2e is at 15 degrees in an individual, it is difficult to say if this is normal, or if the individual used to have the I-2e isopter at 30 degrees and now has a depressed field. Moreover, the visual field normally undergoes a slow generalized depression as one grows older, and a relatively inward position of isopters must be considered normal for older people without its signifying the presence of ocular disease.

However, superimposed on this individual variability and age-related changes are abnormal depressions. For example, cataracts or corneal opacities typically cause a generalized depression along with a reduction of visual acuity. In fact, if a patient with reduced visual acuity does not have a generalized depression of the field, one has an important diagnostic clue, suggesting that a central scotoma is present to account for the reduced visual acuity, and that the reduced acuity is not due to a media (cornea, lens, vitreous) opacity (see pp. 254 and 280-285).

---

*Of course, the II-4e stimulus is larger than I-4e, rather than brighter. However, for the present purpose, we can consider the changing from size I to size II as roughly equivalent to an intensity increase of 0.5 log unit.

Normal

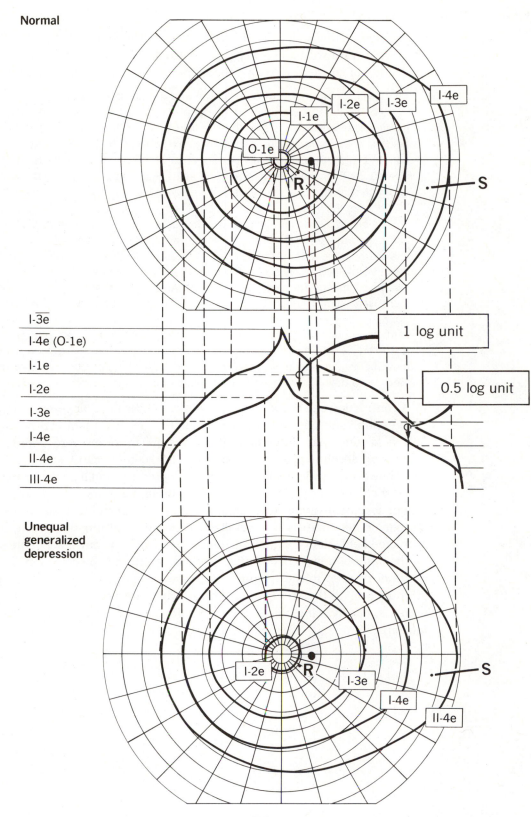

I-3e
I-4e (O-1e)
I-1e
I-2e
I-3e
I-4e
II-4e
III-4e

1 log unit

0.5 log unit

Unequal
generalized
depression

FIG. 13-4

CONTRACTION OF THE VISUAL FIELD

We noted previously (Fig. 13-2) that the extreme boundary of the field does not move inward with an ordinary generalized depression. This contrasts with a contraction of the field in which the extreme boundary does move in.

FIG. 13-5. Comparison of contraction and severe depression.

Above, If visual sensation in the periphery of the field is reduced to the point that *no* stimulus is visible, it is said that the field is contracted. The uninvolved area of the field may have normal visual sensitivity with I-1e and 0-1e isopters in their normal location and all other isopters crowded together at the boundary of the contracted field. The isopter for the strongest stimulus, V-4e, is at 25 degrees. Thus, in this example of a contracted field, visual sensation is severely reduced outside 25 degrees, but inside 25 degrees the visual sensation is normal.

Below, With a severe generalized depression, on the other hand, visual sensation is reduced everywhere so that the seeing part of the field has reduced sensation. In this example the V-4e isopter is at 25 degrees, the IV-4e is at 7 degrees, and the II-4e is not visible at all. This situation represents severe depression of the entire field, not just the periphery. The isopters are not crowded together at the limit of the field, and if there were such a thing as a VI-4e stimulus, we would expect its isopter to be at approximately 40 degrees. Even stronger stimuli would be visible out to the usual extreme boundary of a normal field. By confrontation, in a severe depression (with a restricted field to the strongest test object) there may still be a wide field to hand movements or to light perception with projection. With contraction, an absolute defect, there is no detection of hand movements or light in the periphery (p. 232).

A contraction can be localized (in one area of the field) or generalized just like a depression. The endstage of glaucoma (Fig. 11-3, *D*) is a contraction of the nasal field. Often a contraction simply results from a severe depression that becomes an absolute defect, just as a shallow scotoma can become absolute. At times, however, the distinction between a depression and a contraction is important to the diagnosis (p. 274) because certain diseases produce absolute defects without accompanying or surrounding depression. One clue in such cases can be whether or not there is a generalized depression within the seeing area of a contracted field. Hence, if plotting a restricted field, it is never adequate simply to plot the outer boundary of a contracted field, but it must be determined what can or cannot be seen in the seeing zone. In other words, visual threshold must be determined in all the seeing area. This is important not only in establishing the diagnosis, but in being able to follow the progress of chronic conditions such as glaucoma.

Contraction

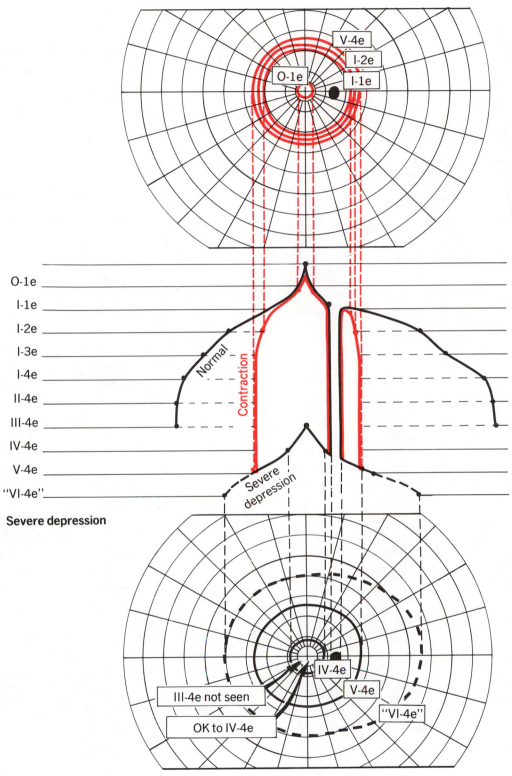

O-1e

I-1e

I-2e

I-3e

I-4e

II-4e

III-4e

IV-4e

V-4e

"VI-4e"

Severe depression

FIG. 13-5

153

CHAPTER 14

Advanced perimetric technique

REVIEW OF BASIC STEPS IN PERIMETRY

Before proceeding to advanced techniques, I will review the important details of the basic steps. Many of the basic rules are in the first portion of this book but are repeated because of their importance.

With the Goldmann perimeter, the visual field examination is performed in a darkened room with the doors closed so that there is no stray light shining in the bowl to create a non–standard background illumination, to cause uneven illumination within the bowl, or to cast shadows within the bowl. The intensity of the projected stimulus and the intensity of the background should be calibrated frequently (p. 138), especially if someone else has used the perimeter since you last used it.

As you may recall from Chapter 8, it is important to educate the patient about his task and to establish a pattern of good fixation and consistent responses. If the patient has not had field testing before, confrontation testing will teach the patient that he is supposed to report what he sees without looking directly at it. At the same time the confrontation testing will give you a general idea of the kind and severity of any major field defects present. At the perimeter, it is wise to start with the patient's better eye if he has not had a field test previously. The patient is shown a large object near fixation, a small object near fixation, a large object farther from fixation, and so on, until the patient understands that there will be several types of stimuli in various locations. This process of using several sizes of objects and making them appear and disappear in various areas should be continued until the patient's responses are consistent. *The perimetrist makes use of this phase of testing to note the consistency of the responses, the response time of the patient, and the general size of the visual field for various stimuli.* Finally, one should map the blind spot as a check on whether or not the patient is ready to proceed. To outline the absolute boundary of the physiologic blind spot, a small bright object (I-4e) should be used. If one is looking for depressed sensation around the blind spot ("enlarged blind spot"), the blind spot can be outlined also with a weaker stimulus. This may not be necessary if static spot checking with the appropriate test object is being used in the region around the blind spot. Of course, a stimulus stronger then I-4e will have to be used to outline the blind spot if the field is so depressed that the I-4e isopter does not enclose the position of the blind spot by a reasonable margin of 5 degrees or more.

It is important to choose the appropriate test stimuli, the areas of the field in which to concentrate your effort, and the strategy of the field examination. These decisions are based on the characteristics of the suspected field defect (that is, the reason for which it was decided to perform a visual field test) as well as on the responses obtained during the phase of education of the patient.

For example, knowing the location of a retinal lesion determines the correct location at which to search for a corresponding scotoma. Knowing that an optic nerve lesion is suspected as the cause of reduced acuity will allow the perimetrist to be particularly careful in seeking a central scotoma (pp. 238, 240 and 254). Knowing that the intraocular pressure is elevated will lead the perimetrist to look especially for paracentral scotomas and nasal steps (Chapters 11 and 18). Knowing that a pituitary tumor is suspected will induce the perimetrist to search for a hemianopia (pp. 200 and 256).

This approach not only saves time and energy of the patient and of the examiner but also makes the test more sensitive by concentrating on the areas where the visual field defects are most likely. One can therefore be more confident when no defect is found that indeed there is no defect, because one is sure that the right areas of the field have been checked carefully.

The small fixation mirror (p. 30) is used whenever it can be seen by the patient and the large fixation mirror is used only when the small one cannot be seen. The small mirror not only holds a steadier fixation but also automatically stimulates the appropriate degree of accommodation by the patient so that the fixation spot and the rest of the bowl will be in correct focus on the retina.

It is important to monitor fixation continuously. In particular, the examiner should be looking through the telescope as the test object is being moved inward kinetically so that the eye is monitored at the time just before the patient responds to be sure that he has not looked away for an instant (p. 36).

Corrective lenses (Chapter 10, p. 98) should be used inside 30 degrees, but loose corrective lenses should not be used outside 30 degrees. However, contact lenses can be used for the entire field. When testing outside 30 degrees, not only the lens but also the lens holder should be removed. (pp. 102 and 281) A common mistake is to believe that certain stimuli require correction and others do not. This is not the case. Correction is used for all stimuli when tested inside 30 degrees, but trial lenses are not used outside 30 degrees for any of the stimuli (p. 102). Of course, contact lenses may be used outside 30 degrees.

NONSEEING TO SEEING

An important general rule in kinetic perimetry is that the test stimulus should be moved from nonseeing areas to seeing areas. This applies to the plotting of ordinary isopters, as well as to the plotting of scotoma boundaries. This permits the greatest consistency of responses because it is physiologically easier for the patient to recognize when something *appears* rather than when something *disappears*.

Moreover, the technique of moving the object from a nonseeing area to a seeing area establishes the signal pattern that the patient responds whenever he sees the object. This pattern also occurs during static suprathreshold spot checking and static threshold perimetry, which also requires the patient to respond each time he sees the stimulus. It would be very confusing if, during kinetic perimetry, the patient were asked to respond when he does not see it and during static perimetry he is asked to respond when he does see it.

FIG. 14-1. Kinetic perimetry. In kinetic perimetry, in order to plot an isopter it is important to turn the stimulus on in a region thought to be nonseeing and then to pause a second to make sure that indeed it is not seen. Once it is certain that the stimulus is indeed not seen at the position where you turned it on, the stimulus is moved inward toward the seeing area. As soon as the patient responds, the stimulus is turned off. If the stimulus is kept on, the patient will be confused, not knowing whether or not he is expected to respond again.

The rate of movement of the stimulus should not be too great. The movement could be 1 degree per second in the central field for careful plotting of isopters and the boundary of scotomas, 2 to 3 degrees per second in the intermediate part of the field for ordinary isopter plotting, and up to 5 degrees per second in the most peripheral field. It is important to guard against moving the stimulus too fast. Those with previous experience at the tangent screen must be particularly cautious to move very slowly within the 30 degrees of the central field, remembering that the perimeter chart is miniaturized compared to the tangent screen, and one must move in miniature. The speed should be even slower than normal if the patient has a long response time, and the position of the isopter should occasionally be checked by static spot checking inside and outside the isopter (p. 174).

The rate of movement should be steady until the patient responds. Avoid slowing down when approaching the expected position of the isopter, as this increases the time interval of the stimulus being in the area where you think the isopter will be, thereby introducing a bias that the responses will occur where you expect the isopter rather than where it really is.

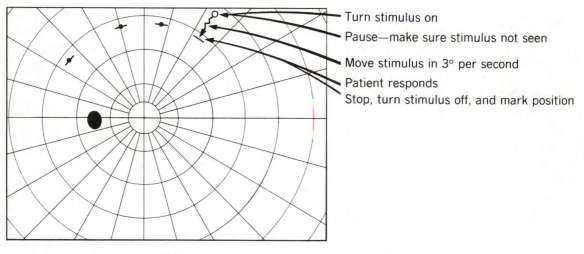

Turn stimulus on

Pause—make sure stimulus not seen

Move stimulus in 3° per second

Patient responds
Stop, turn stimulus off, and mark position

FIG. 14-1

It is a great time saver if the stimulus is turned on close to the expected position of the isopter (i.e., 5 to 10 degrees away) so that there is a short path of movement for only 1 or 2 seconds before the stimulus becomes seen. With a short path, a long wait by the patient between stimuli is avoided. Also, there is less temptation to move the stimulus too fast, the result of which is that the location of the isopter is determined carelessly. Moreover, with slow movement the stimulus approximates a static stimulus and the position of the isopter would closely approximate that which would be obtained if threshold were determined statically.

The danger in starting close to the expected position of the isopter is that you might inadvertently already be within the seeing zone when you first turn on the stimulus. This makes it important that you pause before beginning to move the stimulus (Fig. 14-1) to make absolutely certain that it is not seen before you begin to move it. If you move the stimulus immediately and if you have started inside the seeing zone, the patient will always respond several degrees inside where you started the kinetic paths and you will think you are plotting an isopter, but the true isopter might be much more peripheral. Also, if the patient responds the very instant you start to move it, you are too close to the isopter and you need to back up a little further into the nonseeing area.

You should not allow a long time to go without a stimulus being seen by the patient. Thus, if an isopter is being plotted and a stimulus does not become visible for several seconds, the stimulus should be moved into a position where it is known to have been seen, allowing him to respond, thereby reassuring him that the test is still in progress and keeping him from becoming frightened that he maybe is supposed to be seeing something but is not. It also reassures you that the patient is still alert and responding when he does see the stimulus. Then, continue moving the stimulus along the path in the area being tested until it becomes seen.

FIG. 14-2. An alternate method. When the patient does not respond at the expected position, move the stimulus very rapidly toward the seeing area until it does become visible and the patient does respond. This gives him the needed reassurance of not waiting too long and also saves you time by letting you know the approximate location of the isopter. Then you can back up a short distance along the same path using slower movement to obtain the precise location for the isopter. This method saves time if there are large irregular field defects.

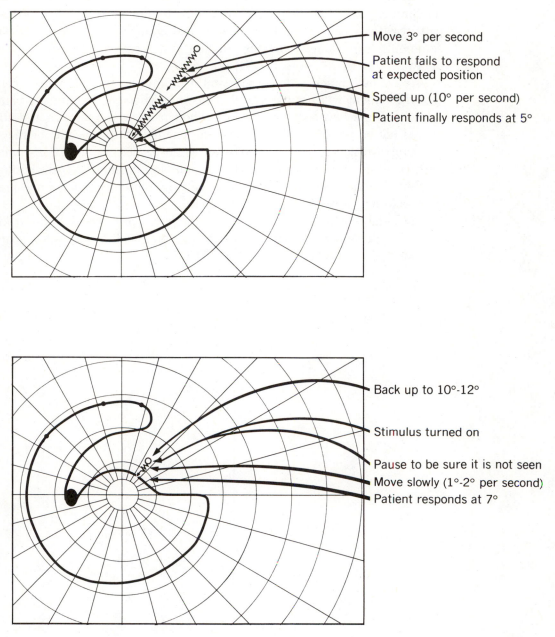

Move 3° per second

Patient fails to respond
at expected position

Speed up (10° per second)

Patient finally responds at 5°

Back up to 10°-12°

Stimulus turned on

Pause to be sure it is not seen

Move slowly (1°-2° per second)

Patient responds at 7°

FIG. 14-2

STATIC SPOT CHECKING

Similarly, during static spot checking, if you find three or four consecutive presentations that the patient cannot see, you should put the stimulus in an area where you know he can see, allow him to respond, and then return to exploring the apparent defect. This will reassure you that the machine continues to function properly and that the patient is paying attention, and equally important, the patient will not become tense waiting for a stimulus that seems quite delayed in coming. In fact, if you handle this situation with finesse, the patient may not even be aware that there are spots he is not seeing.

You should practice depressing and releasing the shutter switch silently, so that the patient will not have an audible clue when the stimulus is being presented. Also, when spot checking or when plotting the isopter, the stimulus should not be presented rhythmically, for example every second, or the patient will simply respond every second, even when he does not see the stimulus, or perhaps even continue to respond after you stop presenting the stimulus. The rhythm should be somewhat irregular, with no more than 10 normal presentations before a pause or break in the pattern.

Remember also that it is important to check *many* spots when looking for scotomas. Resist the temptation to cut corners by checking only a few spots. Spot checking is discussed further on pp. 170-176.

KEEPING THE PATIENT AT HIS BEST

Most patients need continual encouragement with voice contact. At first, you can say "Good!" after each response, and later, after each half a dozen responses or so. Do not be monotonous but on the other hand, do let the patient know you are there and that things are proceeding well. When you need 15 seconds to draw the isopter or to change pencils, take the opportunity to break the monotony by telling the patient to close his eyes and rest a minute. Otherwise he will spend that 15 seconds in a state of alert attention awaiting the next stimulus, fatiguing himself, and worrying about why there is no new stimulus.

The importance of the voice contact cannot be overemphasized. When a person is staring into empty white space with only monotonous brief flashes of light and monotonous buzzing, he will become sleepy. If he is motivated, he will fight to stay awake but in doing so will tire quickly. The examiner, by talking to the patient, can keep him awake just as a passenger talking to the driver on a long automobile journey may help keep him awake.

Encouraging words will also reduce anxiety and improve the quality of the responses. Anxiety may result from concern about whether or not they have lost vision but in addition many people are naturally anxious in any situation of "testing" in which they feel their performance is being judged.

Every person who performs perimetry should undergo visual field testing themselves to see how the light fades in and out and how there may be apparent flashes of light even when the stimulus is not being presented, thereby explaining occasional patient responses when there is no stimulus. The experience of undergoing perimetry will help you to understand and empathize with the patient, to be understanding about their inconsistencies, and to realize the importance of helping them with encouragement.

ADDITIONAL READINGS

Burke, R.M.: Static perimetry. In Thompson, H.S., and others: Topics in neuro-ophthalmology, Baltimore, 1979, The Williams & Wilkins Co., pp. 36-38.

Frisén, L.: Kinetic perimetry: techniques and strategies. In Thompson, H.S., and others: Topics in neuro-ophthalmology, Baltimore, 1979, The Williams & Wilkins Co., p. 21.

VISUAL THRESHOLD AS A ZONE

Until now, we have considered the isopter as the boundary between the seeing and nonseeing regions for the test stimulus. More accurately, there is a narrow zone around the isopter where the stimulus is sometimes seen and sometimes not, because it is barely visible at the isopter.

FIG. 14-3. Visual sensation in the region of an isopter.

In kinetic perimetry, the stimulus may be seen as it first enters the threshold zone or it may, on a second trial, be seen as it has almost passed through the zone. This can account for the patient's responses being somewhat inconsistent.

In static threshold perimetry, definitely infrathreshold stimuli are not seen at all. As the stimulus is made more intense, it becomes visible 10% to 25% of the time. As it is intensified, it is seen 50% of the time and eventually 75% to 90% of the time. Finally, it is seen 100% of the time.

We could define visual threshold as the stimulus intensity at which the stimulus is barely visible and is seen 50% of the time. As the stimulus is made more intense than the threshold stimulus, it seems brighter to the patient. If the stimulus is in the threshold zone it will seem quite dim—in fact, barely visible. When it is more intense, it will seem brighter and easier to see with certainty. If the stimulus is even more intense, it will seem quite bright (very easily seen), and the *apparent brightness is related to how much more intense than threshold the stimulus is* (p. 46). We will see the importance of this fact later (pages 172, 238 and 256). Finally, consider what would happen if the region of the isopter is explored with static spot checking. A short distance inside the isopter the test object should be seen consistently almost every time it is presented. A short distance outside the isopter it should never be seen. In the region right at the isopter there should be a zone within which the stimulus is sometimes seen and sometimes not. In this zone, the responses are not only inconsistent but also sometimes delayed with a long response time. This region is the zone of uncertainty, the zone of inconsistency, or the threshold zone.

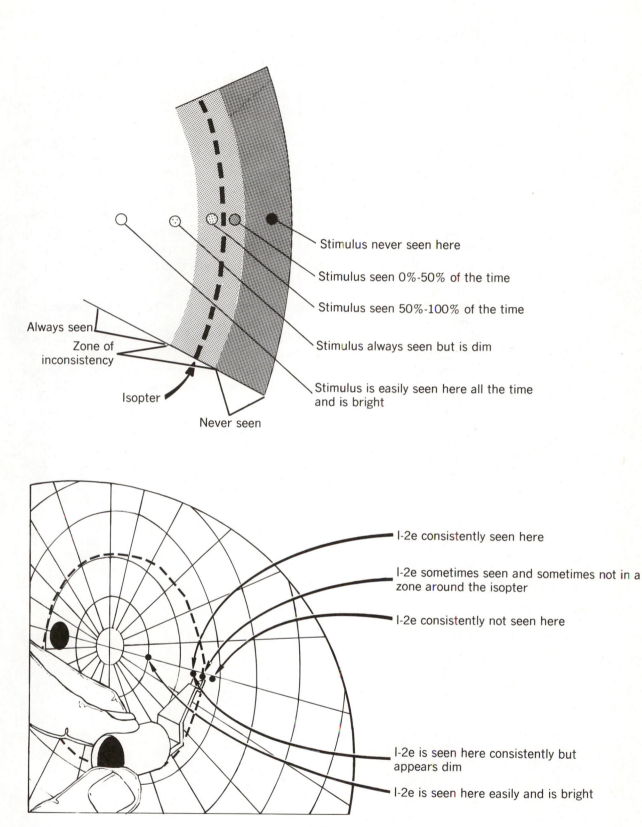

Stimulus never seen here

Stimulus seen 0%-50% of the time

Stimulus seen 50%-100% of the time

Stimulus always seen but is dim

Stimulus is easily seen here all the time
and is bright

Always seen
Zone of
inconsistency

Isopter

Never seen

I-2e consistently seen here

I-2e sometimes seen and sometimes not in a
zone around the isopter

I-2e consistently not seen here

I-2e is seen here consistently but
appears dim

I-2e is seen here easily and is bright

FIG. 14-3

163

CROSSING THE ISOPTER PERPENDICULARLY

FIG. 14-4. Effect of a nonperpendicular crossing on patient response. If the stimulus passes through the threshold zone perpendicular to the isopter, there is only a short distance over which the stimulus goes from definitely invisible to definitely visible. In fact, the patient may give a response within a narrow 2- to 3-degree zone rather consistently.

However, if the stimulus passes through the threshold zone at an angle and if the patient might respond any time while it is still in the threshold zone (after it leaves the definite nonseeing area but before it enters the definite seeing area), it is easy to see how the responses would be at varying locations.

The responses are thus more consistent when the kinetic stimulus crosses into a seeing zone perpendicular to the isopter. Obviously the best tactic in outlining an isopter is to move the kinetic stimulus perpendicular to the isopter, but of course the problem is that one does not know exactly where the isopter is until after it is plotted.

FIG. 14-5. Examples of irregular isopters that may not be crossed perpendicularly.
A, A nasal step may cause responses at 22, 32, and 42 degrees when the stimulus is passed along the horizontal meridian three times.
B, Imagine the perimetrist's confusion when the stimulus is passed along a path three times and three different locations of response are obtained.

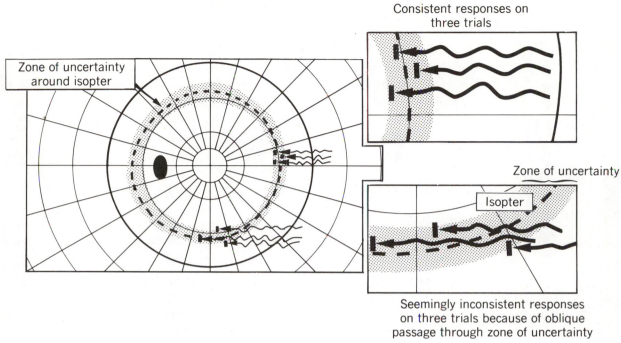

Consistent responses on
three trials

Zone of uncertainty
around isopter

Zone of uncertainty

Isopter

Seemingly inconsistent responses
on three trials because of oblique
passage through zone of uncertainty

FIG. 14-4

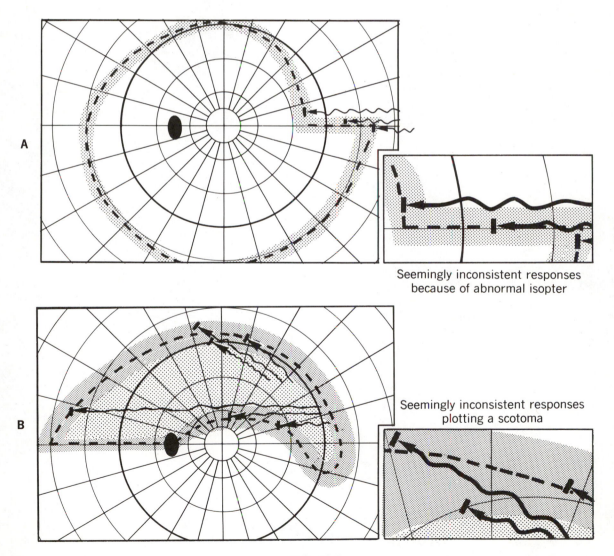

A

Seemingly inconsistent responses
because of abnormal isopter

B

Seemingly inconsistent responses
plotting a scotoma

FIG. 14-5

To achieve a perpendicular crossing of the isopter, the path of the stimulus should be toward fixation for the usual isopters. If a step is suspected because of responses that are different on the two sides of a meridian, the path should be in the path of an arc around fixation in the suspected location of the step, as was utilized to confirm the nasal step in glaucoma (p. 134).

In plotting scotomas, the examiner should move the stimulus away from the center of a round scotoma, perhaps in 8 meridians, as was illustrated previously for plotting the blind spot (p. 66). For arcuate scotomas, the paths could be away from fixation, toward fixation, or in an arcuate path pointed toward or away from the physiologic blind spot.

For plotting irregular isopters and scotomas whose outlines are not yet unfolded in the course of an examination, there is a trick that is helpful in achieving a nearly perpendicular approach to the isopter.

FIG. 14-6. An efficient way to find the contour of an abnormal isopter. The trick is to imagine a line connecting two previous response points and to aim the next path midway between the two points perpendicular to the imaginary line. Any time a region seems abnormal or there is a wide separation between two points on the isopter, more points should be plotted following this rule between each pair of previous points until the exact shape of the isopter is determined. Note that the method to confirm the presence of a nasal step is essentially the same principle of going perpendicular to a line connecting two points already plotted.

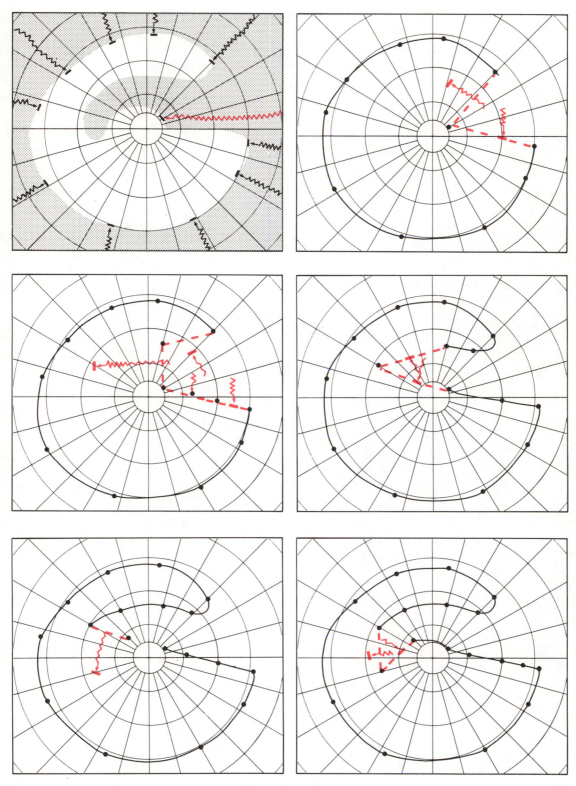

FIG. 14-6

THE SLOPE OF THE HILL OF VISION

We have just seen that there is a zone of uncertainty around the isopter and that in kinetic perimetry a stimulus may become visible at any point within that zone of uncertainty. If there is a long path through the zone of uncertainty, there is a long segment over which the stimulus may become visible and the results will seem inconsistent. The segment of the path within the zone of uncertainty is shortest and the responses are most consistent if the path is perpendicular to the isopter.

The breadth of the zone of uncertainty depends in part on the slope of the hill of vision at the isopter.

FIG. 14-7. Influence of the slope on the width of the zone of uncertainty. In the profile plot, the zone of uncertainty (shaded area) is the same height everywhere. In the isopter plot, the I-2e isopter in this example has a narrower zone of uncertainty than the I-3e isopter because the slope of the profile is steep near the I-2e isopter and flat near the I-3e isopter.

The slope influences the consistency of responses in both normal and abnormal regions of the visual field. In general, the responses during kinetic perimetry will be more consistent with a steep slope (isopters crowded together) than in a flat region of the field (isopters widely separated).

In some instances of a generalized depression (e.g., from cataracts or uncorrected refractive error), the hill of vision also becomes flatter. It also becomes flatter under mesopic or scotopic (dark-adapted) conditions instead of the photopic (light adapted) conditions of background illumination (p. 8) used for Goldmann perimetry. In these instances, isopters will be separated and the patient responses will be somewhat inconsistent with the exact location of the isopters more difficult to determine.

Of course, this is not the only reason for inconsistent patient responses. If the responses are inconsistent throughout all of the visual field with all test stimuli, it could also indicate that the patient is not a good subject for this kind of testing, or else that you have done a poor job of educating him in what is expected.

However, it is good to keep in mind that a flat hill of vision will produce inconsistent responses and inconsistency should be expected when isopters are widely separated (indicating a flat hill of vision).

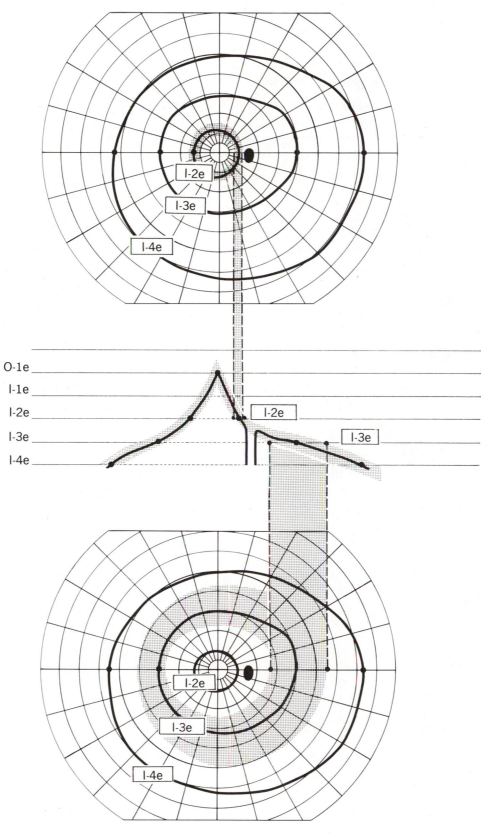

FIG. 14-7

LOCALIZED AREAS OF INCONSISTENT RESPONSES

If a patient has inconsistent responses only in a particular region of the visual field to a particular stimulus, this may indicate that the stimulus is right in the threshold zone for that particular region of the visual field. Often this represents the presence of a subtle abnormality.

FIG. 14-8. Localized inconsistent responses.

A, In this example, the responses are inconsistent just above the horizontal meridian but not below, suggesting an abnormality. Such an area should be labeled "inconsistent" to show that it is definitely an abnormal region, even though an exact isopter is not drawn. The plotting of additional isopters (in this example 0.2 log units above and below the threshold indicated by inconsistent responses) may or may not confirm that the region is abnormal by showing a nasal step.

B, Another example is an apparent scotoma. Static spot checking with I-3e reveals that the stimulus is seen only half the time or with a much slower response time in this particular location. Again, the thing that makes this area abnormal is that in surrounding areas the stimulus is definitely seen. The boundary of the abnormal region can be confirmed with a slightly weaker stimulus, I-3c, that forms an isopter closer to the region of inconsistent responses. With this stimulus the boundary of the scotoma is plotted. Moreover, an even weaker stimulus, I-3a, may show a deviation around the shallow scotoma.

The principle illustrated here is that localized inconsistent responses are a clue to the possibility of subtle abnormality. Inconsistent responses in kinetic plotting (Fig. 14-8, *A*) or in static spot checking (Fig. 14-8, *B*) are each quantitated by plotting additional isopters. If the unusual area is far from the original isopter, the new isopter should be just outside this region so that the weaker stimulus can be used for static spot checking—perhaps to define a scotoma. If, on the other hand, the area of inconsistent responses is nearer the original isopter, a new isopter that would normally pass through the region should be plotted, possibly indicating a localized depression and confirming that the area is, indeed, abnormal. The region of inconsistent responses should at least be indicated on the field diagram as a suspicious region, even if it cannot be defined as a genuine defect.

Another method for defining an area of inconsistent responses is discussed on p. 186.

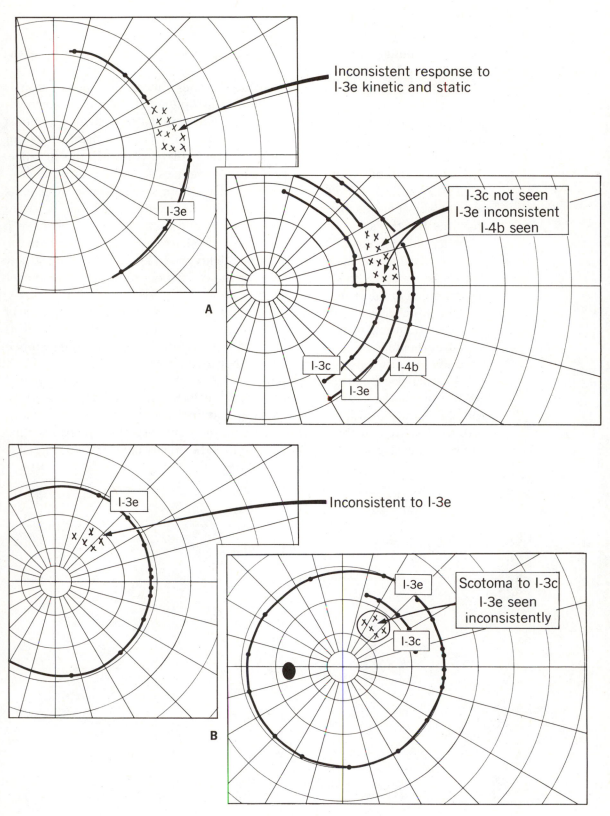

Inconsistent response to
I-3e kinetic and static

I-3e

A

I-3c not seen
I-3e inconsistent
I-4b seen

I-3c

I-3e

I-4b

Inconsistent to I-3e

I-3e

Scotoma to I-3c
I-3e seen
inconsistently

I-3e

I-3c

B

FIG. 14-8

THE DIM AREA

During static spot checking to look for scotomas, the patient may comment that the stimulus seems dimmer in a certain region. This area needs to be explained just like an area of inconsistent responses.

To understand the reason for localized dimness, recall that the stimulus is barely visible near its isopter but is subjectively brighter (more above threshold) in the region nearer fixation (p. 162-163). Conceivably, in a shallow scotoma nearer fixation (such as the one in Fig. 11-13, *A*, p. 127), the object may seem dimmer than in the surrounding region but may still be visible. In this instance, the patient responds with the buzzer because he does see it and, thus, the scotoma is not ordinarily detected. However, if a patient spontaneously comments that the object seems dimmer in a certain spot, the examiner needs to be aware that this has the same significance that slow and inconsistent responses in a particular location have. The patient's comment should alert the examiner to the possible presence of a scotoma. The possibility is explored by plotting a new isopter just outside the abnormal region, and by spot checking with the weaker test stimulus to uncover the scotoma.

The principle is that identical stimuli of the same intensity may seem to be of different brightness inside and outside an area of reduced vision. The stimulus is suprathreshold in both areas, but its apparent brightness depends on how much more intense it is than the threshold in that particular region.

As an analogy, consider a patient who has 20/20 vision in the right eye and 20/50 vision in the left. When asked to read the 20/80 line of letters, he can do so with either eye but will be able to tell you that the letters are blurred when seen with the left eye and sharp when seen with the right eye. Thus, he can see the letters with each eye but can also tell you that the quality of vision is not equal.

THE UPPER EYELID

A frequent problem is that the isopters are flattened more than the normal depression superiorly (p. 46) because of an overhang of the upper eyelid or eyebrow. The field seems depressed superiorly, simulating an altitudinal defect or an upper nasal depression typical of glaucoma (Fig. 21-6, p. 274). The perimetrist must be aware of this problem. Whenever there seems to be a visual depression superiorly, especially if the patient has a droopy upper eyelid or eyebrow, the isopter(s) should be rechecked with the eyelid elevated. Often the patient can simply be instructed to "open wide" while you check half a dozen points in the upper field to determine how much effect the eyelid is having. This extra effort to open the eyes widely may be tiring for the patient and it need not be maintained while the lower half or the lower two-thirds of the field is being tested. Nor is it necessary to continue raising the eyelid to test the upper part of the field once you have determined that the eyelid is not producing a problem in this particular patient. When the upper eyelid *is* being troublesome and the patient cannot open his eyes widely, you may have to have an assistant or the patient himself hold the upper eyelid up manually (without obstructing the field of view, however). Sometimes a small piece of tape is used to hold the eyelid up, but this is uncomfortable and should be used only for a minute or two to plot the upper segments of one or two isopters. The remainder of the field is tested and any necessary spot checking is completed without tape on the eyelids.

THE PROMINENT NOSE

In a similar way, the tip of the nose may interfere with the lower nasal quadrant of the visual field. This problem is overcome by having the patient turn his face slightly to the opposite side, e.g., to the left while testing the right eye. Interestingly, even with the nose well out of the way, there may normally remain a localized contraction of the visual field corresponding to the tip of the nose.

THE CORNEAL REFLECTION

If you look at the cornea carefully through the telescope, you can see the reflection of the test stimulus as you move it. If something, e.g., the nose, eyelid, or rim of the corrective lenses, is obstructing the patient's view of the stimulus, you can tell because there will be no corneal reflection. The reflection will appear on the cornea as soon as the stimulus moves to a position where its view is not obstructed. If the patient's response corresponds to the moment when the corneal reflection appears, you are plotting the boundary of the obstructing object and not an isopter of the visual field. When you are obtaining puzzling responses, observation of corneal reflection is reassuring that the projected test stimulus is actually on.

CREATIVE SPOT CHECKING

In Chapter 7 static spot checking to detect scotomas is discussed. However, there are other uses. For example, spot checking can be used to confirm the exact location of an isopter, especially in puzzling areas. Remember that the isopter separates the region where the stimulus is seen from the region where it is not seen. Therefore, you can use static spot checking to make sure the stimulus can be seen just inside where you think the isopter is, and that it cannot be seen just outside where you think the isopter is. This method can be used in a number of circumstances.

FIG. 14-9. Uses of static spot checking.

A, Checking the size of the blind spot. Sometimes if you are moving the stimulus too fast, the blind spot will be plotted larger than it really is as a result of the delay between the time when the patient sees the stimulus and the time when he responds. Occasionally, as a matter of *routine,* it is good to check yourself after plotting the blind spot kinetically by using static spot checking to see if the blind spot is really as large as you plotted it.

B, Confirming a nasal step. We have already noted (p. 134) that one way to confirm a nasal step is to move the stimulus vertically across the step. Sometimes the situation still may not be clear, especially if the step is not exactly on the horizontal meridian, and static spot checking can be used to locate the isopter.

C, Checking ordinary isopters. Once or twice on each patient you should briefly check one or two of the isopters, even if they seem normal, just to be sure that you are not being fooled by a slow response time, a bias in your technique (pp. 156 and 158), or some other quirk. There is no end to possible quirks. For example, when an isopter is plotted kinetically, the patient may see the stimulus when it is first turned on but may think he is not to respond until it moves: he does not respond during the pause before the stimulus is moved, but does respond after it starts to move but with a delay. The examiner may think he is plotting an isopter.

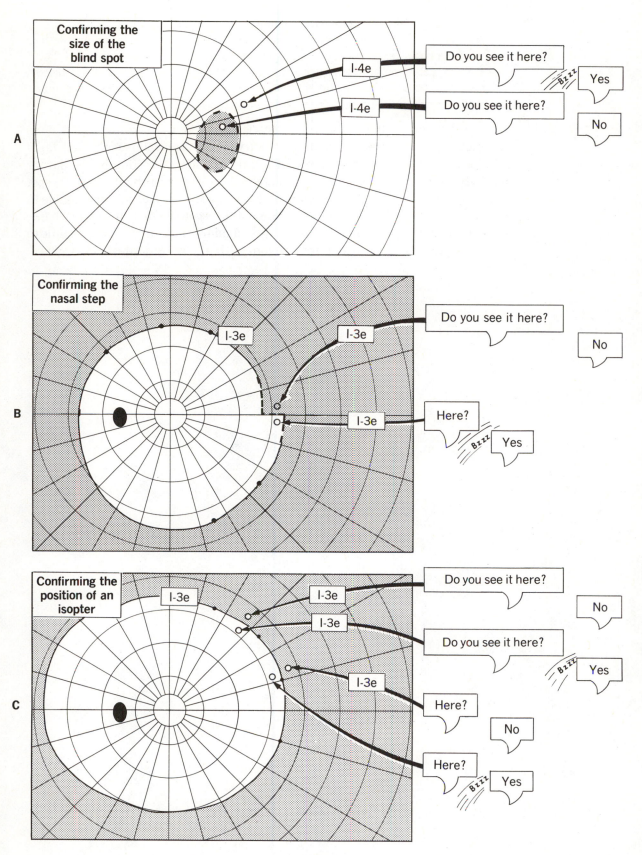

FIG. 14-9

FIG. 14-10. Static spot checking to confirm the boundary of a scotoma.
A, Based on seven patient responses, including one erroneous response, an oval scotoma is outlined instead of the arcuate scotoma that is actually present.
B, With static spot checking, the oval boundary is not confirmed, and it is discovered that the scotoma is larger than had been plotted. Exact boundaries are important in following the progress of scotomas or other abnormalities.

You should not check each point statically—it would take too much time. After all, the reason you use kinetic perimetry to plot the isopters is that it is rapid and for the most part very accurate (if you do not move the stimulus too fast or mark the responses on the chart too sloppily). However, you should do static spot checking whenever you are uncertain of the boundary, such as in this example in which you might reasonably have wondered if this scotoma had an arcuate shape. Occasional static spot checking also lets you monitor the patient's reaction time to near-threshold targets—which may be longer than for suprathreshold targets.

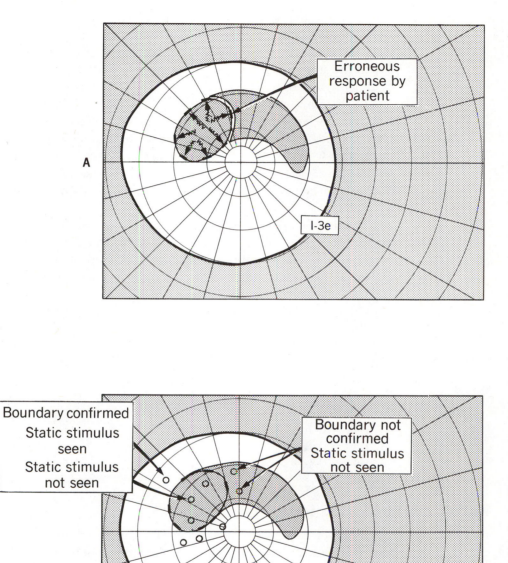

FIG. 14-10

STANDARD STIMULI

Except for very special purposes, only standard stimuli are used: 0-1, I-1, I-2, I-3, I-4, II-4, III-4, IV-4, and V-4. With each of these, the brightness of any of the subdivisions *a* through *e* may be used.

This selection of stimuli derives from the fact that size I is the standard size for Goldmann perimetry and it is used with the entire range of twenty different light intensities from 1a through 4e. The larger sizes *II* through *V* are utilized only if the strongest stimulus of standard size, I-4e, is too weak in a region of the field being tested.

At the other end of the range, if I-1a is too strong for testing near the very center of the field, there are two ways to achieve a weaker stimulus. One method is by use of a 2-log–unit filter (represented by a single bar), beginning the series again at I-4e. Thus, in 0.5 log unit steps, in descending order of intensity, the stimuli are: I-3e, I-2e, I-1e, I-$\overline{4e}$, I-$\overline{3e}$,. . . . In descending order of intensity in 0.1-log–unit steps, the stimuli are: . . ., I-1c, I-1b, I-1a, I-$\overline{4e}$, I-$\overline{4d}$, I-$\overline{4c}$, . . . (see p. 47, Fig. 6-1.)

Should it happen that the I-1a stimulus is still not sufficiently weak, it is possible to place a 4-log–unit filter (represented by a double bar), again beginning at the top of the series with 4e. Thus, in 0.1-log–unit steps, in order of descending intensity, the stimuli would be: . . ., I-$\overline{\overline{1c}}$, I-$\overline{\overline{1b}}$, I-$\overline{\overline{1a}}$, I-$\overline{\overline{4e}}$, I-$\overline{\overline{4d}}$, I-$\overline{\overline{4c}}$, ...

On those perimeters that are not equipped with a 2-log–unit and a 4-log–unit filter, an option is to use the reduced size, *0*, but only with intensities 1e through 1a. Thus, in descending order of stimulus strength, the stimuli are: . . ., I-1c, I-1b, I-1a, 0-1e, 0-1d, 0-1c, 0-1b, and 0-1a. In terms of visibility, 0-1e is roughly equivalent to I-$\overline{4e}$, 0-1d is roughly equivalent to I-$\overline{4d}$, and so on:

. . .

I-1b	I-$\overline{4b}$ = 0-1b
I-1a	I-$\overline{4a}$ = 0-1a
I-$\overline{4e}$ = 0-1e	I-$\overline{3e}$
I-$\overline{4d}$ = 0-1d	I-$\overline{3d}$
I-$\overline{4c}$ = 0-1c	. . .

REPRESENTING THE STIMULI

It is useful to have a color code for the various stimuli, using dense colors for strong stimuli and light colors for weak stimuli, such as:

V-4 black	I-4 red
IV-4 brown	I-3 orange
III-4 purple	I-2 blue
II-4 green	I-1 yellow
	0-1 pink

With these colors, the isopters are drawn and a check mark placed in the appropriate box in the lower right hand corner of the field diagram. A region can be marked "O.K." in the appropriate color, indicating that that region was searched with that test object by static spot checking, and no scotomas were found. Thus, "O.K." written in blue indicates that that region was checked by static spot checking wih the I-2 test stimulus and it was seen throughout that region. If the same color code is used routinely, it makes it easier to compare successive field tests to look for progressive change in the visual field.

To represent scotomas, the nonseeing areas to a particular test stimulus are colored in. Thus, the scotomatous region might be colored red within the region where the I-4 is not seen. The surrounding larger area where the I-2 is not seen would be colored blue. The center would be marked "II-4 seen," indicating that that is the threshold value in this location where the I-4 is not seen. If the blind spot has been plotted with the I-4 test stimulus, it is colored red. For a steep-walled scotoma, the scotoma boundary is outlined with the weakest stimulus and filled in with the color of the strongest stimulus to which there is a scotoma. Areas of inconsistent or slow responses are marked with a cross hatching in the appropriate color, indicating which stimulus was giving inconsistent responses.

LABELING THE CHART

The perimetrist must in some sense interpret the responses of the patient and be sure that the visual field chart correctly reflects what transpired while the visual field test was being performed. Only the perimetrist knows what actually occurred during the field testing and this information must be transmitted on the visual field chart. Areas of inconsistent responses must be so labeled—do not just draw in an isopter where you think it might be without indicating that there was some question about its location, or that there were inconsistent responses in a particular portion of the field. This information could be very important.

The consistency of the responses, the steadiness of fixation, and whether or not the patient was particularly slow in responses, generally, and the overall reliability of the field should be indicated. Obviously it is important to know whether the patient had inconsistent responses everywhere in the field (indicating a flat hill of vision [p. 168] or an unreliable field) or had inconsistent responses only in one place (indicating a localized abnormality). It is important to know these things if diagnostic and therapeutic decisions are going to be made on the basis of the visual field (p. 260). It becomes especially important in clinics where over a period of years the patient may be cared for by several different physicians, where the perimetry is not performed by the physician only, or where the perimetrist might not be the same person each year. The nonphysician perimetrist has a special obligation not only to be knowledgeable, but also to record accurately the results so that the physician can make adequate diagnostic and therapeutic decisions. Labels such as "I-4e seen, but I-1 not seen" or "depression still present when eyelid taped up" shows that the perimetrist was alert, knew to do these extra steps, and actually did them.

Of course, the field chart must also be labeled with the first and last name of the patient, the date, including the year, the examiner's name, whether the eye was right or left, the correction used, the visual acuity, the pupil size, and (if customary to measure) the intraocular pressure.

CHAPTER 15

Static threshold perimetry: the static cut and related procedures

CURRENT STATUS OF STATIC THRESHOLD PERIMETRY

Static threshold perimetry has been used almost exclusively in specialized institutions, mainly research centers. One reason is that only in these centers can be found the expensive Tübinger perimeter of Harms and Aulhorn (Oculus) designed with static perimetry in mind; the commonly available Goldmann perimeter is, in comparison, awkward for this purpose. Another reason is that static threshold perimetry requires a sophistication in comprehension and interpretation of visual fields that is just now becoming prevalent among ophthalmologists. A third reason is that, although the importance of high-quality perimetry is becoming increasingly evident, the role of static threshold perimetry to supplement kinetic perimetry with static spot checking in the everyday ophthalmic practice is not yet certain.

The attitude toward and the usefulness of static threshold perimetry may well change with the increasing emphasis on visual field testing. Moreover, most of the automatic perimeters now becoming available determine visual threshold statically. Therefore, it is important to understand the principles of static threshold perimetry, its relationship to kinetic perimetry, and its potential usefulness, especially if the newer instruments are to be used intelligently.

SUPRATHRESHOLD VERSUS THRESHOLD

In static *supra*threshold perimetry, which we have called "spot checking," an area is explored with a suprathreshold stimulus that is expected to be easily visible. With this method, the exact visual threshold is not determined. What is determined is that in regions where the stimulus is visible the threshold is some stimulus weaker than the one being used. By way of analogy, if a person is asked to read the 20/40 visual acuity line when being tested for a driver's license what is being determined is that that person's visual acuity is either "20/40 or better" or "less than 20/40."

In static threshold perimetry, the exact visual threshold is determined at selected points. If the threshold is determined at a series of points along a line, the procedure is called "static profile perimetry" or a "static cut." The line along which threshold is determined is typically a meridian (meridional static cut) but may be an arc or any other line.

FIG. 15-1. Meridional static cut through a scotoma. Threshold is determined along the 315-degree meridian, from 1 to 33 degrees from fixation at 2-degree intervals.

The static cut along a meridian is but one form of static threshold perimetry.

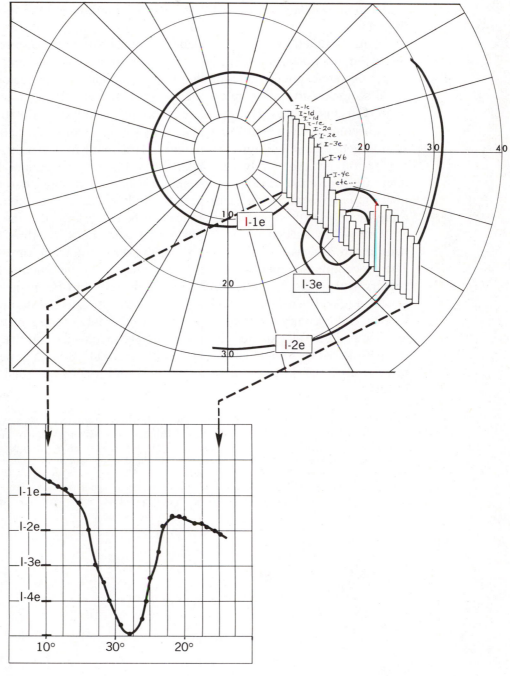

FIG. 15-1

SPECIAL FEATURES OF STATIC PERIMETRY

One helpful feature of static perimetry is that it is not affected by the patient's reaction time. The stimulus is presented and it does not matter if the patient responds ½ second later or 3 seconds later. In kinetic perimetry the examiner wants to know *when* the patient first sees the stimulus and the reaction time is important.

Static perimetry gives a very accurate threshold determination at each point tested, but the price paid is time and a limited number of points can be tested. It is used to good advantage to quantitate very accurately central scotomas or other small scotomas, to explore questionable areas, and in other situations to be described in this chapter. However, the technique of kinetic perimetry with static spot checking is often more efficient in rapidly giving more information about the field in general and outlining the extent of large defects.*Even centers that use static perimetry extensively will use kinetic perimetry to gain general information about the individual's field of vision and to select the locations deserving careful quantitation by static threshold perimetry. Indeed, kinetic perimetry may be required at times to be sure that the static cut is being performed in the right place.†

Once it is decided where in the visual field the static threshold is to be determined, it does not take much skill to perform the static threshold testing. The procedure is rather regimented. In contrast, the technique of kinetic perimetry with static spot checking requires decisions to be made continuously concerning additional points and isopters to be plotted, as the nature of the field unfolds and becomes apparent to the examiner, or for certain apparently normal areas to be less well explored. Thus, kinetic perimetry relies on the judgment of the perimetrist that comes with experience and skill. Automatic perimeters are more easily programmed to examine the field in a regimented fashion by static means.

---

*Aulhorn, E.: Static perimetry, Annee Ther. Clin. Ophthalmol. **25**:164-173, 1974; Aulhorn, E., and Harms, H.: Visual perimetry. In Jameson, D. and Hurvich, L.M., editors: Visual psycophysics, Handbook of sensory physiology, vol. 7, no. 4, New York, 1972, Springer-Verlag, pp. 102-145; Greve, E.L., Furuno, F., and Verduin, W.M.: A critical phase in the development of glaucomatous visual field defects, Doc. Ophthalmol. Proc. Series **19**:127-136, 1979.
†Aulhorn, E., Harms, H., and Karmeyer, H.: The influence of spontaneous eye rotation on the perimetric determination of small scotomas. Doc. Ophthalmol. Proc. Series **19**:363-367, 1979.

TECHNIQUE OF DETERMINING THRESHOLD AT A POINT

After the projector arm of the perimeter is positioned at the desired spot, a stimulus of standard size (I for the Goldmann perimeter) is flashed for ½ to 1 second at a presumed slightly infrathreshold intensity. Provided that the patient, as expected, does not respond to the first stimulus, a stimulus of the next brightest intensity is presented for ½ to 1 second. The stimulus is kept on for at least ½ second to be sure that maximum temporal summation has occurred (p. 8). The duration is no longer than 1 second, with a 2-second pause between stimuli to avoid light adaptation at the site being tested, which would reduce light sensitivity at that spot. Increasingly intense stimuli are presented until the patient finally does see the stimulus. The stimulus first seen can be recorded as threshold. To be sure of the accuracy, it is best if at least two stimuli presentations are invisible (confirming that the initial test stimulus is infrathreshold) before reaching the intensity that becomes visible.

Usually each location is tested in this manner only once, provided the threshold value obtained is in keeping with what is expected, taking into account the threshold value obtained at the adjacent points. However, if there is doubt or if for some reason the visual threshold is to be determined with special care, the stimulus first seen should be presented a second time (double-checking) to confirm that it is visible.* If missed on the second presentation, it is presented a third and a fourth time, and it may be counted as "visible" if it is seen on both the third and fourth presentations. Recall that a stimulus right at threshold (or within the threshold zone) may be seen only a certain percentage of the time. In the double-checking method, a stimulus is counted as threshold if it is the weakest stimulus seen at all and if it is seen more than half of the time, i.e., more than two out of four presentations. If there is doubt, stimuli one or two steps more intense can be presented to confirm that they are suprathreshold. If there is a wide range of stimuli for which the responses are inconsistent only in a specific area this information should be recorded.

---

*Burde, R.M.: Static perimetry. In Thompson, H.S. and others: Topics in neuro-ophthalmology, Baltimore, 1979, The Williams & Wilkins Co., pp. 30-45; Ellenberger, C., Jr.: Perimetry, Int. Ophthalmol. Clin. **17**(1):85-113, 1977.

Greve uses yet another strategy.[1] The stimulus intensity is increased with each presentation until the patient responds. After the first response, the stimulus is increased in intensity one more step and presented again. If the patient also responds for this one, the dimmer one at which the patient first responded is considered the threshold. However, if the patient does not respond to the second stimulus, slightly more intense than the one to which he first responded, then the response is considered to have been a false response. In that case, the process of presenting stimuli in increasing intensity is continued until the patient sees two in a row. The first response of a pair is considered the threshold.

Another strategy is to find rapidly one stimulus that is infrathreshold and one that is suprathreshold to estimate the threshold, and then to approach the threshold in steps from both sides. It is certainly wise to have an estimate of the range in which threshold will be found at a spot. Especially in an abnormal region of the field, estimating may save time by avoiding presentation of many stimuli far below threshold before finally reaching threshold. While narrowing the estimated range, the presentation of some stimuli above threshold may also reassure the patient and the examiner by not having several consecutive presentations that are invisible. However, this is usually not necessary. The usual method is simply to approach threshold from below threshold but to start only slightly below the expected threshold based on the threshold of an adjacent point or determined by a quick estimating technique.[1]

---

[1]Greve, E.L., and Verduin, W.M.: Detection of early glaucomatous damage. I. Visual field examination, Doc. Ophthalmol. Proc. Series **14**:103-114, 1977.

The circumstances will dictate the exactness with which threshold is determined. For example, if it is determined that I-le and I-2e are not seen but I-3e and I-4e are seen in a specific location, it has been determined to the nearest 0.5 log unit that the I-3e stimulus is the visual threshold; actually, the visual threshold is somewhere between I-2e and I-3e, which are stimuli with intensities 0.5 log units apart. However, if it has been determined that stimuli I-1e, I-2a, and I-2b are not seen, while I-2c, I-2d, etc., are seen, the visual threshold has been determined to be I-2c with 0.1 log unit accuracy (or, better stated, the visual threshold is somewhere between I-2b and I-2c, which are 0.1 log unit apart). For convenience, we will simply say that the visual threshold is I-2c, the weakest stimulus visible. It would be usual for the visual threshold to be determined by using stimuli 0.1 log unit apart in intensity.

Note the equivalence here between the accuracy with which threshold is determined by kinetic or static threshold perimetry. If isopters 0.5 log unit apart (e.g., I-2e and I-3e) are plotted, and if the region between them is spot-checked with the stronger stimulus, I-3e in this case, it is known with 0.5 log unit accuracy that the threshold is between I-2e (which is not seen, being outside the I-2e isopter) and I-3e (which is seen, as determined by static spot checking). However, if isopters 0.2 log unit apart (e.g., I-2b and I-2d) are plotted and the region between them is spot-checked with the stronger stimulus, the threshold in this region is known with 0.2 log unit accuracy to be between I-2b and I-2d.

Typically in static threshold perimetry with the Oculus or Goldmann perimeter, threshold is determined to an accuracy of 0.1 log unit. The strategy might be to obtain a gross estimate of threshold in steps of 0.5 log unit (I-2e, I-3e, I-4e). If the I-3e is visible but the I-2e is not, then the sequence I-3a, I-3b, I-3c, and I-3d is presented to determine threshold to the nearest 0.1 log unit. Sometimes, especially in a normal region, the perimetrist has a good idea of what the threshold will be, based on the threshold at an adjacent spot or based on knowing where isopters have been plotted. Then the examiner can start 0.2 or 0.3 log units below the anticipated threshold, confirm that this stimulus is not seen, and increase the stimulus in steps of 0.1 log unit. In this way, threshold may be determined efficiently with only three or four presentations at each location. Estimating the threshold in steps of 0.5 log unit before refining the determination in 0.1 log unit steps becomes necessary only when an unexpected abnormality is encountered.

APPLICATION

In *kinetic perimetry,* it is necessary to choose which isopters to plot, how many to plot, and in what region of the field to concentrate. With *static supra-threshold spot checking,* it is necessary to select a region in the field to be spot-checked, how many points to spot-check, and the proper stimulus to use in specific region.

Similarly, in *static threshold perimetry,* there are choices to make. It is important to select which areas of the field to test, how many points to test, with what accuracy threshold is to be determined at each point, and the distribution of points (e.g., scattered in a grid pattern, along a meridian, or along an arc). Depending on circumstances and the diagnostic information desired, points, 1, 2, 3, or 5 degrees apart may be tested along a straight line, in grid pattern, or along an arc. Examples follow.

Scotoma

A static cut can be used to confirm the presence of and to quantitate a suspected scotoma, for example, the one in Fig. 14-8, p. 171.

FIG. 15-2, A. Static cut through a scotoma. If there is an area of inconsistent responses to static spot checking, it may be faster to perform a single static cut than to plot one or two additional partial isopters plus the boundary of the scotoma, as in Fig. 14-8.

For large scotomas or for elongated arcuate scotomas it may be desirable to plot two or three static cuts along adjacent meridians.

FIG. 15-2, B. Static cuts through an arcuate scotoma.

A static cut may determine the depth and slope of the boundary very accurately. However, several adjacent cuts may be required to determine the boundary or extent of a defect (p. 192) and, especially if the defect is large, it may be more efficiently determined by kinetic means (pp. 58 and 182).

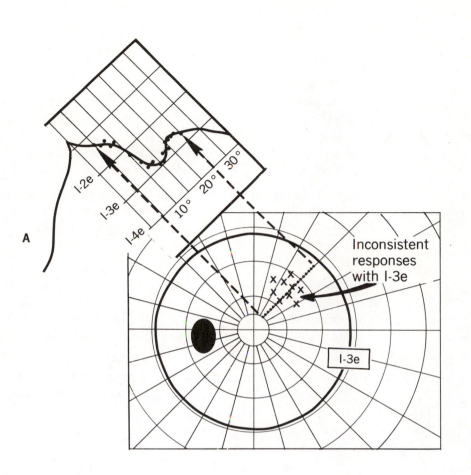

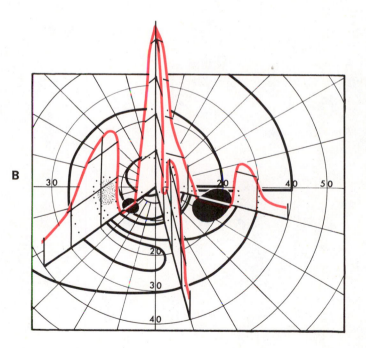

FIG. 15-2

Single point static threshold

We are already familiar with determining static threshold at a single point. When determining the depth of a scotoma, the stimulus strength was increased until it first became visible (p. 60). The point was appropriately labeled to indicate the threshold (i.e., "I-2e seen").

There are other occasions when it may be useful to check the threshold of individual points, for example in the region of an uncertain nasal step.

FIG. 15-3, A. Inconsistent responses to kinetic perimetry above the horizontal meridian between 30 and 40 degrees. If the threshold at 35 degrees is I-4b above the horizontal meridian but I-3b below, the difference in visual threshold is 0.5 log unit. Note how this is equivalent to Fig. 14-8, but the presence of an abnormality is documented by a different technique.

Threshold testing at selected single points may help clarify the nature of the visual field in other situations. For example, in a flat region of the field with widely separated isopters and difficulty in plotting an exact location of the isopters because of inconsistent responses (p. 168), it may be useful to determine that a somewhat stronger stimulus is seen everywhere.

FIG. 15-3, B. Flat depressed field with inconsistent response to I-4e. In the inconsistent area, II-4e is seen everywhere. This type of field is typical of cataract.

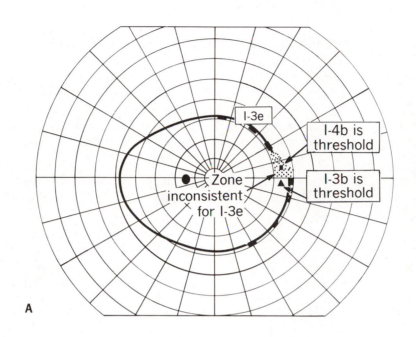

A

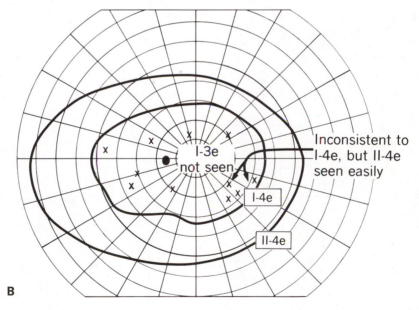

B

FIG. 15-3

Circular or arc cuts

The static cut need not be along a meridian (meridional static cut); it may be along an arc.

FIG. 15-4. Static cut along an arc through a nasal step. There is a sharply demarcated difference in visual threshold above and below the horizontal meridian, whereas normally there is no such difference. This method is a refinement of the single point static threshold perimetry (Fig. 15-3, *A*), and is an alternative method to spot checking (Fig. 14-9, *B*), plotting the isopter kinetically along an arc (Fig. 11-17), or plotting additional isopters (Fig. 14-8). Each method confirms the presence of an abnormality. Artful combination and variation of these methods are useful when there is doubt about the presence or absence of an abnormality such as a nasal step.

Arc cuts can be used in a similar way to confirm or deny the presence of a step along the vertical meridian in the case of suspected hemianopia (see Chapter 16, p. 258).

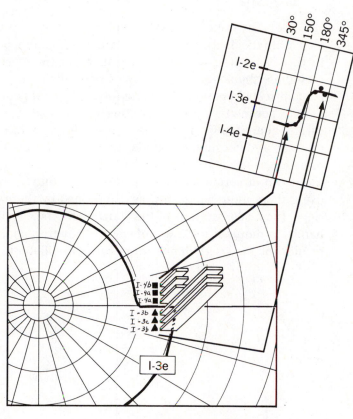

FIG. 15-4

"Scatterplot" threshold perimetry

Threshold determinations can be made in any pattern of locations, not only along a single meridian or an arc but also along several adjacent meridians or arcs.

FIG. 15-5. Scattergram threshold perimetry.

A, Visual threshold has been determined at 64 points 1 degree apart. The results can be represented as a series of 8 meridional cuts or as a series of 8 arc cuts.

B, The scattergram is equivalent to the plotting of multiple isopters.

C, Representation of threshold by symbol can give a visual impression of the varying depth in the scotoma. More examples of scatterplots can be found on pp. 224-225, 263, and 269.

The basic principle of visual field testing (p. 9) is to determine visual threshold within the field of vision. Visual threshold cannot be determined in every point in the visual field—there are too many of them. However, it is important to quantitate the abnormal areas more carefully than elsewhere. Now we see that static threshold perimetry (represented by several cuts or by a scattergram) and kinetic perimetry with the plotting of multiple isopters can each accomplish careful quantitations in regions of special interest. Kinetic perimetry may be more efficient in determining boundaries of large defects than static threshold determination at several points, but static determination may be better for quantitating the depth of certain defects (p. 186). Versatility in understanding both and in using them interchangeably, as determined by the nature of the defect (i.e., its slope, the responsiveness of the patient, and the capabilities of the instrument at hand), is required to be a proficient perimetrist and to be able to compare the results obtained with different machines in different modes.

A

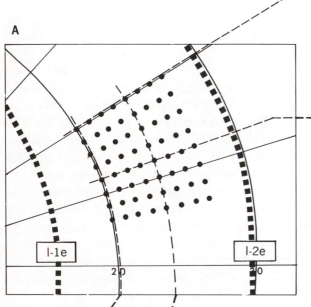

I-1e   20   I-2e

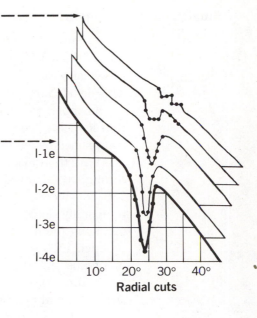

I-1e
I-2e
I-3e
I-4e

10°   20°   30°   40°

Radial cuts

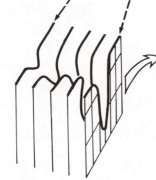

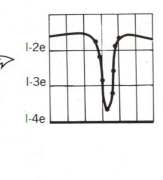

I-2e
I-3e
I-4e

Arc cuts

B

I-2a   I-2c   I-2d
I-2b
I-3e
I-2e

I-1e   0   20   I-2e

C

■ I-4a to I-4e
▲ I-3a to I-3e
⊙ I-2a to I-2e

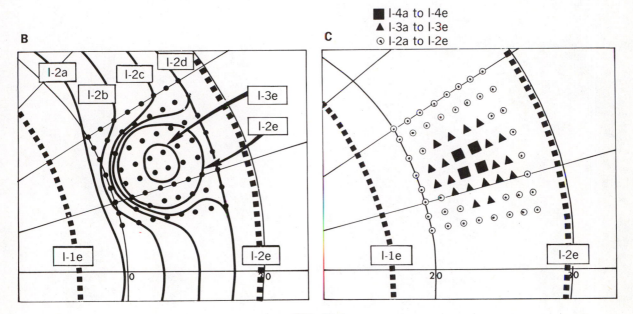

I-1e   20   I-2e

FIG. 15-5

Small island of remaining vision

Because the telescope port occupies 2 degrees around the fixation target, this area of the field cannot be tested with the Goldmann perimeter except by utilizing a special device that projects a fixation target away from the center of the bowl. This device projects a diamond of four red spots, and the patient is told to fixate on the apparent center of the diamond. The visual field chart is slid to one side so that its center corresponds to the position of the projected diamond; this is accomplished by aligning the short line on the bottom of the paper in the V-notch.

With this device, the central 2 degrees can be quantitated, e.g., by a static cut through the central 5 degrees along the 45- to 225-degree meridian and the 135- to 315-degree meridian. Cuts through the 90- to 270-degree meridian and temporally along the 0- to 180-degree meridian can also be performed, although a cut along the nasal side is avoided because it may course along a nasal step and produce inconsistent responses. Of course, plotting along so many adjacent meridians amounts to a static scatterplot. Equally valid is to plot very carefully two or three isopters to weak stimuli. With any technique, or with a combination, one can afford plenty of time to be very accurate, since there is so little field area to quantitate. When such care is exercised, e.g., for a glaucoma patient, very slight changes over a period of time can be detected, perhaps allowing more vigorous treatment to be instituted before all is lost.

FIG. 15-6. The small central island. A multiple isopter plot is compared to a static cut through a small severely contracted field.

ADDITIONAL READINGS

Additional examples in which static perimetry is useful in clinical practice can be found in the following articles:

Burde, R.M.: Static perimetry. In Thompson, H.S., and others: Topics in neuro-ophthalmology, Baltimore, 1979, The Williams & Wilkins Co., pp. 38-44.

Ellenberger, C., Jr.: Modern perimetry in neuro-ophthalmic diagnosis, Arch. Neurol. **30:**193-201, 1974.

Greve, E.L.: Visual fields, glaucoma, and cataract, Doc. Ophthalmol. Proc. Series **22:**79-88, 1979.

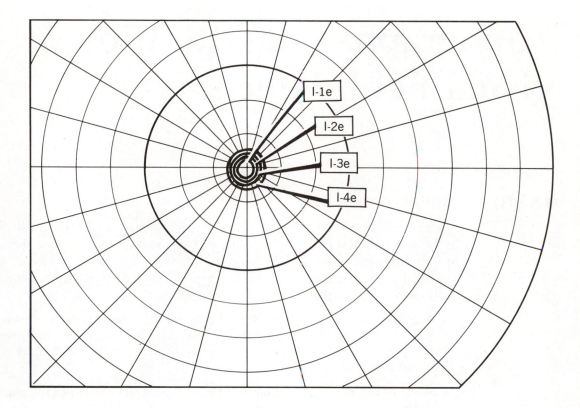

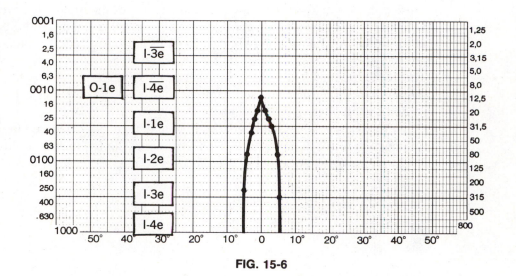

FIG. 15-6

CHAPTER 16

Topographic classification of visual field defects

ANATOMIC BASIS

So far, we have concentrated on the visual field defects of glaucoma because in the usual clinical practice this is the most common type. However, there are many other types of visual field defects. All field defects can be classified topographically as prechiasmal, chiasmal, or postchiasmal, as determined by the anatomic location of the disease that produced the visual abnormality.

FIG. 16-1. Anatomic basis of topographic classification. The optics of the eye (cornea and lens, Fig. 2-1, p. 18) focus an image on the retina. The retina converts the light to nervous impulses that are processed and conducted ultimately to the occipital, or visual, cortex.

Some of the nerve fibers from each eye cross at the chiasm to the opposite side of the brain in such a manner that impulses derived from objects to the right side of the field of vision are received by the left visual cortex and objects to the left, by the right visual cortex. Thus, a stimulus in the right (temporal) visual field of the right eye is seen by the nasal retina of the right eye and nerves carrying these impulses cross at the chiasm to the left side of the brain. However, objects to the left of fixation seen by the right eye in its nasal visual field stimulate points in the temporal retina of the right eye. Nervous impulses from the temporal retina are carried by nerve fibers that do not cross the chiasm, but remain on the right side of the brain. Note that the point that divides the nasal and temporal halves of the retina is the fovea (represented by fixation), not the optic nerve head (represented by the physiologic blind spot).

In this chapter the characteristics of field defects are discussed in relation to the location of the lesion in the visual pathway. The techniques to look for different types of defects are discussed in later chapters.

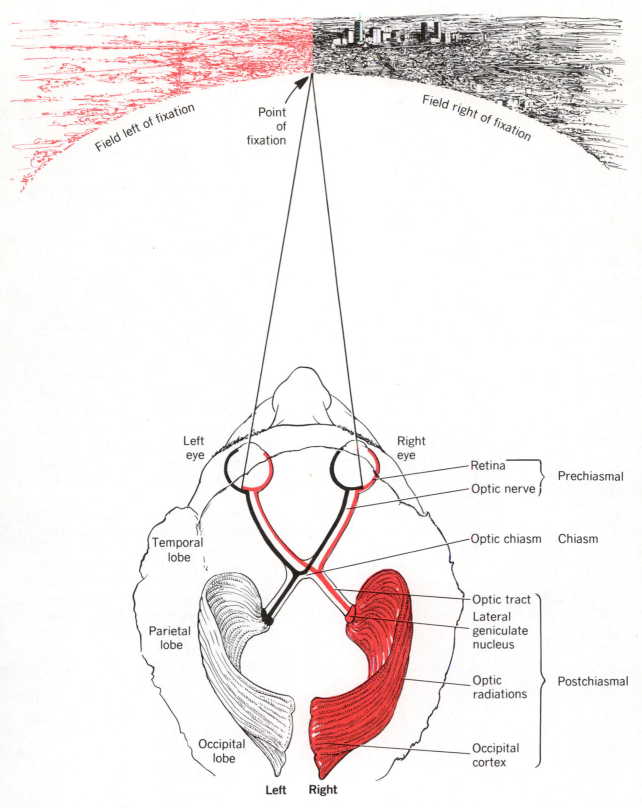

Field left of fixation

Point of fixation

Field right of fixation

Left eye

Right eye

Retina

Optic nerve

Prechiasmal

Temporal lobe

Optic chiasm

Chiasm

Parietal lobe

Optic tract
Lateral geniculate nucleus

Optic radiations

Postchiasmal

Occipital lobe

Occipital cortex

Left   Right

FIG. 16-1

197

PRECHIASMAL VISUAL FIELD DEFECTS

Prechiasmal lesions include abnormalities in the refractive properties and transparent ocular media of the eye (cornea, lens, vitreous), as well as a wide variety of diseases affecting the retina and optic nerve. Glaucoma, a disease characterized by intraocular pressure damaging the optic nerve, is one example of a prechiasmal lesion.

Prechiasmal lesions produce visual field defects with the following characteristics:

1. The defect is in one eye only—unless the disease affects both retinas or optic nerves, in which case both eyes may have visual field defects. Should there be a visual field defect in only one eye and the other eye has no defect at all, the lesion must be prechiasmal. Moreover, if there is no preretinal or retinal lesion (almost any of which would be visible on examination of the eye) to explain the defect, it must be an optic nerve lesion.

2. The defect may extend uninterrupted across the vertical meridian. The diagnostic importance of this fact is that a defect resulting from a postchiasmal lesion does not cross the vertical meridian. Therefore, if a defect crosses the vertical midline uninterrupted, the lesion is not postchiasmal but prechiasmal (or combined chiasmal and prechiasmal).

3. If the result of a lesion of the optic nerve (or the retinal nerve fiber layer), visual field defects in the nasal visual field *may* end abruptly with a straight horizontal border nasal to fixation (i.e., a nasal step or a scotoma with a flat horizontal edge). However, if the result of a lesion in the temporal retina or choroid, a defect in the nasal visual field may extend across the horizontal meridian uninterrupted. If the defect has a sharp horizontal border nasally, it is undoubtedly the result of a prechiasmal lesion. If it does not have a horizontal nasal border, it may or may not be prechiasmal.

4. There are quite a variety of scotomas and depressions produced by prechiasmal lesions. Selected typical examples are shown on the opposite page.

5. A prechiasmal visual field defect may be—but is not always—associated with:

   a. A reduced visual acuity (e.g., generalized depressions resulting from media opacities and central scotomas resulting from macular or optic nerve disease);

   b. An abnormal pupil reaction (afferent pupillary defect);

   c. An abnormality evident on ophthalmoscopy; or

   d. Abnormal color vision.

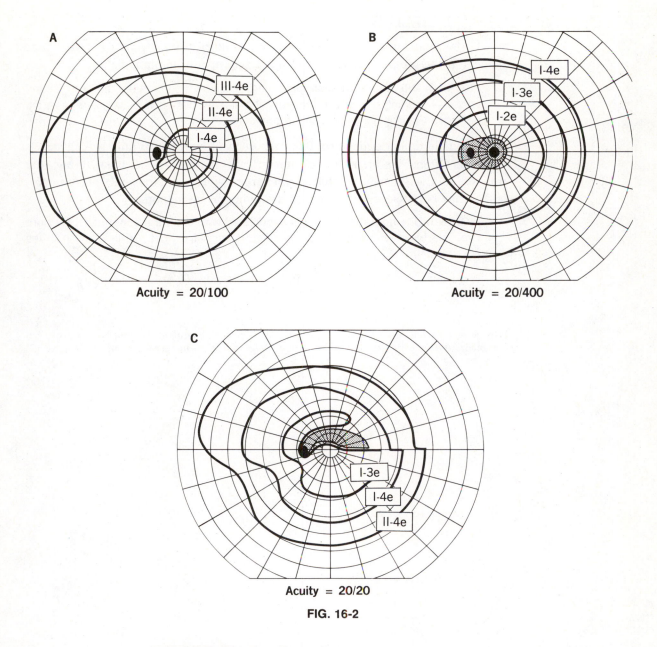

A

III-4e
II-4e
I-4e

Acuity = 20/100

B

I-4e
I-3e
I-2e

Acuity = 20/400

C

I-3e
I-4e
II-4e

Acuity = 20/20

FIG. 16-2

FIG. 16-2. Prechiasmal field defects.
A, Generalized depression with flattening of the hill of vision typically results from opacity of the ocular media. Some diffuse diseases of the retina or optic nerve may also produce generalized depression or constriction of the visual field. The visual acuity is reduced.
B, Central scotomas or centrocecal scotomas may result from lesions of the macula or the optic nerve, particularly the posterior optic nerve, and are associated with a reduced visual acuity.
C, Arcuate or wedge-shaped defects that point toward the blind spot are characteristic of lesions that destroy bundles of nerve fibers in the retinal nerve fiber layers or the anterior optic nerve. Glaucoma is an example. Note that the defect may cross the vertical meridian uninterrupted and may have a sharp horizontal border nasally. The visual acuity may remain normal.

199

CHIASMAL VISUAL FIELD DEFECTS

Lesions affecting the chiasm, e.g., a pituitary tumor, produce visual field defects in the temporal field of both eyes (bitemporal hemianopia*).

FIG. 16-3. Bitemporal hemianopia. The defective vision is in the temporal field of each eye, ending abruptly at the vertical meridian; but, as is usually the case, the defective vision is not to the same extent in the two eyes.

The field defect ends abruptly at the vertical meridian if only the chiasm is affected. Often, one or both optic nerves are affected by the same tumor that presses on the chiasm, so that characteristics of a prechiasmal (optic nerve) lesion may be present in addition to the temporal hemianopia.

FIG. 16-4. Bitemporal hemianopia associated with a central scotoma in the right eye. The tumor is compressing the optic nerve of the right eye in addition to the chiasm.

With chiasmal lesions, the visual acuity is normal unless the optic nerve is also involved.

Hemianopia is defective vision within half the visual field. *Temporal hemianopia* is defective vision confined to the temporal half of the field. *Bitemporal hemianopia* is temporal hemianopia in both eyes.

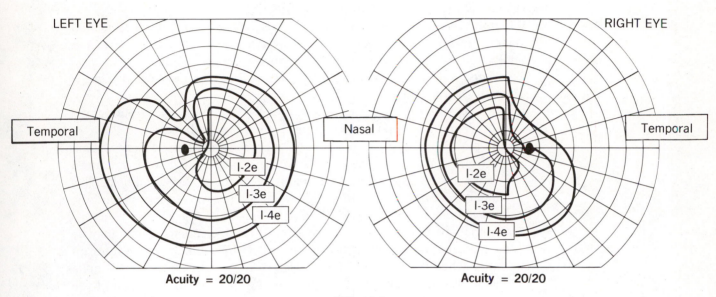

LEFT EYE

Temporal

Nasal

Temporal

RIGHT EYE

I-2e

I-3e

I-4e

I-2e

I-3e

I-4e

Acuity = 20/20

Acuity = 20/20

FIG. 16-3

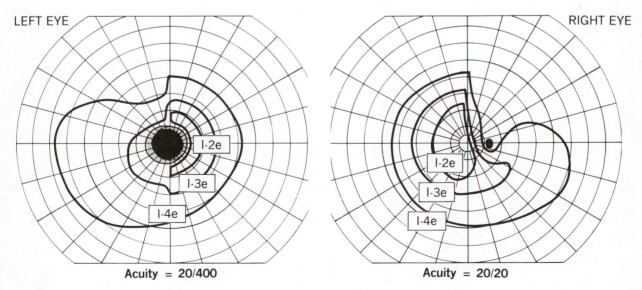

LEFT EYE

RIGHT EYE

I-2e

I-3e

I-4e

I-2e

I-3e

I-4e

Acuity = 20/400

Acuity = 20/20

FIG. 16-4

POSTCHIASMAL VISUAL FIELD DEFECTS

Lesions affecting the postchiasmal visual pathway produce visual field defects in both eyes, but the two eyes may not be affected equally. The field defects are limited to half the field (hemianopia) and end abruptly at the vertical midline.

The hemianopic defects are "homonymous." In homonymous hemianopia, the defects of the two eyes are both to the right or both to the left. Therefore, the defect is nasal in one eye and temporal in the other.

When the lesion is of the occipital cortex (usually vascular), the defects tend to be identical (congruous), but lesions in most other locations (e.g., optic tract or temporal lobe), usually tumors, typically produce incongruous defects.

Associated findings are sometimes important to a diagnosis when there is homonymous hemianopia:

1. With postchiasmal lesions, the visual acuity is almost always normal except when there is postchiasmal involvement on both sides.
2. The pupil reactions are normal (unlike prechiasmal lesions), except that with optic tract lesions there may be a "hemianopic pupil" with a reduced reaction of the pupil to light on the involved side of the visual field. This should occur only with optic tract lesions and not with lesions behind the lateral geniculate body.
3. Ophthalmoscopy is typically normal, with two exceptions. There may be papilledema associated with a brain tumor. In addition, in the rare instance when the hemianopia is caused by an optic tract lesion, the optic disc is pale in a "bow-tie" shape in the eye on the opposite side of the lesion, while the disc on the eye on the same side shows temporal pallor.
4. Opticokinetic nystagmus may be abnormal toward the side of the lesion with postchiasmal lesions.

FIG. 16-5. Postchiasmal field defects.

A, Example of *incongruous right homonymous hemianopia* as would be produced by a tumor of the left temporal lobe, affecting the right side of the visual field in both eyes. Note that the defect ends abruptly at the vertical midline (making the defect a hemianopia), that the right half of the field is affected in both eyes (making it homonymous), and that the defect is not of equal severity in the two eyes (making it incongruous).
B, Example of a *congruous homonymous hemianopia,* typical of occipital lobe lesions, often the result of vascular occlusion.
C, *Congruous homonymous scotomatous hemianopia* as a result of a small occipital lobe infarction.

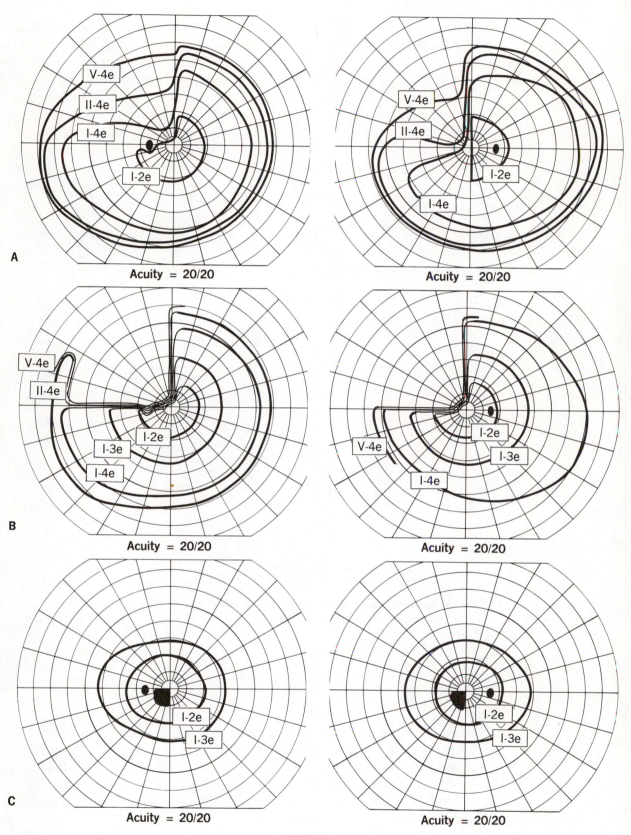

FIG. 16-5

RIDDOCH PHENOMENON

Sometimes within a hemianopic field defect a test stimulus *is* visible if it is moving but is not visible if it is stationary, as if there were a much greater abnormality of visual threshold with static stimuli than with kinetic stimuli. The result is that an isopter for a certain stimulus may be plotted kinetically, but in static spot checking the stimulus will not be visible over a broad area inside the isopter. However, it *is* visible inside the isopter if the stimulus is moving.

This marked difference in visibility between moving and nonmoving stimuli within an abnormal region of the visual field is known as the Riddoch phenomenon. When such a region is encountered by an unsuspecting perimetrist, it can be very confusing because it appears, with the usual combined kinetic and static spot-checking technique, as though the patient is being inconsistent. However, once it is realized that the field defect is displaying the Riddoch phenomenon, it is possible to outline a normal seeing area, an area inside the kinetic isopter within which the stimulus is seen only if moving, and a nonseeing area outside the kinetic isopter where the stimulus is not seen, whether moving or not.

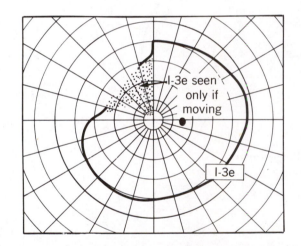

FIG. 16-6. Hemianopic field defect displaying the Riddoch phenomenon.

It is sometimes difficult in the presence of the Riddoch phenomenon to outline isopters accurately. Fortunately, when dealing with hemianopias, it is often necessary only to know that there is a definite abnormality, but its exact boundary is less important. If quantitation is required, it may best be achieved by static perimetry, which will show a denser abnormality than the kinetic stimulus and will give the most consistent patient responses.

ADDITIONAL READINGS

For those who wish more details on the topographic approach to visual field diagnosis as relevant especially to neurologic conditions, considerable information can be found in the following:

Duane, T.D., editor: Clinical ophthalmology, vol. 2, New York, 1976, Harper & Row, Publishers.

Ellenberger, C., Jr.: Perimetry: principles, technique, and interpretation, New York, 1980, Raven Press.

Glaser, J.S.: Neuro-ophthalmology, New York, 1978, Harper & Row, Publishers, pp. 47-167. [This is almost the same as the Duane, reprinted with slight modification.]

Harrington, D.O.: The visual fields: a textbook and atlas of clinical perimetry, ed. 5, St. Louis, 1981, The C.V. Mosby Co.

Huber, A.: Eye signs and symptoms in brain tumors, ed. 6, St. Louis, 1976, The C.V. Mosby Co.

Hughes, B.: The visual fields. A study of the applications of quantitative perimetry to the anatomy and pathology of the visual pathways, Springfield, Ill., 1954, Charles C Thomas, Publisher.

Traquair, H.M.: An introduction to clinical perimetry, ed. 6, St. Louis, 1949, The C.V. Mosby Co. [It is hard to beat the valuable information found in this great classic.]

Walsh, F.B., and Hoyt, W.F.: Clinical neuro-ophthalmology, vol. 1, ed. 3, Baltimore, 1969, The Williams & Wilkins Co., pp. 43-97.

CHAPTER 17

Purposeful examination of the field

TYPES OF FIELD EXAMINATIONS

There is no such thing as a standard visual field examination, but a technique must be chosen according to the purpose at hand. There should always be a specific question in mind to be answered in the time available. There are four general types of examinations:

1. GENERAL SCREENING EXAMINATIONS. General screening examinations are performed in general populations (e.g., all patients seen in the office, all individuals renewing their driver's license, and all individuals entering the U.S. Air Force) to detect any kind of field defect that might be present. Applicable techniques may range from simple finger-counting confrontation fields to the kinetic plotting of a central and a peripheral isopter with static spot checking centrally, or simply static spot checking without plotting an isopter. The choice depends on the sensitivity desired and the types of defects that are most important to detect in the group being tested.

2. SPECIFIC SCREENING EXAMINATIONS. Specific screening examinations are directed at deciding whether or not a specific type of field defect is present. For example, for an individual with poor visual acuity, the question may be whether or not a central scotoma is present. For another individual with medical evidence of endocrine abnormality suggesting a possible pituitary tumor, the question may be whether or not a bitemporal hemianopia is present. For a person who has elevated intraocular pressure, there may be a question of whether or not a glaucomatous type of visual field defect is present. Such glaucoma screening examinations could also be directed toward people at retirement centers.

Obviously, the exact nature of the screening examination may depend on the type of defect for which one is looking: the screening examination performed to look for a central scotoma will not be the same as one performed to look for hemianopia or a glaucomatous defect.

In addition, even for a single condition such as glaucoma, there may be several different methods for screening, which may differ in ease and in accuracy (sensitivity and specificity). The choice of instrument and technique may depend on the setting in which the screening examination is performed—the number of people to be screened, the amount of time that can be devoted, the accuracy desired, and the likelihood that a defect is present in any one individual.

3. **DIAGNOSTIC EXAMINATIONS.** Diagnostic examinations are those that establish, or help to establish, a diagnosis. At times there is not much distinction between a screening examination and a diagnostic examination. For example, if a pituitary tumor is suspected because the patient has endocrine abnormalities and a field examination shows a bitemporal hemianopsia, the presence of a pituitary tumor is both detected (screening) and established (diagnosis). Another situation in which screening and diagnosis are performed at the same examination is when a screening strategy is used with a sophisticated machine (Chapter 11) and the perimetrist proceeds immediately to define in detail the nature of any defect that has seemingly been detected, thus performing the screening and diagnostic functions simultaneously. In these examples, an accurate diagnostic test is performed at the onset and used as a screening test because the likelihood of a defect is great. In this setting, the screening examination becomes a diagnostic examination as soon as the presence of a defect is documented and they really are one and the same.

However, in another setting it may be efficient to use a relatively rapid general screening technique (perhaps with a large number of false positive results) to look for glaucoma in a large general population in which only a few people will actually have glaucoma. Then one can use a more time-consuming but more accurate technique for diagnosis on those who seem to have a defect with the screening technique. The purpose of the second diagnostic examination is to screen out those individuals who had false positive results on the first test from those individuals who truly do have defective vision.

The distinction between screening and diagnosis in such an example is that a rapid screening examination detects the *possible (or probable)* presence of an abnormality, while the diagnostic examination establishes the presence of a certain type of defect with sufficient certainty that a diagnosis can be made, perhaps indicating the need for treatment.

Occasionally a diagnostic examination takes the form of distinguishing between two types of defects. For example, in the case of reduced visual acuity, it may be of diagnostic utility to know whether the visual reduction is the result of a generalized depression or a central scotoma. Such a diagnostic test consists of looking for both of the suspected defects, expecting one or the other to be found but not both.

4. **QUANTITATIVE EXAMINATIONS OF THE ABNORMALITIES.** These are often not necessary in order to establish a diagnosis; however, quantitation of the defects is important if the patient has a condition that may worsen or improve, and if it is important to follow the progress of the patient's condition in order to make therapeutic decisions. Glaucoma, used as an example throughout most of the book, is a typical example. Field testing to look for recurrence of a brain tumor after irradiation is another.

PRACTICAL APPLICATIONS

From the preceding, it is evident that some instrumentation and technique may apply at one time and place to a particular patient but not to another. There is no point in going through a fully quantitative visual field examination for half an hour when the question at hand is simply whether or not there is a hemianopia—a question that can be answered rather quickly with a less elaborate technique. Similarly, if finding a central scotoma is the only goal in performing the visual field examination, this may be accomplished rather quickly without the need to examine quantitatively the entire field, or even the entire central field. Moreover, a highly quantitative field test covering the entire area may be less accurate for specific purposes: one may do a fairly extensive quantitative visual field test and miss a small central scotoma accounting for 20/60 vision unless the examiner has in mind that the goal of performing the field test in this patient is to look for a central scotoma and concentrates efforts at the central 2 or 3 degrees of the field.

Thus, before performing a field examination, the examiner needs to know the context in which the examination is being performed and the type of possible defects (e.g., central scotomas, paracentral scotomas, or hemianopias) according to the disease suspected. When a defect is uncovered in the course of a screening examination and a diagnostic evaluation is indicated, it is important to have in mind which diagnoses are under consideration and the features of the field defect that will help distinguish one kind of visual field defect from another (e.g., a quadrantic defect pointing toward fixation versus one pointing toward the disc, or the presence or absence of a strict limit of the defect at the vertical meridian). Finally, when doing the assessment or descriptive phase of the examination, it is necessary to decide whether the defect should be quantitated carefully (because the condition is going to be checked at intervals to detect a worsening severity of the defect) or whether the only purpose at hand is to have the presence or absence of the defect convincingly demonstrated.

The same considerations are important for automatic perimetry. Certain automatic perimeters with specific standard programs are appropriate for certain specific purposes only. The person deciding which perimeters or which programs to use must do so after careful consideration of the goal in a specific setting for a particular patient. It is particularly important to know which goals will *not* be served by particular instruments and programs.

We will now proceed in the next several chapters to explore various strategies, methods, and instruments for field examination and the roles for each.

CHAPTER 18

More about testing for glaucoma

INTRODUCTION

We have just seen that a visual field examination should be done in different ways, depending on whether one wants (1) only to screen for a defect, (2) to characterize the nature of a defect in order to establish a diagnosis, or (3) to quantitate a defect in order to follow its progress.

In Chapter 11 is described an approach to the visual field that includes screening, diagnosis, and quantitation for glaucoma all at one time. This approach certainly applies to the usual clinical setting where the diagnostic screening examination is performed with patients in whom there is already some sign of glaucoma, e.g., an elevated intraocular pressure or an abnormality of the optic disc. In such a setting, the likelihood of a defect being present is greater than in a general unselected group of people and a careful method requiring moderate expenditure of time is warranted. Moreover, if a defect is found, it needs to be described quantitatively, since the progress of the glaucoma patient will need to be checked at intervals to judge the adequacy of the treatment. It makes sense to use a strategy and an instrument that will allow one to proceed for a quantitated examination as soon as a defect is discovered.

The technique presented in Chapter 11 is a good basic technique to be mastered by everyone who performs visual field examinations for several reasons.

First, in the usual clinical practice in which glaucoma patients abound, it is the most frequent examination performed. Second, with slight modification (such as checking for steps along the vertical meridian or checking for brightness differences across the vertical meridian [p. 238]), the method can be used for field defects other than glaucoma. Even without modifying the method, the alert perimetrist will recognize that some type of defect other than glaucoma is present. The major problems with using this technique for nonglaucomatous defects are:

1. It is inefficient in those diagnostic settings in which it is not necessary to examine as many regions of the field or to be quite so quantitative,
2. Some important defects, especially central scotomas, will escape detection because the strategy is not directed toward these defects.

A third reason the glaucoma technique in Chapter 11 is a good basic technique is that for general use it is a reasonable compromise between accuracy and efficient use of time. It is fairly rapid, as long as no field defects that need quantitation are present, and hence serves as a good screening test. However, there are other equivalent approaches. Some are more accurate and others are less accurate but require less time. These alternative methods that have utilities in various settings are the subject of this chapter.

THE BASIC ARMALY-DRANCE TECHNIQUE

Armaly described the basic method of suprathreshold static spot checking to detect scotomas, and he simplified it to a rapid technique for use in his scientific study of glaucoma in the general population. He called his method "selective perimetry." Drance studied the accuracy of the technique and made certain modifications. Both Armaly and Drance have, through the years, used several variations but the basic nature of the technique, as it has evolved, includes the following steps:

Static spot checking

Static spot checking is the single most important component of the glaucoma screen. The first step is to select the stimulus for spot checking.

The stimulus for spot checking can be simply a standard stimulus, such as a 1W/1000 at the tangent screen or an I-2e on the Goldmann perimeter. The 2W/1000 or I-3e is used if the weaker stimulus forms an isopter smaller than 20 degrees. It is better to determine the approximate visual threshold at 25 degrees and use that stimulus.

> **FIG. 18-1. Stimulus selection.** The visual threshold is determined at four locations where the horizontal and vertical meridians cross the 25-degree circle. Traditionally, the threshold is determined for this purpose in 0.5-log–unit steps (e.g., I-1e, I-2e, I-3e, I-4e, II-4e). The selected stimulus will be I-2e most often, I-3e less often, etc. Therefore, choosing a target usually is a matter of determining that I-1e is not seen and that I-2e is seen. A more compulsive and more time-consuming method would be to determine threshold to the nearest 0.1 or 0.2 log unit.

Practice varies with regard to using (1) the strongest of the four threshold stimuli, which is the weakest stimulus that is seen in *all* four locations; (2) the weakest of the four threshold stimuli, which is the weakest stimulus seen at *any* of the four locations; or (3) the threshold at 25 degrees temporally (near the blind spot), ignoring the other three locations. The easiest, and perhaps the best overall, is simply to use the stimulus that is threshold at 25 degrees temporally, without bothering to determine the threshold at the other three points (p. 120).

There is no "best" way for choosing the stimulus. It all depends on the clinical setting. The weaker stimulus, seen only at one of the four locations, has the advantage that it will allow detection of shallow scotomas. However, it will be barely visible even in normal regions of the field. Therefore, the patient may miss seeing it once in a while, falsely giving the impression that there is a scotoma. For example, with a certain weak stimulus 5% of those screened may falsely appear to have a scotoma, but the field will turn out to be normal on more careful examination. This 5% "false positive" rate may cause a problem when screening a group of people in a retirement center where only one in 200 people have glaucoma. The weak stimulus that yields 5% incorrect diagnoses will yield 10 false diagnoses in 200 people along with one correct diagnosis. This may be acceptable if one has the time and facilities to perform a more detailed ocular examination, including a more

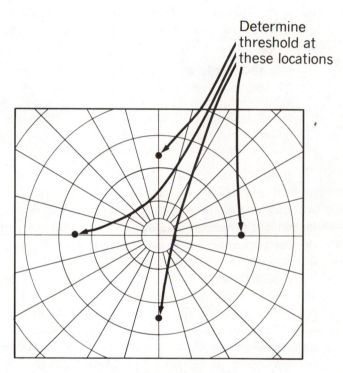

Determine threshold at these locations

FIG. 18-1

detailed visual field examination, to sort out the 10 "false positives" (normals) from the one "true positive" (glaucoma). Usually, however, in such a setting one would rather use a slightly stronger stimulus in order to have fewer "false positives," knowing that some shallow defects might not be detected, but knowing also that the defects *not* detected will be milder—not of as much consequence as the deeper defects that *are* detected.

The situation is different among a group of patients with other signs of glaucoma, perhaps 20% or more of whom really do have a field defect. The proportion of 20 "true positives" (those with a defect) to 5 "false positives" (normal people who just *seem* to have a defect) while using a weak stimulus is acceptably high. Moreover, the extra effort to sort out the true from false positives is worthwhile in this group that is overall at greater risk than the general population and in whom one is anxious not to miss detecting a shallow defect.

Once the stimulus is selected, static spot checking is performed at 76 locations. These locations are every 15 degrees along the circles 5, 10, and 15 degrees away from fixation where the circles intersect the meridians, and at four locations inside the 5-degree circle.

FIG. 18-2. Static spot checking at 76 points. The standard technique when testing manually is a 1-second presentation of a selected stimulus once, and only once, at each location in an orderly sequence—e.g., around the 5-degree circle, then around the 10-degree circle, and finally around the 15-degree circle. Some automated methods will present the stimulus in a random sequence but still only once at each location. The location of each missed point is marked.

If four or more adjacent points are missed, an arcuate scotoma is probably present and the field is probably abnormal. If the only purpose is to determine whether or not there probably exists a field defect, the screening test can be terminated as soon as a definite defect is detected, and a more thorough diagnostic test performed later. Or one can proceed immediately to plot isopters and quantitative defects as outlined in Chapter 11.

If fewer than four adjacent spots are missed, any missed points are checked a second time with the same stimulus (p. 122). A paracentral scotoma is probably present at any spots where, on the second presentation, the stimulus is again not seen; but any spots where the stimulus is seen on the second presentation are ignored. (In some clinics points that were missed only on the first presentation are considered significant if several are clustered together.) Any time the criteria show that the field is probably abnormal, the screening examination can be terminated and the quantitative examination can be deferred for another occasion, or one can proceed immediately to determine the depth of the scotoma and outline its boundary kinetically.

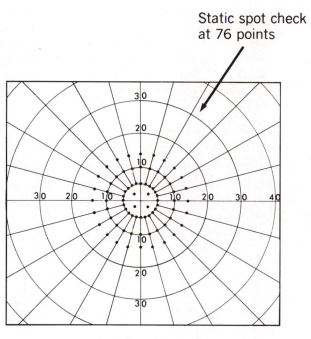

Static spot check
at 76 points

FIG. 18-2

Central kinetic plotting

The stimulus selected for static spot checking is also used to plot the blind spot kinetically by moving the stimulus in eight directions outward from the center of the blind spot. Actually, this step is usually performed prior to the static spot checking. In addition to detecting arcuate field defects, the plotting of the blind spot, as always, ensures that everything is in order; if the blind spot cannot be plotted, something may be wrong (p. 72). The same stimulus is also used to plot an isopter.

FIG. 18-3. Kinetic plotting. First, the blind spot is plotted. Then, the selected stimulus is used to plot part of an isopter on the nasal side to look for a nasal step. Eight points are plotted at 5, 10, 15, and 30 degrees above and below the nasal horizontal meridian. A 10-degree nasal step is considered diagnostic by itself. A 5-degree nasal step may also be significant, but is usually considered a definite diagnostic sign only if there is also a paracentral or arcuate scotoma.

Finally, the selected stimulus is used to plot two points kinetically on the temporal side of the field 30-degrees above and below the horizontal meridian. These two points along with the eight nasal points give a partial representation of the isopter. However, the two temporal points are marginally informative and could be omitted, especially if the Drance method of checking the temporal field statically (see below) is used.

In some descriptions of the Armaly-Drance technique the entire isopter is plotted by determining points kinetically along every 15-degree meridian; but if the purpose is only to screen, this can be reduced to eight points nasally and perhaps two points temporally as a method of saving time. The rest are not needed except to help in interpretation if the results of static spot checking suggest the presence of an abnormality.

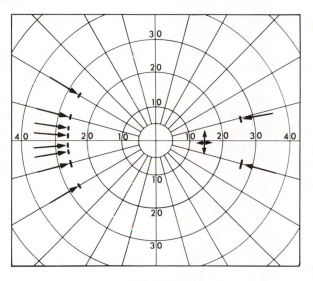

FIG. 18-3

Peripheral field

To check the peripheral field, the location of an isopter is checked at eight points nasally to look for a peripheral nasal step—similar to plotting the central isopter but using a stronger stimulus. In a more complete technique the entire isopter is plotted.

In the original technique, when the I-2e is used routinely as a standard central isopter, the I-4e is used for the peripheral isopter. In a more refined technique, the weakest stimulus seen nasally at 55 degrees either above or below the horizontal meridian is used for the peripheral field. If no stimulus is seen at 55 degrees nasally, the absolute periphery of the field is determined with the V-4e stimulus and the threshold is determined 5 degrees inside the absolute periphery.

FIG. 18-4. Checking the peripheral field.
A, Position at which threshold is determined (55 degrees nasally) to select peripheral stimulus.
B, Selection of stimulus if V-4e is not visible at 55 degrees nasally. The absolute nasal periphery of the field is found with the V-4e, and threshold is determined 5 degrees inside the periphery.
C, Plotting the peripheral field with the selected peripheral stimulus. In this example, I-2e was used to plot the central isopter and I-4e was chosen to plot the peripheral isopter. The essential minimum is a search for a nasal step by plotting eight points nasally (solid arrows), but a complete plot of other meridians around the periphery (dashed arrows) may be made.

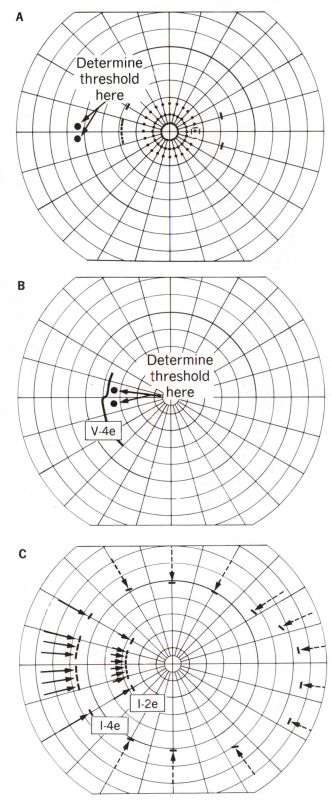

FIG. 18-4

THE BASIC ARMALY-DRANCE TECHNIQUE: SUMMARY

To review, the sequence of testing is as follows:

1. Select a stimulus for the central field by determining threshold at 25 degrees temporally, adjacent to the blind spot. Alternately, also take into account the threshold 25 degrees above, below, and nasal to fixation; or simply use the I-2e routinely.
2. With the selected stimulus:
   A. Plot the blind spot.
   B. Check statically 76 points.
   C. Plot the isopter at least nasally (eight points) and temporally (two points). Additional points all the way around are optional.
3. Select a stimulus for the peripheral field by determining threshold at 55 degrees nasally above and below the horizontal (or simply use an I-4e) or, if necessary, determine threshold 5 degrees inside the absolute nasal periphery.
4. With the peripheral stimulus, plot eight points of the isopter nasally and (optional) two points temporally, or the whole isopter.

ADDITIONAL READINGS

For those interested, the original descriptions of the method and its modifications can be found in the following references listed in chronological order so that the reader can follow the historical development:

Armaly, M.F.: Ocular pressure and visual fields: a ten-year follow-up study, Arch. Ophthalmol. **81**:25-40, 1969.

Armaly, M.F.: Visual field defects in early open angle glaucoma, Trans. Am. Ophthalmol. Soc. **69:** 147-162, 1971.

Rock, W.J., Drance, S.M., and Morgan, R.W.: A modification of the Armaly visual field screening technique for glaucoma, Can. J. Ophthalmol. **6**:283-292, 1971.

Armaly, M.F.: Selective perimetry for glaucomatous defects in ocular hypertension, Arch. Ophthalmol. **87**:518-524, 1972.

Drance, S.M., and others: A screening method for temporal visual defects in chronic simple glaucoma, Can. J. Ophthalmol. **7**:428-429, 1972.

Rock, W.J., Drance, S.M., and Morgan, R.W.: Visual field screening in glaucoma: an evaluation of the Armaly technique for screening glaucomatous visual fields, Arch. Ophthalmol. **89**:287-290, 1973.

ARMALY-DRANCE TECHNIQUE: APPLICATION

The Armaly-Drance technique is an accurate and rapid (7 minutes per eye) method for determining whether or not a glaucomatous field defect is present. It can be easily taught to someone who is not a fully trained perimetrist and used to screen large numbers of people. The regimented sequence of stimuli presentation can be made easily by an automatic perimeter.

Confirmation that the defects are real (diagnosis) and quantitation (for later checking) can be accomplished subsequently. If the Armaly-Drance technique is performed manually with the Goldmann perimeter and followed immediately by quantitation, one has essentially the technique described in Chapter 11. One difference, however, is that the technique in Chapter 11 allows freedom to decide the number and location of points to explore and to recheck areas with combined static and kinetic stimuli. This will allow a good perimetrists to do a better job (sometimes at the expense of taking longer) or poor perimetrists to do a poorer job (e.g., if they do not check enough points carefully). One advantage of a regimented system, whether with a manual or with an automatic perimeter, is its usefulness in a research study. A regimented method ensures that every field examination is uniformly consistent, even if performed by different people or in different clinics.

Thus the Armaly-Drance screening method is useful:
1. By itself in screening large numbers of people, perhaps by relatively inexperienced perimetrists (manually or with an automatic perimeter), with the plan being to perform on a subsequent occasion the definitive diagnostic and quantitation steps on individuals with possible defects.
2. As the first visual field technique to teach those in training before going on to quantitation steps.
3. As the essential base of a full quantitative field examination (Chapter 11). Experienced perimetrists must realize that despite the freedom that comes with experience, they must not spot-check fewer than the prescribed 76 points centrally, or they will be doing a poorer job than a novice who simply follows directions.
4. As the basic program for automatic perimeters.
5. In research studies where it is important that all fields are performed in an identical manner, either manually or with automatic perimeters.

ARMALY-DRANCE TECHNIQUE: REFINEMENTS AND VARIATIONS

It is tempting to attempt to improve the basic technique to improve its sensitivity in picking up mild defects. Each "improvement" may complicate the technique and may lengthen it.

1. The number or distribution of spots to be checked in the central field could be changed. Because of the shape of the arcuate regions involved in glaucoma (Fig. 11-10), it is logical to check the nasal field at 20 and 25 degrees in addition to the prescribed 5, 10, and 15 degrees.

FIG. 18-5, A. Additional nasal points (large dots). Of course, it is not abnormal to miss these points if the isopter falls between 20 and 25 degrees without producing a nasal step.

For any pattern, it is important to check a sufficient number of spots, including the area near fixation. With too few points, it becomes possible for a small scotoma (e.g., 5 degrees in diameter) to escape detection because it falls between the points checked (p. 122).

2. An additional isopter can be plotted nasally (eight points) with a stimulus that forms an isopter at approximately 40 to 45 degrees (e.g., I-3e or the threshold stimulus at 40 degrees nasally). This yields a total of three isopters plotted at approximately 25 to 30 degrees, 40 to 45 degrees, and 50 to 55 degrees across the nasal meridian to look for nasal steps.

FIG. 18-5, B. The nasal field explored with three nasal isopters instead of two. Note the similarity to the basic method described on p. 128.

3. Instead of an isopter plotted kinetically across the horizontal meridian nasally, an arc static cut across the meridian at 25, 40, and 55 degrees may be used to look for nasal steps. A 0.5 log unit difference above and below is considered significant.

FIG. 18-5, C. Arc static cut. The threshold is I-4b at three points above the horizontal meridian and I-3a at three points below the nasal meridian. Because there is more than 0.5 log unit difference, a nasal step is present. In this example the nasal step is also shown kinetically with the I-3e stimulus, in order to show that the two methods are equivalent (see also Fig. 15-4, p. 191).

4. In Drance's second modification of the Armaly technique, additional attention is given to the temporal field. Suprathreshold static spot checking is performed at 24 midperipheral points along the 30-, 40-, and 50-degree circles.

FIG. 18-5, D. Location of the 24 temporal points checked in Drance's modification of the testing technique.

The stimulus used is the weakest stimulus seen at 30 degrees from fixation superiorly, 35 degrees from fixation inferiorly, or 55 degrees from fixation temporally.

FIG. 18-5, E. Locations where threshold is checked temporally. The threshold stimulus at these points is used for static suprathreshold spot checking of the temporal field at the points indicated in Fig. 18-5, *D*.

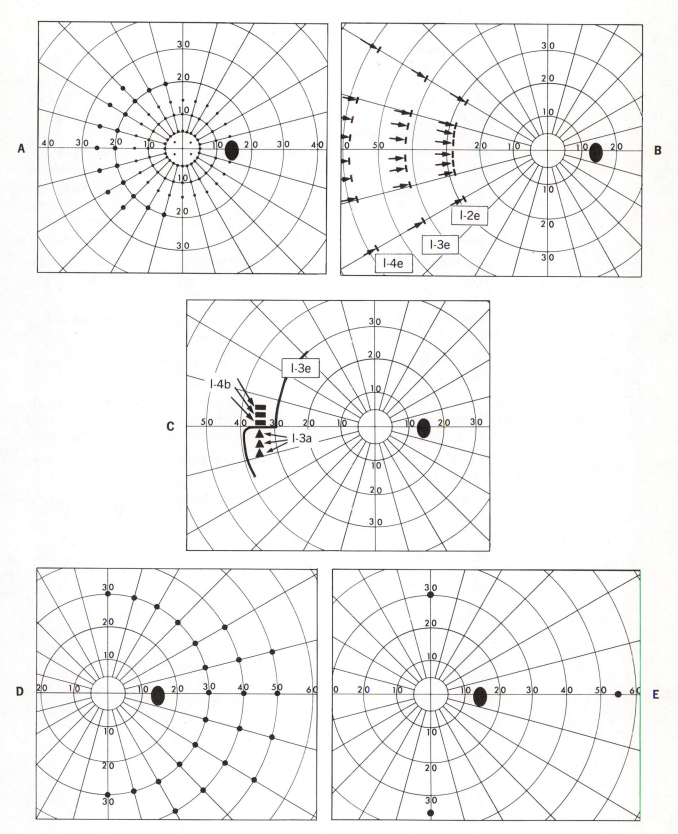

FIG. 18-5

5. We noted earlier (p. 126) that when a stimulus that is threshold at 25 degrees is used for spot checking, a shallow scotoma near fixation might be missed because the stimulus is too strongly suprathreshold close to fixation. To overcome this problem, when extra sensitivity of the techniques is required, the central 10 to 15 degrees is spot-checked with a stimulus that forms an isopter at 10 to 15 degrees, and the usual slightly stronger stimulus is used elsewhere in the central field (Fig. 11-13, *B*).

In order to spot check for shallow scotomas near fixation without plotting several isopters, Drance's department now uses the following method. Threshold is determined along the horizontal meridian 5 degrees temporal to fixation. A stimulus 0.2 log unit brighter than this is used to check the 5-degree circle and four points within the 5-degree circle. For example, if the threshold is I-1b, then I-1d is used.

FIG. 18-6, A. Checking the central 5 degrees. Threshold is determined at *A* and a stimulus 0.2 log unit more intense is used for spot checking along the circle 5 degrees from fixation.

In a similar way, threshold is determined 10 degrees temporal to fixation and a stimulus 0.2 log unit brighter is used for the 10-degree circle.

FIG. 18-6, B. Checking the 10-degree circle with a stimulus 0.2 log unit more intense than the threshold at *B*.

Finally, the 15-degree circle is checked with a stimulus 0.2 log unit brighter than the threshold 20 degrees temporal from fixation (the 15-degree location cannot be used to determine threshold because it usually would fall within the blind spot).

FIG. 18-6, C. Checking the 15-degree circle with a stimulus 0.2 log units more intense than the threshold at *C*.

See pp. 242-245 on the Friedmann analyzer for another approach to this problem.

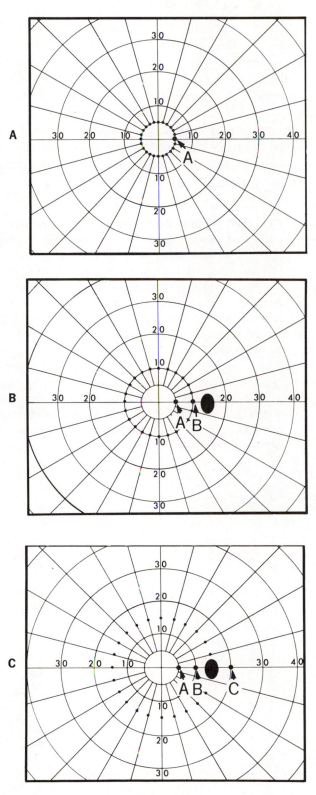

FIG. 18-6

QUANTITATION IN SPOT CHECKING

After confirming that a stimulus is not seen at a certain location, it is possible to increase the strength of the stimulus until it is seen, thereby confirming that the defect is real and determining exact threshold at all locations where abnormalities have been detected. After the threshold of all abnormal points has been quantitated, the size of the defect is revealed. However, if the defect is large and deep it may be more efficient to plot the boundary of the defect kinetically (p. 58), rather than to determine the threshold at many adjacent points. It is difficult to record the results of the resulting scatterplot of visual threshold in a form that is as readable as the isopter plot that results from kinetic quantitation of the defects. However, the information about the visual field is more or less equivalent (see p. 192).

FIG. 18-7. Hypothetical examples of visual field defect represented as isopter plots and scatterplots. The small dots represent points where I-1e is visible. The open circles represent where I-2e is visible, but not I-1e (that is, threshold is between I-2a and I-2e). The triangles are points where I-3a through I-3e is threshold, and the squares represent points where I-4a through I-4e is threshold.

A, Paracentral scotoma, represented to the left in an ordinary isopter plot. To the right is a plot in which threshold is determined statically at several points and no isopters were plotted kinetically.

B, Nasal step, similarly compared as an isopter plot and as a scatterplot.

C, Arcuate defect. *Right,* A combined representation resulting from an isopter plot in which all points that were missed on static spot checking were quantitated statically without kinetic plotting of the scotomatous area. The regions without symbols were checked by static spot checking and the stimulus was seen, meaning that that region was normal. Thus, the isopters are plotted and the scotomatous region is represented with symbols that indicate the threshold at each point.

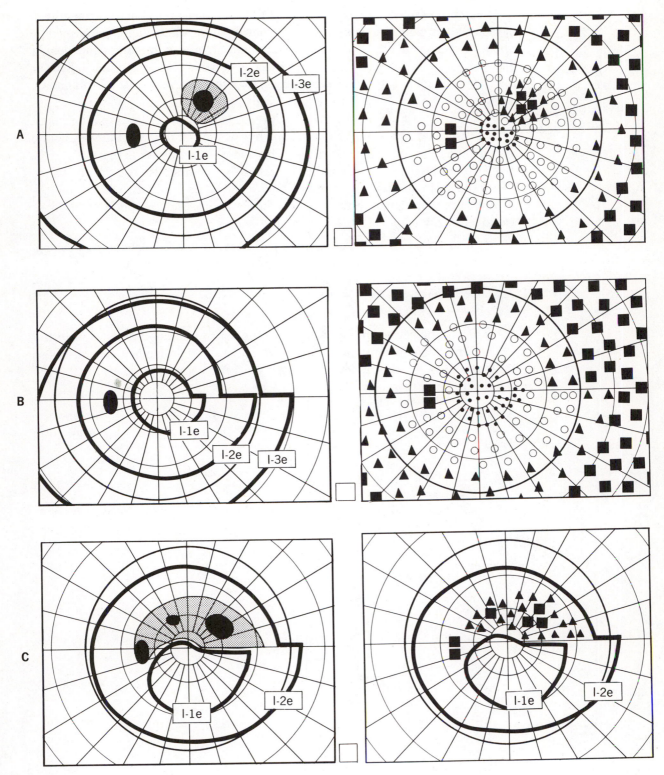

FIG. 18-7

STATIC CUT FOR GLAUCOMA SCREENING

A static cut in the 45-225-degree and 135-315-degree meridians is sometimes performed for glaucomatous screening. Such a pair of static cuts, if performed by themselves, may not be more time consuming than other screening strategies. At present, this method is not widely used because personnel in very few offices or clinics are facile with static perimetry. However, the use of some automatic perimeters may make such static cuts easily available.

Obviously, a pair of static cuts provides very accurate information about visual threshold along the two meridians but would not detect scotomas that do not lie along the meridian (see p. 14). The underlying premise is that only rarely would there be a scotoma elsewhere without there being also some disturbance along the entire arcuate region that would be detected by the two static cuts. As always, a screening test shows only whether or not the field is abnormal but does not necessarily demonstrate all the abnormalities.

FIG. 18-8. Hypothetical example of a pair of static cuts for glaucoma screening. The pair of static cuts shows that the field is abnormal, but not all the defects are detected. For example, the scotoma inferiorly is not detected. The 45-225 degree cut shows the upper nasal depression, and the 135-315 degree cut shows the scotoma above the blind spot.

The criteria devised by Greve[1] are that the defect must be 3 degrees wide and 0.5 log unit deep. Because of the appearance in a static profile plot, he calls these "wedge-shaped defects." However, Greve does not use the static cut as the primary screening method.[2]

ADDITIONAL READING

To supplement the references already given on pp. 116 and 218, additional information about distribution of glaucomatous field defects and screening strategies can be found in Appendix B.

---

[1]Greve, E.L.: Single and multiple stimulus static perimetry in glaucoma: the two phases of visual field examination, Doc. Ophthalmol. **136:**1-355, 1973.

[2]Greve, E.L., Furums, F., and Verduin, W.M.: A critical phase in the development of glaucomatous visual field defects, Doc. Ophthalmol. Proc. Series **19:**127-135, 1979.

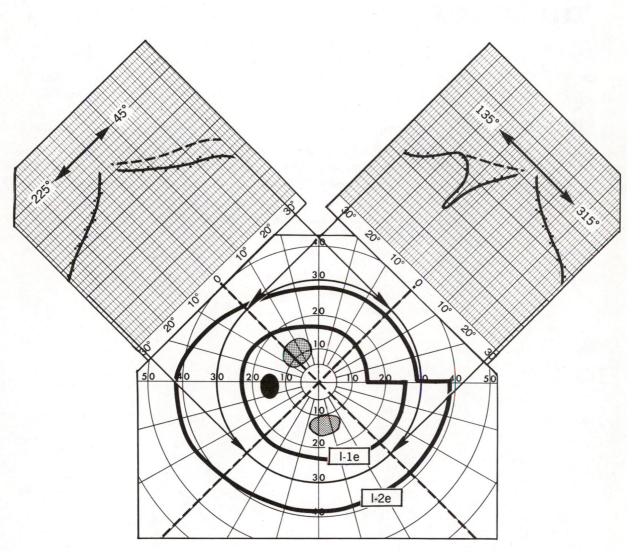

FIG. 18-8

CHAPTER 19

Alternate and supplemental methods

INTRODUCTION

Until now, we have dealt mainly with kinetic and static perimetry as performed with the Goldmann projection perimeter and the tangent screen. To know these methods is not enough. There are alternatives to the Goldmann perimeter that are advantageous for certain purposes. Certain clinical situations will, in fact, *require* other methods, either instead of or in addition to projection perimetry.

CONFRONTATION TECHNIQUES: INTRODUCTION

Confrontation techniques for evaluating the visual field are often very useful:

1. To screen for the presence of unsuspected field defects as part of a routine eye examination that would not ordinarily include formal field testing. We include a quick confrontation finger-counting field in every complete eye examination but of course do not do formal perimetry on every patient.

2. To educate the patient about field testing before performing perimetry (see p. 70).

3. To determine approximately the type and extent of a field defect to be expected on perimetry.

4. To confirm or deny perimetric findings. For example, extreme contraction of the field by perimetry may or may not be present on confrontation and the perimetry may be wrong. Likewise, confrontation comparison tests may suggest a hemianopia not discovered by perimetry or may confirm the perimetric findings.

5. As the only type of field examination that is feasible for some patients. One should not underestimate the amount of valuable information that can be obtained by a careful confrontation method, even for patients who cannot perform well on the perimeter.

The basic confrontation techniques to be described on the following pages are the finger-counting method and the comparison method.

CONFRONTATION: SCREENING WITH THE FINGER-COUNTING METHOD

This method of screening was originally described by Welsh.[1] As in all field testing, each eye is tested separately. The patient should use his palm, not his fingers, to occlude the other eye. The palm is used to be sure that he cannot peek between fingers and that he does not exert pressure on the covered eye, blurring his vision and making subsequent testing of this eye difficult. There should be no glare, but the examiner's back, ideally, should be toward a blank, evenly illuminated wall without windows or other bright sources of light.

Next, the patient is asked to fixate on the examiner's face (usually the nose) and report how many fingers the examiner holds up in the peripheral field. Each quadrant is tested separately by placing the hand 3 or 4 feet away from the patient, about 45 degrees from fixation. Normally, a person with a normal pupil size and without opacity in the media or other visual abnormality should be able to count fingers at 6 to 10 feet away, out to 60 degrees temporally and 45 to 50 degrees nasally. Therefore, counting fingers 3 to 4 feet away at 45 degrees should be achieved comfortably if the visual field is normal.

The examiner can hold up either one finger or two and the patient can report how many fingers he sees. One can also present four fingers or a whole hand, so that the patient has a choice of one, two, or all. A closed fist (no fingers) can also be used. Never use three fingers because three is exceedingly difficult to differentiate from two or four.

Especially if the patient is having trouble fixating, you can hold up both fists in a manner that will not allow the patient to tell which hand you will be using. Then, elevate one, two, or four fingers on one hand or the other and lower them again before the patient shifts his fixation to look directly at them.

FIG. 19-1. Finger-counting confrontation field.

---

[1]Welsh, R.C.: Finger counting in the four quadrants as a method of visual field gross screening, Arch. Ophthalmol. **66:**678-679, 1961.

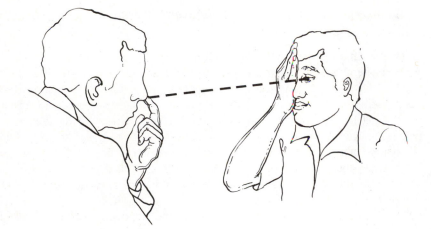

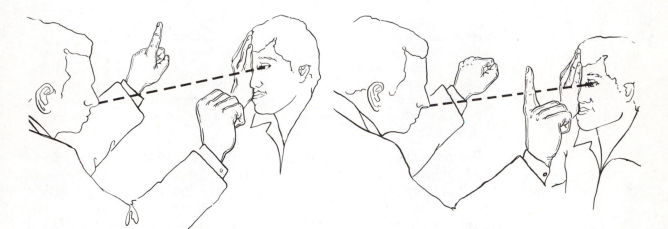

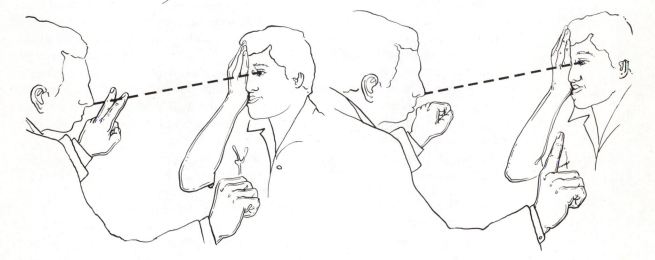

FIG. 19-1

CONFRONTATION: QUANTITATION IN THE FINGER-COUNTING METHOD

If the fingers cannot be counted in a given quadrant at 45 degrees, there are two helpful maneuvers.

FIG. 19-2. Quantitation by confrontation.

A, In the first quantitative maneuver the hand with upheld fingers can be moved transversely in an arc toward fixation, staying 2 to 3 feet from the patient. The procedure resembles kinetic perimetry and the idea is to determine how close to fixation the hand must be before the fingers can be counted. Similar to the technique when plotting an isopter, the direction of movement need not be toward fixation. For example, if there is marked difference between two quadrants, one may be able to confirm dramatically the presence of a hemianopia or a nasal step if the patient is suddenly able to count the fingers as the hand crosses the vertical meridian or the horizontal meridian nasally.

B, In the second quantitation maneuver, the hand is moved toward the patient along the line 45 degrees from fixation until the fingers can be counted (or start at 6 feet away and back away until the fingers cannot be counted) and the minimum closeness required to count fingers is compared between the four quadrants. This maneuver resembles static perimetry.

In the segments of the field where fingers cannot be counted, it should be determined whether or not the patient can distinguish if the fingers are wiggling or holding still. If he cannot make that distinction, it should be determined whether or not he can, with correct projection, detect the presence or absence of a light. This will help make the distinction between a severe depression and a contraction of the field, which is an absolute defect (p. 152).

When the visual sensation is so poor that one is looking for the presence or absence of light perception in different areas of the field, it is important to make note of whether or not the patient can accurately tell you where the light is located. Only if the patient can tell you where the light is located can you be sure that that area of the field is intact to light perception. For example, suppose a patient has a contracted field with only a temporal island of vision remaining from glaucoma and also has a cataract (which diffuses light within the eye). When you place a light in the nasal field, the patient may be able to tell you correctly that the light is on as a result of diffusion of the light by the cataract onto the seeing retina. The patient may tell you either that he sees that there is light temporally, or that he sees the light but is not sure where it is located. However, with the light on the temporal side, he may be able to tell you where the light is located and report that he now sees it brightly, whereas when the light was on the nasal side he was only aware of a dim glow. Sometimes it is quite striking that as you move the light around, the patient can suddenly localize the light accurately, letting you know that you have crossed the boundary into the seeing portion of the field. In a patient with cataract and glaucoma, it may be very encouraging if the patient can project light not only on the temporal side but in a region around fixation, even though he cannot accurately localize light seen in the nasal quadrant. The finding of accurate projection around fixation suggests that there is an intact central island of vision, perhaps with the potential of good acuity when a cataract is removed. The outlook is not so good if accurate light projection exists only in the temporal field, or if the patient reports that the light is dimmer at fixation than it is in the temporal field.

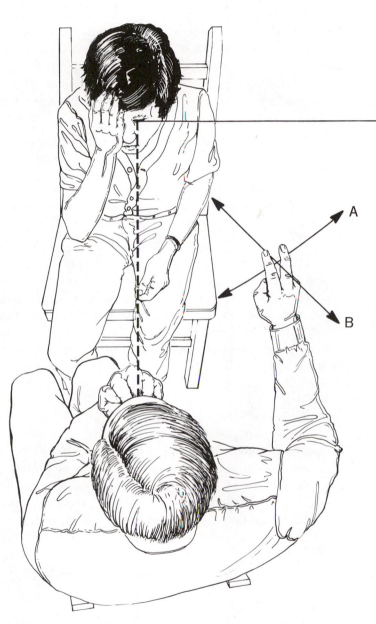

FIG. 19-2

DIAGRAMMING CONFRONTATION FIELDS

The conventional method of diagramming all visual fields is "as the patient sees it," the right eye to the right, the left eye to the left, the nasal side of the field toward the center, and the temporal side toward the edge. This diagramming is easy to accomplish with a technique such as the tangent screen and the perimeter, but with confrontation methods it is necessary for the examiner to invert right and left from his perspective so that it ends up on the paper "as the patient sees it." In doing so, it is well to label the diagram with an "N" between the two eyes and a "T" on the two edges, marking the right and the left eye, so that there is no ambiguity. This is particularly important because some experienced individuals intentionally diagram their confrontation findings in the unconventional manner, "as the examiner sees it."[1]

FIG. 19-3. Diagram of hypothetical visual fields by confrontation. In the first example, as might occur in a patient with both glaucoma and cataract, there is generalized depression and reduced activity, especially in the left eye, and the upper nasal depression. In the second example, as might occur in the presence of retinal detachment, there is very localized visual loss. HM indicates the region where the vision is limited to the detection of hand movements, and FC indicates the region where fingers can be counted at the indicated distance.

Considerable qualitative and even semiquantitative information can be obtained from a carefully performed finger-counting confrontation field with quantitation of abnormal areas. With care, one may be able to determine whether there is a central scotoma or not, or if a patient with glaucoma has a central island of vision remaining or only a temporal island. This can be done even when the vision is so poor because of cataracts or fixation is so poor because of reduced vision that an adequate examination with a perimeter or tangent screen cannot be accomplished. For such occasions, one needs to be experienced in performing confrontation fields.

It is also useful to perform confrontation field testing as a matter of routine in conjunction with perimetry to confirm or to deny the perimetric findings on the occasions when there may be a fault in perimetric technique and also for the examiner to learn through experience how to do a better perimetric examination. For example, if the confrontation technique does not reveal a defect and the perimetric examination shows a reasonably dense defect in one quadrant, the examiner should repeat the confrontation field, both to corroborate the presence of a defect and to learn why the presence of the defect was missed initially by confrontation. With such experience, the use of the confrontation field routinely on all patients seen in the office becomes a quick but reasonably accurate technique.

---

[1] Welsh, R.C.: How to quanti-tate and unconventionally diagram finger-counting confrontation visual fields, Ophthalmol. Times 5(4):17, 19, 30, 34, 48, 53, 1980.

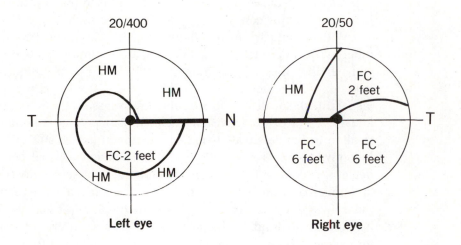

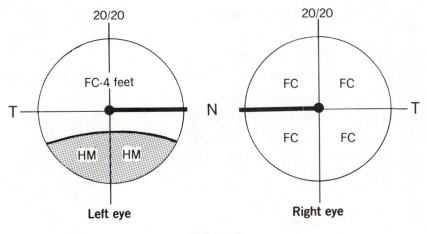

FIG. 19-3

CONFRONTATION: COMPARISON TECHNIQUES

With all the techniques described so far, one always asks the patient whether or not he is able to see a certain stimulus (e.g., a light or wiggling fingers). Even with the finger-counting technique, basically one is asking whether or not the patient is able to see the fingers; asking him to tell you how many fingers you have up is simply confirming that he can see them.

With a comparison technique, one is asking the patient a fundamentally different question. He is asked to compare a stimulus in two locations and to tell you whether they are the same or different. The usefulness of the technique depends on the fact that if visual sensation is reduced because of a change in visual threshold, all stimuli are subjectively less bright in that region (pp. 46, 162, and 172). For example, visual sensation is depressed on one side of the vertical midline in hemianopias, whether bitemporal as a result of chiasmal lesions or homonymous as a result of postchiasmal lesions. Usual perimetric techniques detect this depression in terms of detecting light sensitivity (or visual threshold) and finger-counting confrontation may also detect a depression in terms of acuity (sharpness of vision). However, the hemianopic depression is also reflected in the brightness of stimuli in that area and in color saturation. Thus a red object may, for example, seem maroon to the right and bright red to the left of fixation.

To detect this difference, one can take a red object of reasonable size, ½ to 2 inches in diameter (such as a top of a cycloplegic bottle), have the patient fixate on your nose, and ask him if the red object has the exact same color 3 to 6 inches to the right of fixation as it does 3 to 6 inches to the left of fixation. This can be done somewhat above fixation and again somewhat below fixation.

You should pay the greatest attention to the patient's first response. The color difference should be instantly obvious to him. If he has to think about it, he may be reporting some subtle lighting difference or something else and the test is unreliable.

FIG. 19-4. Searching for quadrant differences in color saturation.

One can ask the patient to compare the two sides with the red object shown in sequence, as illustrated, or one can hold up two red objects simultaneously, one on each side, and ask him to compare them.

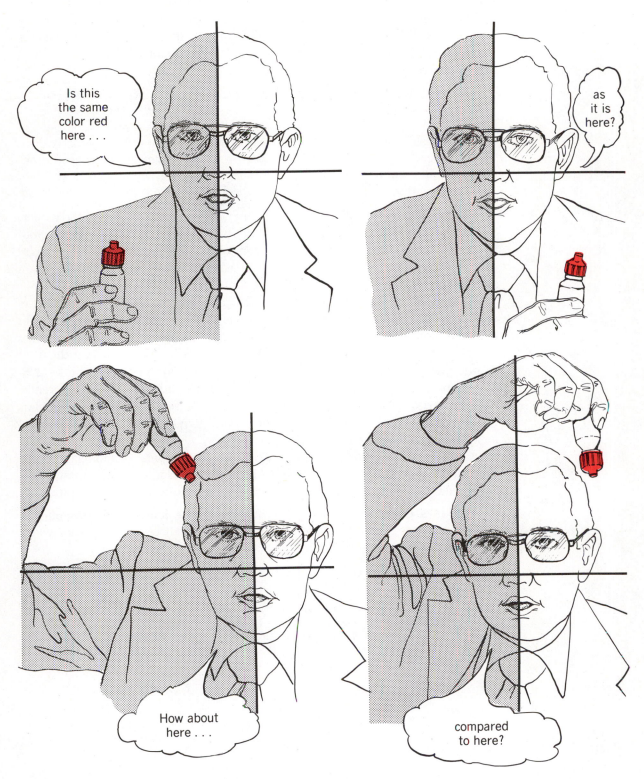

FIG. 19-4

If the patient reports that the color is different (or to confirm in your own mind that there is no difference), one should move the object horizontally and ask the patient to tell you when it changes color, moving it across the vertical midline above fixation and then repeating the process below fixation. The importance of this maneuver will be explained later (p. 272).

FIG. 19-5. Confirming a hemianopia. If the patient reports that the object changes color exactly at the vertical midline, there is strong evidence that a hemianopia is present. A definite absence of a color difference is strong evidence that there is no hemianopia. This test is so sensitive that it should be done whenever a visual field test is performed in search of a hemianopia, even if the perimetric or tangent screen examination has not revealed hemianopia. If hemianopia is not revealed by perimetry but is found by a color comparison test, one should do the perimetric testing again.

The same principle of having the patient compare the two sides of the vertical meridian can be used to compare the clarity with which the patient can see your two palms as you hold them on the two sides of fixation. He may be able to report that the two palms seem different after you ask him if they appear equally bright and equally distant.

This principle can also be used at the perimeter by asking the patient to compare the brightness of the test stimulus to the right and to the left. For example, the brightness 10 degrees from fixation along the 45-degree meridian can be compared with the brightness 10 degrees from fixation along the 135-degree meridian. This can also be done 10 degrees from fixation along the 225-degree meridian and the 315-degree meridian. If the patient detects a difference, the stimulus can be moved horizontally to see if the brightness changes just as the stimulus crosses the vertical midline. Application of the technique in neurologic testing is discussed on p. 256.

Comparison methods can also be used to check for central scotomas (p. 254). The patient may find that the red object has a duller color at fixation than it does at the side. In a normal field, color, brightness, and acuity are greatest at fixation.

FIG. 19-6. Checking for a central scotoma by color comparison techniques. A central scotoma is present if the patient reports that the color is brighter away from fixation than it is at fixation.

ADDITIONAL READING

Some additional information about confrontation testing can be found in:

Frisen, L.: A versatile color confrontation test for the central visual field: a comparison with automatic perimetry, Arch. Ophthalmol. **89:**3-9, 1973.

Glaser, J.S.: Neuro-ophthalmology, New York, 1978, Harper & Row, Publishers, pp. 12-20.

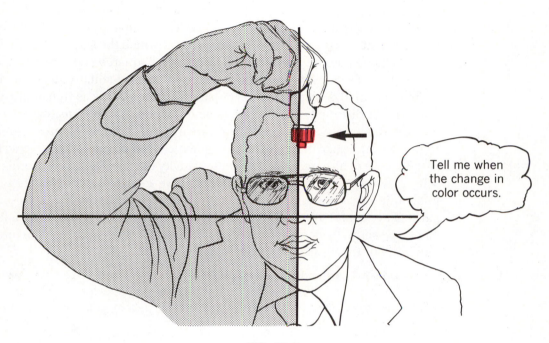

FIG. 19-5

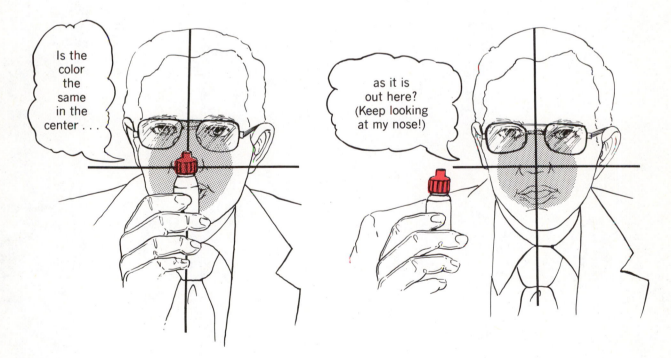

FIG. 19-6

AMSLER GRID

The Amsler grid is a method of testing approximately the inner 10 degrees of the central visual field. The standard chart consists of a grid of white lines on black paper held at a reading distance of 28 to 30 cm. The size of each square is 5 mm, which occupies 1 degree of the field. The complete set of Amsler grids has six other patterns useful in special situations in which the standard chart does not suffice. The patient is asked to look at a grid of squares and describe the areas where the lines are either missing or distorted. It is a qualitative test, but one that is quite useful in detecting central or paracentral scotomas as well as areas where the vision is distorted even if there is no reduction in light sensitivity. Distortion (as opposed to absence) of the grid squares (or metamorphopsia) suggests a retinal lesion rather than a central scotoma caused by an optic nerve lesion.

Because of its ease, rapidity, and sensitivity the Amsler grid is useful in those settings where one does not want quantitative information but wants simply to know quickly and accurately whether or not a central scotoma is present. It is particularly useful as an adjunct to perimetry with the Goldmann perimeter because the central 2 degrees cannot be adequately tested on the Goldmann perimeter without the special projection device.

FIG. 19-7. The standard Amsler grid. The patient is asked if he sees the white dot at the center. Then he is asked if, while continuing to stare at the dot, all four corners of the grid are visible, there are absent areas in the pattern, or the squares are distorted or blurred anywhere.

ADDITIONAL READINGS

Amsler, M.: L'Examen qualitatif de la fonction maculaire, Ophthalmologica, **114**:248-261, 1947.

Amsler, M.: Quantitative and qualitative vision, Trans. Ophthalmol. Soc. U.K. **69**:397-410, 1949.

FIG. 19-7

FRIEDMANN VISUAL FIELD ANALYSER

The Friedmann analyser[1], though not yet commonly in use deserves special attention because it has a unique approach and is incredibly simple in concept, accurate, and rapid.

This instrument consists of a strobe light (discharge tube) that flashes for about half a millisecond and evenly illuminates a translucent screen (diffuser). The intensity of the flash is controlled with filters in 0.2 log unit steps. A pair of opaque black plates with 98 holes (46 holes in the original model) sits in front of the screen as the patient sees it. An external illuminator provides an even illumination of the front plate surface and represents the "background illumination" (p. 8). The test is conducted in the mesopic, almost scotopic, range of background illumination.

A lever controlling the rear plate can be placed in 31 positions (designated *A* through *Z* and *a* through *h*). In each position two, three, or four of the holes is open so that two, three, or four spots of light can be seen when the strobe is flashed. The number of open holes for each lever position is indicated on the machine so that the perimetrist can know how many spots the patient should see at any lever position. Thus, for example, with the lever in position *A*, there are four open holes (there are three open holes with the lever in position *B*, two in position *C*, three in position *D*, etc.). When the strobe is flashed with the lever in position *A* and the patient reports seeing all four spots, one has performed static suprathreshold spot checking at four spots simultaneously. The lever is moved to position *B* and the strobe is flashed again. If, for example, the patient reports seeing only two spots, the operator flashes the strobe a second time with the lever in position *B*. If the patient still sees only two of the three spots, the operator determines which spot the patient did not see and records it. The process continues with the lever in positions, *C*, *D*, *E*, *F*, etc., until all 31 lever positions (*A* through *Z* and *a* through *h*) have been tested. By utilizing several simultaneous spots, all 98 spot positions are tested in 31 static presentations. This may take only 1 or 2 minutes per eye, especially if the field is normal.

FIG. 19-8. The Friedmann Analyser.

Simultaneous presentation of several stimuli is a great time saver but this is not the only unique feature. The rapid flash is over before the patient can shift fixation to look for the spots and there is little motivation to shift fixation because the stimuli are in several directions at the same time. This is fortunate because fixation is difficult to monitor: the patient's face is not well illuminated for the examiner to see.

---

[1]Clement-Clark International Ltd., 16 Wigmore Street, London W1H ODH, England.

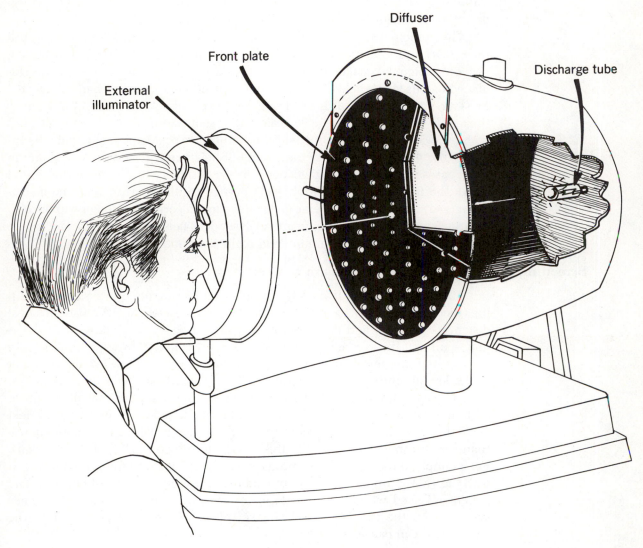

External illuminator

Front plate

Diffuser

Discharge tube

FIG. 19-8

Another unique feature is that the holes are not all the same size: they are larger toward the edge of the plate and smaller near fixation. Therefore, a specific stimulus intensity that is threshold at 20 degrees will also be threshold (not suprathreshold) at 5 degrees because the size of the spot is smaller by an appropriate amount. When a given stimulus intensity is determined to be 0.4 log unit suprathreshold at one location, it should be approximately 0.4 log unit suprathreshold at all locations; therefore, it can be used for static spot checking throughout the entire central field without fear that it will be too strong for the detection of shallow scotomas near fixation (pp. 126 and 222).

The combination of several stimuli presented simultaneously (making it a rapid test) and gradations of size of the hole (making it sensitive to detecting shallow scotomas) make the analyser a quick and very accurate screener for glaucomatous visual field defects, as well as all other defects that can be detected by static spot checking. It is even possible to spot-check the point of fixation as the ninety-ninth location. The 98 positions for spot testing are quite adequate, but with a device for eccentric fixation the number of positions can actually be increased to 490 or more. Only the central 25 degrees is tested, however, and in some cases where there is a defect only in the periphery (but none in the central field), the field test would falsely yield normal results. Fortunately, the instrument is so sensitive that it seems to be rare to find a peripheral defect without *any* central defect, and if the Friedmann analyser does not reveal a defect, one can be reasonably certain that the entire field really is normal.

Screening procedure with the Friedmann analyser

The analyser (Mark II model) can be used in a number of ways. For screening, the following may be a useful approach. First, determine the patient's best distance correction and use a +4.00 D near add or less according to age. It is important that the eye being tested be accurately centered by adjusting the chin rest—a step easy to overlook. It may be necessary to allow a few minutes to adapt to the low illumination level, especially if the patient has been in a brightly lit waiting area. With the lever in position H, the weakest stimulus that allows any or all four spots to be seen (threshold stimulus) is determined. For a visual field screening test, the filters are set so that the stimulus is 0.4 log unit more intense than the threshold stimulus, and this is used to screen at all 31 lever positions. For example, if the threshold stimulus at h is the 2.0 log unit filter, the test is run with the 1.6 log unit filter (0.4 log unit more intense than the threshold at h). The patient is asked with each flash to state how many spots he saw. Sometimes scratches on the front of the plate give reflections that are perceived by the patient and can cause confusion.

Any time the patient reports seeing fewer spots than there actually are, the same spots are flashed a second time, and the miss is not counted if he gives the correct number the second time (compare pp. 122 and 212). On the other hand, if he again sees only some of the spots, he is asked in which quadrants he did see spots and the examiner records the spots that he did not see.

As a screening test, nothing more is done except to record the regions where a defect is found. It is possible to quantitate the threshold at all missed spots, increasing the intensity (reducing the filters) until it is determined at what intensity each of the missed spots does become visible. Quantitation is achieved nicely, but (as always with a scatterplot of threshold determinations) recording of the threshold at each spot in an easily readable format is a problem.

ADDITIONAL READINGS

Bedwell, C.H.: Recent developments in investigations of visual fields, Am. J. Optom. Physiol. Opt. **55**:681-699, 1978.

Friedmann, A.I.: Serial analysis of changes in visual field defects, employing a new instrument, to determine the activity of diseases involving the visual pathways, Ophthalmologica **152**:1-12, 1966.

Friedmann, A.I.: Experiences with a prototype 100-hole front plate for the visual field analyser in glaucoma, Doc. Ophthalmol. Proc. Series **14**:87-92, 1977.

Friedmann, A.I.: Outline of visual field analyser Mark II, Doc. Ophthalmol. Proc. Series **22**:65-67, 1979.

Greve, E.L., and Verduin, W.M.: Mass visual field investigation of 1834 subjects with supposedly normal eyes, Albrecht von Graefes Arch. Klin. Exp. Ophthalmol. **183**:266-293, 1972.

Pashley, J.C.: Assessment of the Friedmann visual field analyser, L'Annee Ther. Clin. Ophtalmol. **25**:536-541, 1974.

AUTOMATIC SCREENING PERIMETERS

Automatic and semiautomatic perimeters and tangent screens are being developed at a rapid rate, and each year brings new models with various changes and improvements; therefore, it is not possible to discuss specific instruments or to give an evaluation of the latest models. However, it is possible to discuss the general nature of automation as used to test visual fields and the features of automatic perimeters that would be important for specific roles.

The easiest task to achieve by automation is suprathreshold static spot checking. In a number of automatic perimeters, a stimulus of a specific intensity is presented at each of 75 to 100 locations within the central field, perhaps extending somewhat into the peripheral field. Typically the operator manually selects the intensity to be used for spot checking. The automation consists of monitoring fixation, presenting the stimulus in some sequence at the various spots, and recording for each spot if the patient did or did not respond. The instrument then produces a field diagram on which is indicated each of the spots at which the patient did not respond. In some instruments, a different threshold value is chosen for the central field (which has the majority of points to be tested) and for the peripheral field (where a few points are checked). Also, with some models, points where the patient did not respond can be checked a second time.

Such instruments are useful to screen for glaucoma and for most other types of visual field defects. They can do an excellent screening for visual field defects—perhaps as well as most experienced perimetrists, provided the operator follows certain important principles (not always mentioned in the instructions provided by the manufacturer), such as selecting a stimulus value that is threshold at 25 degrees for that particular patient and re-checking missed spots if this is not done automatically. The advantage of the automatic perimeter is that any office assistant, even without training in perimetry, can be shown how to select a threshold stimulus and set the machine in operation. The test is rapid and efficient and the results are recorded automatically. Moreover, for research purposes, one can be more confident that each field examination is performed in a standard manner.

A nonautomatic instrument, such as the Friedmann analyser, can also be used by a relatively untrained office assistant. It is more rapid by virtue of multiple simultaneous stimulus presentations but requires the operator to monitor fixation and to record those spots that are not seen, since this information is not recorded automatically.

In principle, it is possible to quantitate the field defects with the automatic spot-checking instrument by rerunning the program at each of several stimulus intensities. Some instruments allow the operator to check with a more intense stimulus only the spots previously missed. Either way, by looking over the several charts generated, one can determine the weakest stimulus seen at each location, or at least at each abnormal location. However, if the screening program must be repeated several times, the total field examination becomes lengthy and it is difficult to record the scatterplot results in a manner that is easily readable. For a skilled perimetrist, it becomes more efficient to do the entire field examination manually on a Goldmann perimeter.

The most efficient use of the automatic instrument is for screening by relatively untrained personnel of a group in which only a few will have a defect. This could include such settings as screening all driver's license or pilot's license applicants or screening for glaucoma in a retirement center. In a clinical office, a low prevalence of defects might be found in patients with elevated intraocular pressure but no cupping, or those with endocrine abnormalities suggesting a pituitary tumor but no optic atrophy or other sign of chiasmal involvement, and a screening instrument might be used. Confirmation of any uncertain defects and quantitation of defects discovered are performed manually on another instrument at some later time by a person knowledgeable and experienced in perimetry. If a patient is very likely to have a defect—for example, if there is marked cupping of the disc, or if a confrontation test has shown a defect to be present—and if the defect will require quantitation, it is more efficient to go directly to manual perimetry, or to use an automatic perimeter that can quantitate defects.

Of course, all screening examinations could be performed manually by an experienced perimetrist, probably as rapidly as with an automatic perimeter. However, in a practice where the majority of people suspected of having field defects will, in fact, not have field defects, and where the ophthalmologist or the visual field technician is unable to handle the entire load of screening field examinations, the automatic perimeter can be used by a less experienced assistant, with the ophthalmologist or the skilled perimetrist performing diagnostic and quantitative examinations only on those who seem to have a defect with the screening instrument.

The automatic perimeter that utilizes suprathreshold static spot checking may also be of particular advantage in certain research studies where statistical analysis is to be performed on visual function according to whether or not a given stimulus is visible in a selection of points throughout the visual field. The automatic perimeter in such a setting, if there are several collaborating clinics, assures that the examination would be performed in the same manner for everyone in all clinics, and in both the treated and untreated groups.

AUTOMATIC PERIMETERS THAT QUANTITATE

Another class of automatic perimeters can actually determine the static threshold at each point automatically. Because it does take several stimulus presentations at each point to determine the threshold, it becomes a more lengthy procedure than suprathreshold static spot checking with only one stimulus presentation at each point, the stimulus being either seen or not seen. While not so efficient for screening purposes, the instrument that determines actual threshold at each point becomes a quantitative visual field examination that would be suitable for following the progress of a chronic condition such as glaucoma, provided enough points are tested.

Representation of the results in a readable format is a problem. A series of numbers at the tested point in the visual field is difficult to interpret until it becomes familiar. A printout with symbols of various densities to represent different stimuli is helpful, similar to the scatterplots already illustrated (pp. 192 and 224). Sometimes many points more are represented on the printout than were actually tested in order to give a better sense of isopters (pp. 263 and 269). In reading these printouts, one must keep in mind that only some of the points have been tested and that each of the other points is an assumed interpolated value. Thus, a certain amount of skill is required to interpret the results, even though the test, while lengthy and highly quantitated at the tested points, has been performed automatically.

At least one automatic perimeter attempts to perform a kinetic visual field examination, or actually a combined kinetic and static examination similar to the manual techniques described in this book. Kinetic perimetry is advantageous in gaining an overview of the field rapidly and outlining larger defects (pp. 182 and 186). It is less efficient to determine threshold at many points in order to outline the boundary of a large dense defect. With skillful use of kinetic perimetry, combined with static spot checking for occasional determinations of threshold statically, the skilled perimetrist manually derives considerable information about the visual field in a very efficient use of time. If it can be duplicated, it may also prove to be efficient for an automatic perimeter.

The difficulty with kinetic perimetry to be performed automatically is that the usual manual examination involves considerable reasoning and decision making on the part of the perimetrist who may have some prior information about the type of visual field defect suspected, may recognize areas where the patient is responding more slowly or with hesitation, or, based on some irregularity in one isopter, may decide to explore more carefully a certain area but to ignore another, and so on. Because of this, an efficient and accurate quantitative visual field by means of automatic kinetic perimetry has been difficult to achieve. However, in principle, kinetic perimetry combined with other modes may eventually be the most efficient way to obtain a completely quantitative visual field. After all, even when static perimetry is used in specialized university clinics, the experienced perimetrist will still rely heavily on kinetic perimetry to map out the hill of vision.

Perimeters that quantitate have different programs for different uses, including rapid screening strategies such as suprathreshold static spot checking. Thus, these perimeters, capable of automatic quantitation, can also be used to screen without quantitation of defects. An automatic perimeter may be used to also provide for storage of visual field information on each patient, so that retesting on subsequent occasions can be more efficient because the testing strategy can take into account the known previous threshold at each point in this individual. Statistical analysis of the change in threshold could also be performed so that some aspects of interpretation can be achieved automatically.

For selected readings on the rapidly developing field of automatic perimetry see Appendix B.

CHAPTER 20

Selection of instruments and techniques

INSTRUMENTS

For general use, the combination of a Goldmann perimeter, the Amsler grid, and confrontation techniques seems to cover most, if not all, visual field testing needs. The Tübinger or Harms (Oculus) perimeter is a less common projection perimeter that is particularly designed for static perimetry and its telescope port does not interfere with testing the central 2 degrees of the visual field. It may be used in place of or in addition to the Goldmann perimeter in specialized clinics that perform static profile perimetry often.

In offices where many visual field tests are being performed and, thus, where a second instrument (in addition to a manual bowl perimeter) becomes necessary, it may make sense to obtain an instrument that can perform static spot checking. It is a reasonable investment if a fair proportion of the field tests being performed are for screening (to determine whether or not a defect is present) and if many of these have normal results or do not need quantitation. Among the options are the Friedmann analyser and several of the automatic perimeters.

The classic tangent screen with standard test objects or projected stimuli (Auto-plot by Bausch & Lomb) is an alternative to the Goldmann perimeter. It is simple and inexpensive and, when used with skill, can provide entirely adequate screening, diagnostic, and quantitative field examinations. With a good room arrangement (i.e., with the screen on the wall 1 meter away from a rotating examining chair), a field examination can be performed quickly with almost no fuss or bother. The practical convenience may be a definite advantage in clinical offices where quick diagnostic examinations predominate and quantitated field examinations are less often needed. Moreover, a skilled perimetrist will find the ability to change the testing distance from 1 to 2 meters helpful in the diagnosis of functional (hysterical) visual loss.

The tangent screen has two problems, neither fatal. First, strict quantitation is more difficult to achieve, particularly if attention is not given to a standard level of even illumination (classically, 7 foot-candles of daylight) and to keeping the test objects clean. Second, another instrument is needed when the peripheral field needs testing, although admittedly it is quite often sufficient to examine only the central field. For the second instrument, an arc perimeter (e.g., the Aimark[1]) is a convenient companion to the tangent screen but shares the difficulty in

---

[1]Clement-Clark International Ltd., 16 Wigmore Street, London W1H ODH, England.

achieving appropriate background illumination. This combination of the tangent screen and the arc perimeter is preferred by some because with both instruments the patient and examiner are in full view of each other, giving less sense of isolation to the patient than occurs when using a bowl perimeter like the Goldmann. Others find that with the bowl perimeter voice contact is usually sufficient and they prefer the ability to perform both central and peripheral field tests with the same instrument, as well as the confidence of a standardized quantitation.

TECHNIQUE AND STRATEGY SELECTION

There are many other visual field testing devices available and some may be quite satisfactory alternatives, provided the device is convenient and allows quantitation by use of controlled background and several standard stimuli. In the end, the perimetrist who chooses the right technique and strategy at the right time is more important than the instrument.

Perimetry is done by the perimetrist, not the perimeter.—*Traquair*

There is no such thing as Goldmann perimetry, only a Goldmann perimeter.

—Goldmann

Also important is the perimetrist's ability to put the patient at ease and obtain the best results that the patient can give. Even the automatic perimeters require someone to choose the right program for the circumstances at hand and the operator must provide warmth and encouragement as needed.

We will now discuss the time and place for using the various techniques described earlier in the book.

ROUTINE OFFICE VISITS

Formal visual field testing is not routinely part of a complete eye examination in most offices and clinics. Probably a routine complete eye examination should include a rapid determination by confrontation that the patient is able to count fingers 3 or 4 feet away, 45 degrees from fixation in each of the four quadrants, along with an examination of the pupils, an alternate cover test, and other components of a complete routine eye examination. Such a quick confrontation examination is routine in our institution and may pick up such things as a glaucomatous visual field defect in the upper nasal quadrant, an unsuspected hemianopia, or a field defect as a result of an unsuspected retinal detachment (although the existence of these conditions may also be detected in the course of the remainder of the eye examination).

With the availability of automatic screening devices, it will be tempting to incorporate a screening visual field examination routinely into every complete eye examination. It remains to be seen if this will be cost effective and how often such an examination will detect the existence of a condition that did not become apparent in the course of the remainder of the eye examination, including ophthalmoscopy.

MASS VISION SCREENING

The screening visual field examination—e.g., with an automatic perimeter that uses static spot-checking strategy—may be useful, along with determination of visual acuity, to look for defects within large groups. The main consideration in judging such screening projects is whether or not a sufficient number of visual defects are detected to be worth the effort and expense. This obviously depends on how many defects exist in the population (prevalence), how serious the existing defects are, and how effectively the testing time can be kept acceptably brief without losing sensitivity in detecting the people who have abnormalities.

An important consideration in choosing a testing strategy is the rate of false positive results (the percentage of people with normal vision who miss a few spots and seem to have a field defect but do not) compared to the prevalence of true visual field defects. It is very discouraging if the prevalence of true defects is quite low (1% or less) and most positive results uncovered during a screening project are false alarms. This will happen if the rate of false positives exceeds the prevalence of true defects in a population. Moreover, the additional time that it takes to do more definitive examinations on the false positives must be taken into account when judging the time expended in detecting the people with true defects.

The rate of false positive results can be reduced by retesting any missed points (pp. 122, 212, and 245) and also by using a somewhat stronger stimulus for spot checking. To reduce the number of false positives while keeping the testing time reasonable, the best strategy in mass screening would seem to be to test a reasonable number of points (between 50 and 100) with a stimulus that ought to be suprathreshold at all points in virtually all normal people (but not too strong a stimulus or it will also be seen too often within moderately deep field defects and these defects would escape detection). All missed points must be retested and must be missed a second time to be considered an abnormality. If it is obvious during the test that the field is abnormal, the screening test can be stopped because it has been determined that a definitive field test is necessary. The Friedmann visual field analyser and most of the automatic perimeters can be used for this type of screening.

It is important to realize that using a stronger stimulus to lessen false positive results and limiting the number of locations to be tested to keep the time acceptable means that small or shallow defects may not be detected. In a screening program this deficiency is accepted with the realization that the defects missed are less important or even inconsequential, being small or shallow. Hopefully, all the more important defects that exceed a certain size and density will be discovered.

GLAUCOMA SCREENING PROGRAMS

Glaucoma screening projects in the general population have generally consisted of measuring the intraocular pressure. It is known that many individuals with glaucoma are not detected by single pressure readings. To supplement the pressure readings, examinations of the optic disc or screening visual field examinations would improve the detection rate. However, since most screening projects are not conducted by highly trained personnel, disc examinations and field examinations have not been considered feasible. Now, with the Friedmann visual field analyser and automatic instruments that use a suprathreshold static spot-checking strategy, which can be operated by personnel without perimetric training, it may become feasible to incorporate field testing into the standard glaucoma detection projects.

The glaucoma screening program differs from the mass screening program in that it is aimed specifically at glaucomatous visual field defects. However, the same considerations apply as in mass screening programs discussed on the preceding page. It is important to use a screening technique that has a low false positive rate. Otherwise it will be too time consuming to do a thorough eye examination (not just of the field, but a complete eye examination) on all who seem to have a defect—most of whom would turn out to be normal. A suitable protocol might be simply to spot-check the central 25 degrees with the I-3e stimulus or a stimulus that is threshold at 30 degrees. In order to achieve a quick, simple screening test without too many false diagnoses some early field defects will escape detection.

GLAUCOMA DETECTION IN THE CLINICAL OFFICE

In an ophthalmologist's office, the combination of pressure measurement and careful examination of the optic disc constitutes an efficient method for glaucoma detection in patients who come for a complete eye examination. Ophthalmoscopy is about as sensitive as visual field testing but faster and, thus, is better for glaucoma detection when expert ophthalmoscopy is available. In this setting, visual field screening for glaucomatous field defects would be performed on individuals who have a particular sign of glaucoma, perhaps an elevated pressure (whether or not the disc appears to be damaged) or an excavated disc (whether the pressure is elevated or not), or some other clinical finding. A standard spot-checking technique can be used, but because the patient is already definitely suspected of having glaucoma, it would be sensible to do a more careful screen than would be used to screen the general population. For example, one could use one of the modifications that uses a weaker stimulus to spot-check in the center 10 or 15 degrees than is used between 15 and 30 degrees, and also to look for nasal steps and temporal wedges. Even if there is a slightly greater rate of false positive results, the number of cases of true glaucoma detected will outnumber the false positive results because the prevalence of glaucoma is high in the group. The subsequent extra effort to confirm equivocal defects by quantitative perimetry is a worthwhile price to pay in order to improve the sensitivity and to detect field defects at the earliest possible stage.

If any defect is found on screening, the boundaries of the defect and its depth need to be determined as a diagnostic examination, to be sure that the defect is real. If a manual technique such as the Goldmann perimeter was used for screening, this can conveniently be accomplished immediately. If other instruments that are only capable of static presentations were used, it is best to switch to an instrument with capabilities to quantitate as soon as it becomes apparent that the field is abnormal.

PATIENTS WITH POOR VISUAL ACUITY OR DISTORTED VISION

Reduced visual acuity should always be associated with an abnormal visual threshold at fixation. Either (1) there is depression of the whole visual field (all isopters are moved inward); (2) there is a central scotoma (or some other pre-chiasmal lesion involving fixation); or (3) both are present.

Therefore, for all patients with reduced acuity who are undergoing visual field examination:

1. Look for presence or absence of generalized depression. Do not make the mistake of plotting only a large isopter (e.g., V-4e) just because the visual acuity is poor. Determine whether moderate stimuli (I-2e, I-3e) are in their normal location, moved inward, or perhaps cannot be seen at all.

2. Look for a central scotoma. Unfortunately, on the Goldmann perimeter, the inner 2 degrees of the field is occupied by the fixation spot and telescope port. Therefore, the very center of the field cannot be tested on the Goldmann perimeter without a special device. However, one should look to see if a central scotoma larger than 2 degrees is present. If none is found—and if the special device for the Goldmann perimeter (or a Harms perimeter that does not have the central port) is not available to explore within the central 2 degrees—the Amsler grid, the tangent screen, or the confrontation test with a red test object should be used to find a central scotoma that cannot be detected within the perimeter. In the presence of very poor vision, ask the patient to compare the brightness of a penlight at fixation to the brightness at other locations in the field. The search for a central scotoma even in the presence of a generalized depression may help determine whether or not a patient with cataract also has macular disease, glaucoma, or optic atrophy that would prevent a good visual return with cataract extraction.

There are additional visual tests that may be used to analyze the cause of reduced acuity:

1. Look for temporal hemianopia, especially superiorly in both eyes, not just the eye with poor acuity. If there is a unilateral unexplained central scotoma, both eyes are tested because chiasmal lesions may involve the optic nerves and produce a central scotoma in one eye associated with a temporal field defect in both eyes.

2. Look for abnormal pupil reactions, especially with the swinging light test. Central scotomas resulting from optic nerve disease will typically have an afferent pupillary defect or Marcus Gunn's pupillary sign. Central scotomas resulting from macular disease will typically not have an abnormal pupil reaction, and neither will a generalized depression resulting from a cataract or other opacity of the normally transparent ocular media.

3. When checking central vision with the Amsler grid, ask if the central region is blurred or absent and also whether or not it is distorted with wavy lines. Distortion of the image, called "metamorphopsia," suggests the presence of macular disease as the cause for poor central vision.

4. If the visual acuity is reduced but still better than 20/80, a photo stress test can be performed by having the patient look at a bright penlight for 10 seconds and then having him look at a visual acuity chart to determine how long it takes for the visual acuity to return to the level he had before staring at the light. If macular disease is present, recovery may take longer than 30 to 50 seconds, or the recovery time in one eye may be more than 20 seconds longer than in the other. However, patients with central scotomas as a result of optic nerve disease, like those with normal eyes, will recover to their usual acuity sooner.

5. If there is reduced acuity but no scotoma under the usual monocular testing circumstances, there may be amblyopia, perhaps as a result of monofixational phoria that can be discovered by stereopsis testing. Another way to determine whether or not a reduced acuity is the result of amblyopia is with a 2.0–log-unit filter. Such a filter placed before a normal eye will reduce the acuity two lines (20/20 to 20/40). When the filter is placed before an amblyopic eye, the vision is affected less than two lines and may even improve; however, when placed in front of an eye with vision reduced organically (retinal or optic nerve disease), the visual acuity will be worsened by at least two lines and sometimes dramatically more.

The visual acuity should always be recorded on the visual field chart—especially if the acuity is reduced.

THE NEUROLOGIC FIELD

The emphasis in this book has been on quantitative visual field examination as performed for detection of glaucoma, based on the assumption that glaucoma is more common in the usual clinic office than neurologic and other conditions that require visual field examinations. Second, if one performs a glaucoma-type examination as outlined in Chapter 11, the visual field examination will be more than adequate for all other purposes, provided that one pays special attention to the vertical meridian of the field of patients who may have a chiasmal or postchiasmal lesion, and that one is alert to the need to look for a central scotoma in the presence of reduced visual acuity.

However, the complete quantitative visual field examination that is necessary to follow patients with glaucoma is far more extensive than is required in many clinical situations. Not only is it a waste of effort but sometimes, particularly in a neurologic or feeble patient, a simple examination can provide more diagnostic information than a quantitated visual field examination, which is difficult for the patient. Therefore, it is necessary to look carefully at the techniques that might be used to test the patient with a suspected neurologic lesion.

Chiasmal and postchiasmal lesions

Techniques for detecting chiasmal and postchiasmal lesions include:

1. **Comparison techniques.** When searching for evidence of a hemianopia, and particularly a bitemporal hemianopia, the strategy of asking the patient to compare the two sides of the vertical meridian by confrontation is a very helpful method. To review what was expressed earlier (pp. 236-240), the patient may be asked to compare the quality of vision with respect to two hands held to the right and left of the vertical meridian, or to compare the color of a sizable red object when held to the right and left of the vertical meridian. In using this technique diagnostically when the patient reports having dimmer vision on one side than on the other, it is very important that the object be moved across the vertical meridian from one side to the other and that the patient report when the change occurs. If the change occurs gradually, the presence of a hemianopia is not convincingly demonstrated; but a hemianopia is demonstrated if the patient reports a sudden change in visibility precisely when the vertical meridian is crossed.

The comparison tests are very good because they are quite sensitive in detecting hemianopias: if an alert patient is quite certain that there is no difference in visibility on the two sides of the vertical meridian, it is quite unlikely that a hemianopia is present. On the other hand, a convincing difference of visibility across the vertical meridian is quite specific, meaning that a hemianopia is almost certain to be present.

Because important neurosurgical diagnostic decisions may be based in part on the field examination, it is well to have corroborating evidence of the hemianopia by one of the other methods given below, especially because some patients give uncertain responses when tested with comparison methods by confrontation. Nonetheless, the color comparison by confrontation is so accurate, despite its simplicity, that it might be used routinely to double-check the findings with other perimetric methods.

2. **Isopter plotting.** A second method for demonstrating a hemianopia is to plot isopters, paying particular attention to the isopters as they cross the vertical meridian. Dr. J. Lawton Smith performs this kinetic examination on the tangent screen, but instead of using the regular test objects, he uses a projected spot of light from a focused flashlight, controlling the intensity of the spot by partially covering the end of the flashlight with his hands.[1] In essence, he dims the stimulus on the tangent screen until it is of appropriate intensity to form an isopter somewhere between 15 and 30 degrees from fixation and uses this projected stimulus to plot the isopter kinetically. The advantage of this method is the simplicity of the equipment and simplicity in performing the test itself. The point is that nothing more elegant is required, since one is simply asking whether or not a hemianopia is present. Dr. Smith's technique need not be performed in an ophthalmologist's office. With the appropriately focused flashlight the technique can be demonstrated in a classroom against a chalkboard or performed in almost any hospital room on a blank wall. Therefore, one does not need to move a debilitated patient to a room with special perimetry equipment.

Of course, if the patient happens to be in a clinical examining room equipped for visual field testing, one can use the ordinary tangent screen method, an Auto-plot, or a Goldmann perimeter, provided it is convenient and comfortable. With the perimeter, one can plot several isopters, particularly across the vertical meridian, and also ask the patient to compare the intensity of the stimulus to the right and to the left of the vertical meridian. One might as well use a sophisticated instrument to plot isopters, if it is convenient and available. Not only is the presence of a hemianopia demonstrated by plotting isopters but also the extent and depth of the defect is demonstrated.

3. **Static spot checking.** The third basic method to find a hemianopia would be by means of static spot checking. The Friedmann visual field analyser or an automatic perimeter that uses static spot-checking strategies would uncover a hemianopia, provided the stimulus is appropriately chosen so that it is supra-

---

[1]Smith, J.L.: The optic nerve, Miami, 1977, Neuro-ophthalmology Tapes (9820 S.W. 62 Court, Miami, Fl. 33156), pp. 55-57.

threshold on one side of the vertical meridian but infrathreshold on the other. In the hands of an experienced person with the appropriate equipment, this method could be rapid and efficient as well as accurate, provided the operator chooses the test stimulus correctly. Spot checking can also be performed at the Goldmann perimeter, but with the perimeter it would, in fact, be more convenient to plot several isopters across the vertical meridian.

4. **Static cut.** Finally, a static cut along an arc crossing the vertical meridian (p. 272) would show the presence of a vertical step, confirming a hemianopia. This method is practical only for those facile in performing static cuts or who have an automatic perimeter with this capability; for an individual with the appropriate equipment and experience, the technique is not difficult because it involves checking only three to five points on either side of the vertical meridian for each static cut.

In most clinics and offices, the static cut methods are not available but could be performed by the quantitating automatic perimeter. Static cuts are certainly not necessary, and the simpler methods may be better, especially if the diagnostician performs the test personally, knowing precisely for what he is testing. There is certainly an advantage in knowing, according to the clinical circumstance, what kind of hemianopia you are looking for, and there is nothing like doing the test yourself to know how subtle or definite the findings are.

Prechiasmal lesions

An optic nerve lesion may produce a central scotoma and poor visual acuity (see pp. 198 and 254) or nerve fiber bundle defects that are similar to glaucoma defects. Nerve fiber bundle defects can be examined by the technique used for glaucoma.

Retinal lesions may produce many different defects. With standard equipment the defects can be detected and outlined with tailor-made strategies to look for such defects as a scotoma corresponding to a choroidal mass or a ring scotoma resulting from retinitis pigmentosa. The location, site, and nature of the field defect are so varied among the many retinal diseases that it is necessary for someone acquainted with the disease under consideration to decide in what location to look for a defect and whether to plot isopters, spot check for scotomas, or perform a static cut.

CHAPTER 21

Interpretation of visual fields

Interpretation of visual field defects is a skill that depends on a knowledge of the many diseases that affect visual function as well as on the personal experience of visual field testing in the various diseases. This chapter is not intended to provide a detailed exposition of this subject but only to introduce the subject by highlighting selected problem areas and principles. The reader will have to gain his ultimate skill of interpretation through clinical experience by applying these principles and his knowledge of the ocular diseases that affect visual function (see references on pp. 205 and 290).

JUDGING THE ADEQUACY OF THE TEST

The first step in interpretation is to make a judgment about the thoroughness and appropriateness of the examination with regard to the nature, size, and depth of the defects being looked for. If no field defect was detected, the questions are, "What defects could have escaped detection by the technique used?" and "Is the defect that could have been missed one that I am interested in?" If hemianopia was suspected, were the proper examination strategies (p. 256) performed to detect a hemianopia? If a central scotoma was suspected, was the appropriate testing (p. 254) performed? To detect scotomas, was the relevant region explored, were a sufficient number of points tested to detect a small scotoma (pp. 122, 160 and 220), and was the stimulus used appropriate to detect shallow scotomas? Were enough points plotted on an isopter in the areas where a defect might exist?

FIG. 21-1. Limits of detectability.
A, Shallow scotomas near the isopter will be detected but scotomas further inward must be deeper to be discovered. Only two of the three scotomas would be discovered with the I-3e stimulus. The shallower scotoma near fixation would escape detection. The interpreter must be conscious of the fact that when spot checking is done with only one stimulus, scotomas less than 0.5 log unit deep might escape detection in the region of the field close to fixation (pp. 126 and 222).

B, Example of an isopter plot based on six points. One must realize that only the six points at which the patient responded to a stimulus were actually tested (see p. 14) and that the line connecting the points may or may not be a smooth curve. Additional points must be plotted to determine that a nasal step is or is not present.

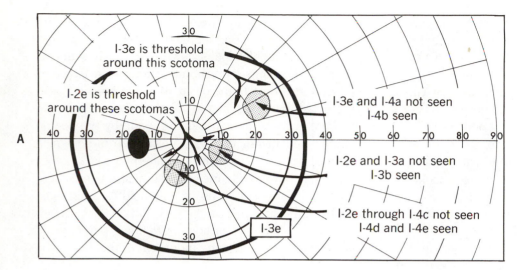

I-3e is threshold
around this scotoma

I-2e is threshold
around these scotomas

A

I-3e and I-4a not seen
I-4b seen

I-2e and I-3a not seen
I-3b seen

I-2e through I-4c not seen
I-4d and I-4e seen

I-3e

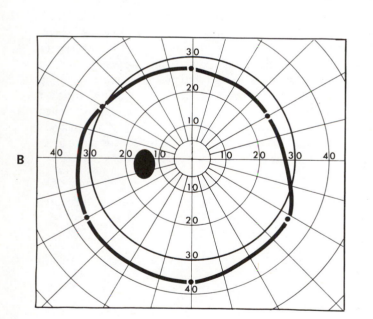

B

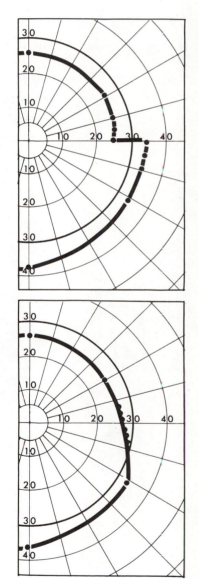

FIG. 21-1

In kinetic perimetry it is a wise practice to mark each point where the patient responds so that the exactness of the test and the degree of variability in patient responses can be judged by another person who looks at the diagram subsequently. In clinics where it is a practice to show only representative points, the isopter is drawn with or without a nasal step according to the perimetrist's impression as to whether there is or is not a demonstrable nasal step. In essence, an interpretive judgment of whether or not there is a real defect is being made by the person performing the examination. In such instances, if no nasal step is shown, a sufficient number of representative points should be indicated so that another person later looking at the chart may have confidence that sufficient points were plotted to have detected a nasal step if one were present. The field diagram must indicate the areas spot-checked and the stimulus used ("O.K. to I-3e"), the steadiness of fixation, and the perimetrist's overall confidence in the examination's reliability (see p. 179). All these factors enter into the judgment of the diagnostic quality of the examination.

With automated perimetry, as with manual perimetry, it is important to know the methods of field testing used by the machine, such as the number of points tested, the strategy of selecting the test stimuli, and so on. Only then can the diagnostic and qualitative limitations of a given field test be appreciated by the interpreter. This knowledge of how the instrument functions is important even for interpreting the output of the most sophisticated perimeters.

FIG. 21-2. A normal visual field represented in the printout scatterplot of the Octopus.[1] The threshold at 2821 points is represented by circular and square symbols of various sizes. It is important to know that only a certain number of points (usually 72) is actually tested and that all the other points are assumed values, calculated by interpretation from the known nearby points. The boundary of the blind spot is fuzzy. This occurs because of the 72 spots actually tested only one was in the blind spot. All surrounding nontested points are assigned thresholds by interpolation, including some points that are actually within the blind spot. The result is a graded transition between the absolute density of the center and the surrounding normal region. The "isopters" (boundaries between areas with different levels of sensation) are plotted irregular even in a normal field because of varying responses close to the isopter (in the zone of inconsistency, see p. 162). (Courtesy of Dr. Jess Smith.)

----

[1]Hitron Corporation, 20 Risho Avenue, Westminister Industrial Park, East Providence, R.I. 02914.

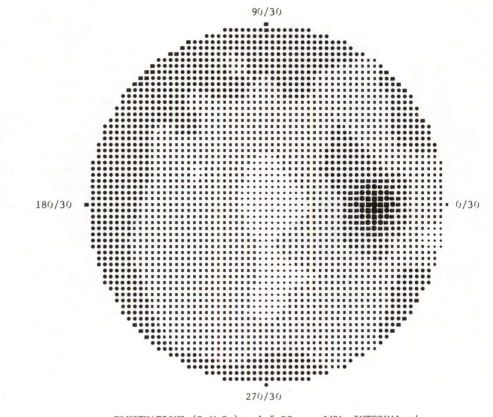

90/30

180/30

0/30

270/30

FLUCTUATIONS (R.M.S.): 1.5 DB   LUM. INTERVAL: 4

Symb.	⣿	⣿	⣿	⣿	⣿	⣿	⣿	⣿	⬛
dB	51−36	35−31	30−26	25−21	20−16	15−11	10−6	5−1	0
asb	0,008−0,25	0,31−0,8	1−2,5	3,1−8	10−25	31−80	100−250	315−800	1000

1 asb = 0,318 cd/m²

FIG. 21-2

CONFIRMING THE PRESENCE OR ABSENCE OF A DEFECT

With static threshold perimetry or static threshold spot checking, sometimes the patient may not respond to an individual stimulus presentation simply because one is working near the zone of uncertainty (zone of inconsistent responses) and the stimuli are barely visible. In a similar way, there may be a delayed response to a kinetic stimulus, suggesting a localized inward deviation of the isopter that may simply be a response at the innermost portion of the zone of uncertainty. This is particularly a problem when the zone is broad because that region of the field is rather flat (pp. 168 and 188). In addition, there may be occasional missed or delayed responses in both static and kinetic perimetry resulting from lapses of attention by the patient.

Therefore, a missed or delayed response in either kinetic or static perimetry may result from the normal variability of responsiveness but, of course, could also represent a real visual field defect. It is obvious that no real conclusion can be drawn on the basis of one or two presentations to which the patient did not respond when it seemed that he should have. There must be some confirmation of the "defect" before concluding that it really does or does not exist.

This confirmation may take the form of repeated presentations of the kinetic or static stimuli in the region until a more accurate idea of visual sensitivity in the region of suspected defect becomes apparent. An experienced perimetrist does this reflexly: any time a response is obtained that is out of keeping with the expected response it is natural to repeat it.

For example, in kinetic perimetry, if a patient responds 10 or 15 degrees closer to fixation than the preceding two or three points that were plotted, the perimetrist will naturally repeat the presentation to see if the isopter really is deviated inward or if the second response obtained is in keeping with the expected location based on the previous two or three points that were plotted. To judge whether or not there really is a visual field defect, the interpreter of the field, if not the same person who performed the field testing, must consider how many points were plotted in the seemingly abnormal region. If only one point is deviated inward and the perimetrist has not rechecked the finding, the defect may or may not be real.

Similarly, during static threshold perimetry, there is a tendency for an experienced perimetrist to retest the threshold at a spot if, and only if, the response is out of keeping with the expected response, based on the previously plotted adjacent point (p. 183). If the region is *not* retested, usually the interpreter will not accept a "defect" as genuine unless it is 0.5 log unit deep. Essentially this 0.5 log unit requirement allows 0.3 log unit for a normal variability of responsiveness and requires that at least one more stimulus (0.1 log unit brighter) was not seen before finally a response was obtained. Obviously, if there is a genuine defect 0.3 or 0.4 log units deep, it might be ignored when the 0.5 log unit criterion is used. A defect only 0.2 to 0.4 log unit deep could be documented only by testing the location in question repeatedly and comparing the average or usual value obtained with a similarly obtained average or usual value in the adjacent regions.

When accuracy is desired, the principle of performing repeated measurements is certainly a valid one. Any kind of measurement is more accurate if it is checked several times, taking the most frequent value or the average value to be the correct one. The average location of a response during kinetic perimetry will be at the center of the zone of uncertainty (the isopter) and not toward the edges. The average response will thus be a more reliable indication of the position of the isopters than any of the individual responses.

Ordinarily the perimetrist does not retest every point. Only when the response is out of keeping with the expected response will the perimetrist retest a given location. It would be very time-consuming to repeat every determination (kinetic or static) three to five times to obtain an average at each point. Therefore, a single response is usually accepted as representative without retesting if the response is as expected, i.e., if it is in keeping with adjacent points. In this manner of working, the confirmation that an individual response is valid is the fact that it is in keeping with adjacent points, rather than the fact that it was repeated several times.

We have already seen several examples in which the principle of repeated measurements has been applied:

For example, in an effort to determine nasal steps, presentations are performed kinetically—three just above and three just below the horizontal meridian nasally. This maneuver essentially constitutes three repeated measurements above and three below the horizontal, increasing the accuracy in each location. The method both increases the chances of discovering a nasal step and decreases the risk of a false response suggesting the presence of a defect that does not exist.

The Armaly-Drance suprathreshold testing technique is a second example. If there is a missed response, the validity of the "defect" is confirmed only if the stimulus is not seen on the second presentation in the same location or if there are missed responses in adjacent locations (see pp. 122 and 212). The same principle should be applied with the various modifications of the technique. For example, with the Friedmann visual field analyser or with automatic perimeters that use a suprathreshold static presentation, the same criteria should be used. Missed points must be retested manually if they are not retested automatically.

A third example is the procedure used in static threshold perimetry. It has been advocated that threshold be confirmed in each instance (1) by insisting that at least two stimuli be *not* seen (confirming that they are infrathreshold) before accepting a positive response and (2) by presenting the stimulus first seen on a second occasion to be sure that it is seen a second time before considering it to be visible (p. 183). In Greve's method (p. 184) the validity of the response is confirmed by response to a stimulus 0.1 log unit brighter. The criteria devised by Greve that a defect must be 0.5 log unit deep and 3 degrees wide is, in essence, demanding that each missed response be confirmed by a second missed response before accepting a pair of positive responses, and also that the apparent defect be confirmed in an adjacent location.

In addition to rechecking the response in the area of suspected abnormalities, the perimetrist may decide to use other means to confirm the presence of an abnormality, such as plotting of a smaller isopter close to the region and using a weaker stimulus to spot-check (p. 170) or doing a static cut through the suspected area (p. 186).

The accuracy of the test is also influenced by the closeness of the test points (e.g., every 1, 2, or 3 degrees) along a meridian. Another factor that must be taken into account by the interpreter is whether successive presentations at each point were 0.1, 0.2, 0.3, or 0.5 log unit apart. Only by knowing the intervals of brightness between stimuli and the strategy of repeating or not repeating stimuli can it be judged whether a specific suggested defect is likely to be real or is within the range of expected response variability. Of course, the greatest accuracy (testing many points 1 degree apart with 0.1 log unit brightness intervals and a strategy of repeat testing) is obtained at the expense of a longer testing time. The expenditure of time may not be worth the greater accuracy depending on the clinical situation. The only point here is that the interpreter of the field test results must know exactly how accurately the examination was performed if the certainty of the results is to be judged accurately.

By deciding when to perform repeated measurements, where to draw the isopter, and what the threshold is on a static cut, the person performing the visual field test makes an interpretive judgment. Obviously there is an opportunity to introduce a bias. On one hand, the perimetrist may be too zealous and indicate as a defect every little area of inconsistency in responses that normally occurs in every field test. On the other hand the perimetrist may be strongly inclined to accept or encourage responses indicating normalcy, slowing down to encourage a response in the expected region (p. 156), or overlooking areas where there are several abnormal responses because there are also a few normal responses. The perimetrist should be looking for areas in which the responses are more inconsistent than elsewhere. A specific region where the responses are particularly inconsistent while in other regions there is no great variability of responsiveness can certainly indicate the presence of a mild visual field defect.[1-3] Such a localized area in which the response is repeatedly inconsistent should be noted. In reaching the decision to indicate a certain area of inconsistent responses, the examiner is again making an interpretation that takes into account the responsiveness of the patient in the other regions of the field. Of course, such a judgment is difficult in those patients who are inconsistent in all areas of the field.

---

[1]Werner, E.B., and Drance, S.M.: Increased scatter of responses as a precursor of visual field changes in glaucoma, Can. J. Ophthalmol. **12**:140-142, 1977.

[2]Werner, E.B., and Drance, S.M.: Early visual field disturbances in glaucoma, Arch. Ophthalmol. **95**:1173-1175, 1977.

[3]Holmin, C., and Krakau, C.E.T.: Variability of glaucomatous visual field defects in computerized perimetry, Albrecht von Graefe's Arch. Klin. Ophthalmol. **210**:235-250, 1979.

Automatic perimeters do not make interpretive judgments as the test is being performed. For example, stimuli may be presented with increasing brightness and the first stimulus seen may be recorded as the threshold without regard to whether or not it is in keeping with the responses at an adjacent point. Such a result is recorded without bias, but also without the benefit of selective repeat testing. The problem is that it would be too time-consuming to repeat all test points and it is difficult for a computer to judge when a given kinetic or static stimulus presentation should be repeated.

FIG. 21-3, A. A static cut performed by the Perimetron.[1] This cut shows a possible 0.3–log-unit scotoma, not confirmed when the static cut is repeated four times. At any given location, the threshold determined by a single stimulus presentation varies about 0.3 log units. It can be seen that any of the individual static cuts (e.g., the one in red) varies above and below the average and may simply by chance seem to show a shallow defect with a depth of 0.3 log unit. Because of this one cannot be certain of a defect on a single testing unless it has a reasonable depth (say 0.5 log unit or more), especially if the defect is represented by only one test point.

Fig. 21-3, B, Apparent scotoma within a field tested by the Octopus.[2] At each of 72 points, a single threshold determination was made to the nearest 0.2 log unit. The scotoma is only 2 decibels (0.2 log unit) deep and is unconfirmed by adjacent points that were tested. So the apparent defect represents one missed response by the patient. The presence of the defect would be more certain (1) if a single point had a depth of 4 or 6 decibels (0.4 or 0.6 log unit), meaning that the patient missed several levels of intensity; (2) if the finding was confirmed by there being several adjacent points with a low threshold; or (3) if the test is repeated several times and an apparent defect is always demonstrated. (On the intensity scatterplot the apparent defect is represented by a cluster of points. However, all but one of these points are interpolated values based on the one point at the center that was actually tested.) (Courtesy of Dr. Jorge Alvarado.)

The point of these two examples is that with automatic perimetry, as with manual perimetry, the interpreter must know exactly how the test was performed in order to judge the presence or absence of a defect.

---

[1]Coherent Medical Division, 3270 West Bayshore Road, Palo Alto, California 94303.
[2]Hitron Corporation, 20 Risho Avenue, Westminster Industrial Park, East Providence, R.I. 02914.

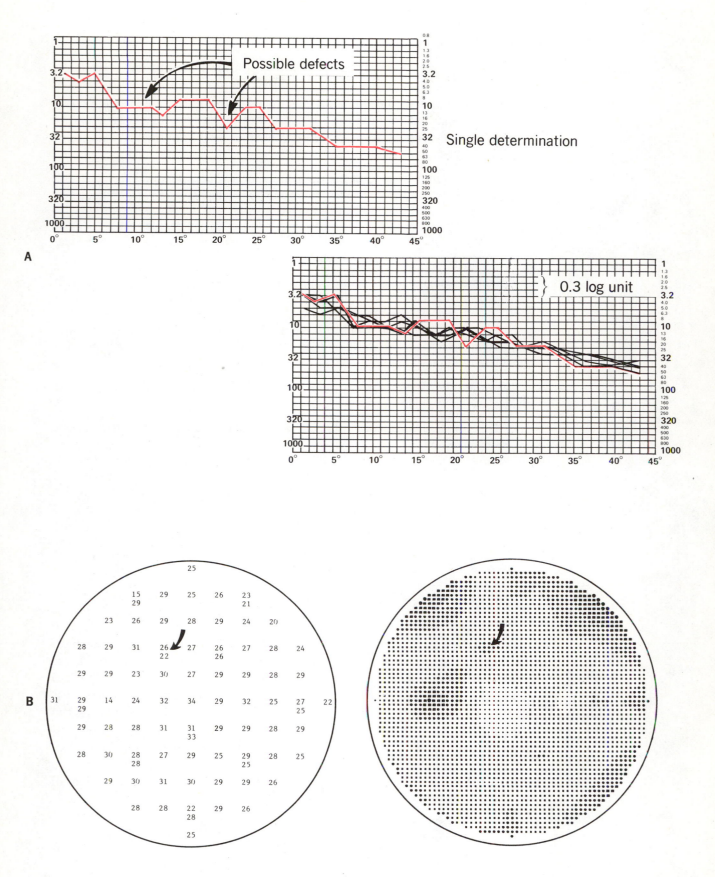

FIG. 21-3

IS A REAL DEFECT ABNORMAL?

Reproducibility of the finding means that the threshold in one area differs from the threshold in another area and that the difference is real. However, it does not necessarily mean that an area of reduced sensation is abnormal. Certain shallow irregularities may exist in the contour of the normal hill of vision and be impossible to distinguish from shallow defects resulting from the early stage of a disease.

FIG. 21-4, A. Visual field of the normal eye of a young person. Every isopter of stimuli 0.1 log unit apart is plotted from I-e to I-3e. Temporally 25 to 50 degrees from fixation the hill of vision is very flat. The I-1e and the I-2e isopters (which differ by 0.5 log unit) are separated by 30 degrees temporally but only 15 degrees nasally. Indeed, the I-2b and the I-1e isopters (only 0.2 log unit apart) are separated by 25 degrees temporally and only 5 degrees nasally.

In this area an irregular contour is apparent in the I-2a isopter in the lower quadrant. Enough points were plotted to be sure that the defect is reproducible with several adjacent points consistently deviated inward. The amount of reduced visual sensation is small. At point R the visual sensation is only 0.1 log unit less than it is at point S. A very slight decrease in visual sensation resulting from disease might start as a shallow abnormality difficult to distinguish from this one.

On the other hand, shallow defects can also be the result of early stages of disease.

FIG. 21-4, B. Hypothetical example of a shallow depression in the arcuate Bjerrum region. In this case, the I-2e isopter superiorly is deviated 10 degrees inward toward fixation compared to the field inferiorly. Visual sensation at point S is reduced (I-2e is not visible but would be if the I-2e isopter were in the proper position at 23 degrees), but the defect is not in a flat region of the field. Therefore, in the preceding figure the inward deviation of the isopter in the flat region of the field represents at most a 0.1 log unit reduction of visual sensitivity. In the present example, visual sensation is reduced as much as 0.4 log unit and the depth of the cliff may be more than could reasonably be attributed simply to a ripple in the contour of a normal hill of vision. The defect can be accepted as pathologic if combined with elevated intraocular pressure and mild glaucomatous cupping. Eventually, with further reduction in visual sensation, the defect could become an arcuate scotoma.

The more carefully the visual field is examined, the more likely one is to find a subtle defect resulting from the early stage of a disease. The problem in interpretation is that the likelihood of finding a seeming defect in a normal field is also greater. If it is an isolated finding, it may be best not to be convinced of an apparent abnormality that is less than 0.3 or even 0.5 log unit deep unless it is reproducible and there are other clinical signs (e.g., cupping of the disc) to confirm that there should be a pathologic defect in the area. Sometimes it is impossible to decide if a defect is really an abnormality, and one must depend on the subsequent clinical course to decide if a shallow defect is real. For example, a shallow defect can be considered to have been real if a deeper scotoma develops in the same location as time goes on.

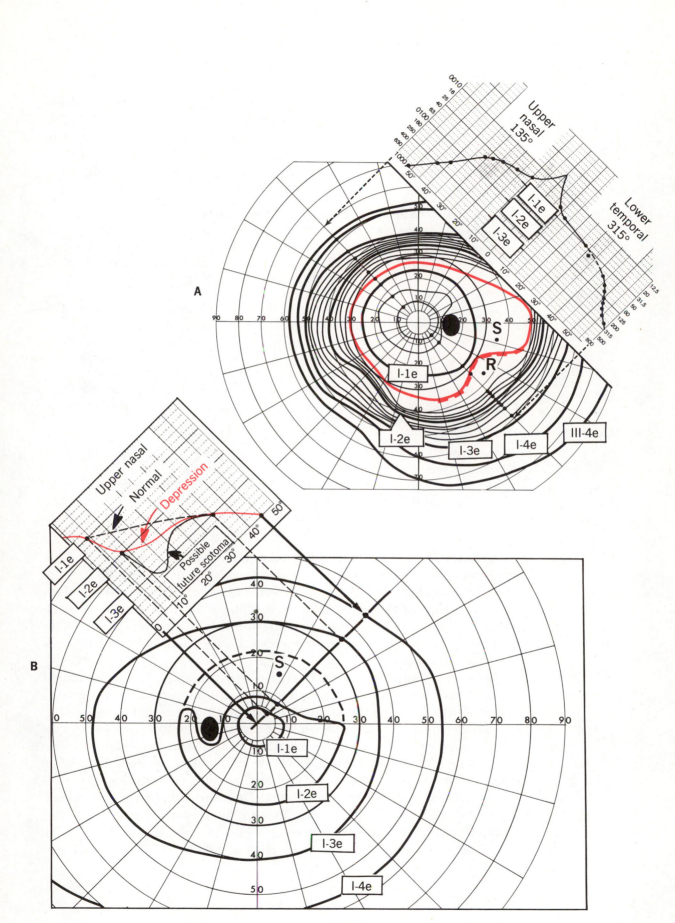

FIG. 21-4

IS THE FIELD DEFECT THE RESULT OF THE SUSPECTED DISEASE?

Once it is decided that the presence of a defect is definite, it must next be decided if the defect is the result of the suspected disease or some other disease. Let us suppose, for example, that an isopter passes along the vertical meridian, suggesting the presence of a hemianopia. The defect is real: there is an undeniable abnormality. However, diagnostic interpretation ("Is it hemianopia?") requires more information than can be provided by a single isopter.

FIG. 21-5. An isopter that suggests a hemianopia. In the course of quantitating the depression (p. 84), additional isopters are drawn, and one of two patterns may emerge. In a hemianopia, other isopters will also show a demarcation along the vertical meridian. In a depression resulting from a prechiasmal lesion, it becomes evident that the initial isopter by happenstance falls along the vertical meridian, but other isopters do not.

In the hemianopia, the depressed visual sensation is only on one side of the vertical meridian: point *M* has a reduced visual sensitivity, but point *N* does not. In contrast, the prechiasmal lesion produces a depressed sensation on both sides of the vertical meridian. Both point *M* and point *N* are in an area of reduced visual sensation (compared to an equivalent spot in the inferior field).

Another criterion sometimes applicable is that the apex of the contour of depressed isopters may point at the blind spot in prechiasmal lesions, whereas in hemianopia the apex (if any) points toward fixation.

The arc static cut (another way of obtaining the information required for diagnostic interpretation) shows that in hemianopia there is a sharp demarcation at the vertical meridian separating the two areas, with 0.5 log unit difference in visual sensation on the two sides. Visual sensation is reduced only on one side of the vertical meridian but not on the other. In the prechiasmal lesion, however, there is a depression on both sides of the vertical meridian. The depression is more marked nasally than temporally, but with a gradual change in threshold as the vertical meridian is crossed.

As can be shown by both the isopter plot and the static cut, a hemianopia has a steep margin along the vertical meridian (several isopters coincide). For this reason, if suprathreshold stimuli are presented just to the right and left of the vertical meridian in the hemianopia, they will be of different subjective brightness to the individual, being more above the threshold on the one side than on the other. Therefore, brightness comparison testing is useful in confirming the presence of a hemianopia.

In the prechiasmal depression, there is also a difference in sensation nasally and temporally but as the object passes from nasal to temporal, there is a gradual increase in visibility rather than a sudden change at the vertical midline (see Fig. 19-5). Hence the technique of crossing the midline is essential in confirming the diagnostic meaning of any seeming abnormality in comparison testing.

In any event, this particular example shows that the interpreter must be on guard not to accept an inadequate field test, a single isopter, as showing the presence of a suspected defect (hemianopia). One must judge whether the abnormality could be the result of another cause, e.g., prechiasmal defect, demanding additional testing (Fig. 21-5) or other confirmation of a defect (pp. 256 to 259). Of course, the same care is required for all types of defects, not just hemianopias.

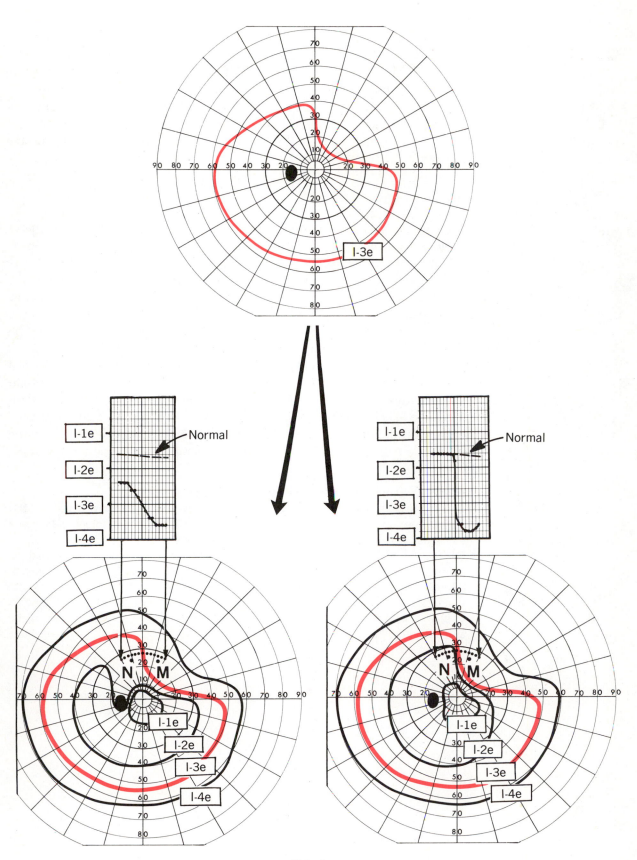

FIG. 21-5

Even if the defect is consistent with the disease under consideration, other causes must be considered. For example, in a patient with elevated intraocular pressure, a localized prechiasmal defect could be the result of a past retinal detachment, branch retinal vascular occlusion, ischemic optic neuropathy, or cataract, instead of the suspected glaucoma. Such things as the exact location and shape of the defect whether the defect is an absolute contraction (p. 152) or a depression, and the presence of other ocular signs may enter into the diagnostic decision.

LOCALIZED DEPRESSION

Most localized depressions (hemianopias, wedge-shaped defects, or nasal depressions with nasal steps) are easily recognized and interpreted. However, some depressions are subtle and require careful evaluation by comparing one part of the field with another, of course taking into account the normal difference between the nasal and the temporal fields, and between the superior and inferior fields. For example, the upper field is normally very slightly depressed compared to the lower field (p. 46) but a superior altitudinal depression may also be the result of glaucoma, a drooping eyelid, or a prominent eyebrow. If the eyelid is interfering with the upper field, the field improves at least partly with special efforts to lift the eyelid (p. 173). Generally, it is not glaucoma if the depression affects the entire superior half (both temporally and nasally) evenly; but glaucoma is more likely if the depression is of greater degree nasally than temporally, if there are any definite nasal steps, or if there is definitely more depression in the upper arcuate region than is evident more peripherally in the superior half of the field.

FIG. 21-6. Examples of depressions in the superior field.

A, A prominent eyebrow or drooping eyelid may produce a relatively generalized depression superiorly all the way to the periphery of the field. It is a sloping defect, as if the upper field were shaded, in effect making every stimulus less bright.

B, Glaucomatous depression is typically more marked on the nasal side than on the temporal side and may or may not be associated with a nasal step. In glaucoma, depressed visual sensation not yet reduced enough to produce a scotoma can produce a localized depression in the upper arcuate region. This can be represented by a flattened region of the field only in the arcuate region (not in the periphery superiorly) as seen in Fig. 21-4, B.

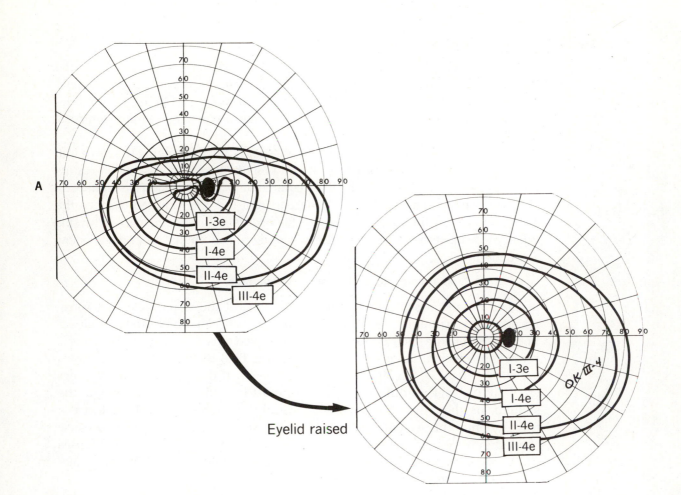

Eyelid raised

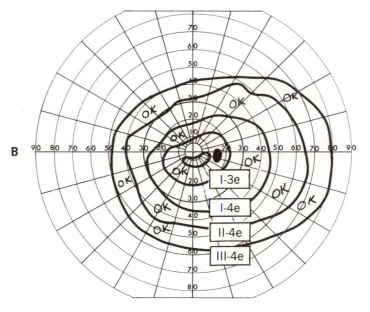

FIG. 21-6

REFRACTION SCOTOMAS

Another localized defect that can be a pitfall of diagnostic interpretation is the "refraction scotoma," which can be either a scotoma or a localized depression, typically within a wedge-shaped zone above the physiologic blind spot. A refraction scotoma can be mistaken for either an arcuate scotoma or an upper temporal hemianopia.

Usually the lens that provides the best visual acuity by bringing the fovea into focus also brings the rest of the retina into focus. A refraction scotoma results when this is not the case and the lens required to focus an eccentric stimulus on the retina away from the fovea is different from the one required to focus the fixation point on the fovea. Typically, this occurs with astigmatism or myopia when the back of the eye is not perfectly round but has a bulge around and below the optic nerve.

FIG. 21-7. Anatomic cause of refraction scotomas.

The refraction scotoma appears in the zone of the visual field that corresponds to the part of the retina not in proper focus because a blurred stimulus is not as visible as a focused one. If a specific scotoma is suspected of being a refraction scotoma, the lens being used for the field testing can be varied by a -1.00 D, -0.50 D, $+0.50$ D, or $+1.00$ D sphere. If the test stimulus becomes visible in the region of the scotoma, there must be an improved focusing of the stimulus on the retina. If the stimulus was already in focus and the defect is a true scotoma, the scotoma would remain the same or become deeper because changing the lens would make the stimulus less visible. Remember that lenses can be used only within the central 30 degrees; thus testing for refractive scotomas in this manner is possible only within the central field.

FIG. 21-8. Example of a refraction scotoma. Visual sensation improves in the region of the refraction scotoma with a change of the lens. At the same time, visual sensation worsens in the region around the fovea because it is being placed out of focus by the lens that brings the region of the refractive scotoma into focus. Because of this, the central isopter (I-2e) moves inward ("becomes smaller").

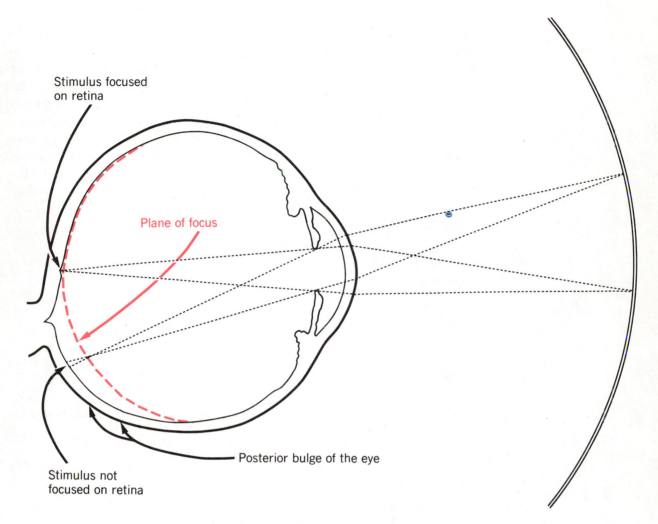

Stimulus focused
on retina

Plane of focus

Posterior bulge of the eye

Stimulus not
focused on retina

FIG. 21-7

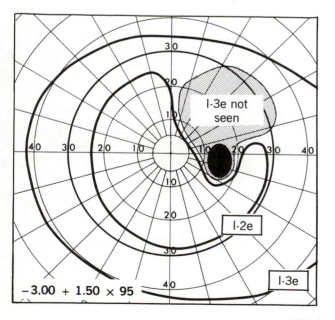

I-3e not
seen

I-2e

I-3e

−3.00 + 1.50 × 95

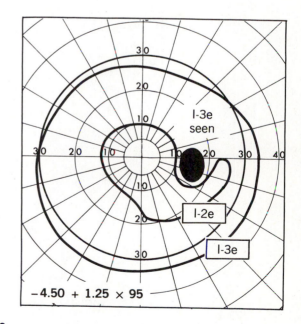

I-3e
seen

I-2e

I-3e

−4.50 + 1.25 × 95

FIG. 21-8

Apart from the fact that lenses are able to eliminate or at least reduce the refraction scotoma, the defect is sometimes distinguished from a typical arcuate scotoma because the wedge-shaped defect goes straight upward and is only vaguely arcuate. Similarly, it may be distinguished from a hemianopia by the fact that it crosses the vertical midline and by the usual means for confirming hemianopias (pp. 256-258). At least some refraction scotomas have been recognized to correlate with the presence of a tilted disc or a wedge of pale color in the lower nasal retina, emanating from the optic disc. Such defects may be an exaggeration of the normal superior "baring of the blind spot" in which visual sensation is slightly reduced above the blind spot so that the isopter may curve around the blind spot without enclosing the region just above it.

FIG. 21-9. Normal or "false" baring of the blind spot. This contrasts with pathologic baring of the blind spot in which a depression or scotoma in the arcuate Bjerrum region causes an isopter to skirt around the blind spot without enclosing it. Examples of pathologic baring of the blind spot can be seen in Figs. 11-3 (p. 113), 11-6 (p. 117), 14-2 (p. 158), 16-2 (p. 199), 16-3 and 16-4 (p. 201), 21-10 (p. 283), and 21-11 (p. 285).

ADDITIONAL READINGS

For more information on refraction scotomas and on tilted discs see:

Aulhorn, E.: Visual field defects in sellar and parasellar processes, Annee Ther. Clin. Opthalmol. **25**:424-434, 1974.

Fankhauser, F., and Enough, J.M.: The effects of blur upon perimetric thresholds: A method for determining a quantitative estimate of retinal contour, Arch. Ophthalmol. **68**:240-251, 1962.

Goldmann, H.: Lichtsinn mit besonderer Berüclksichtigung der Perimetrie, Ophthalmologica **158**: 362-386, 1969.

Kommerell, G.: Binasale refraktionsskotome, Klin. Monatsbl. Augenheilkd. **154**:85-88, 1969.

Riise, D.: The nasal fundus ectasia, Acta Ophthalmol. [Suppl.] **126**:4-108, 1975.

Rucker, C.W.: Bitemporal defects in the visual fields resulting from developmental anomalies of the optic disks, Arch. Ophthalmol. **35**:546-554, 1946.

Schmidt, T.: Kurzes Repetitorium der klinischen Perimetrie, Ophthalmologica **149**:250-265, 1965.

Schmidt, T.: Perimetrie relativer skotome, Ophthalmologica **129**:303-315, 1955.

Young, S.E., Walsh, F.B., and Knox, D.L.: The tilted disk syndrome, Am. J. Ophthalmol. **82**:16-23, 1976.

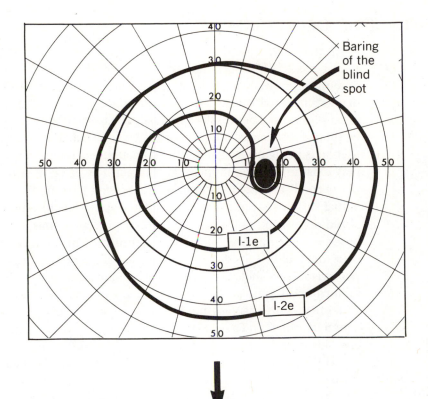

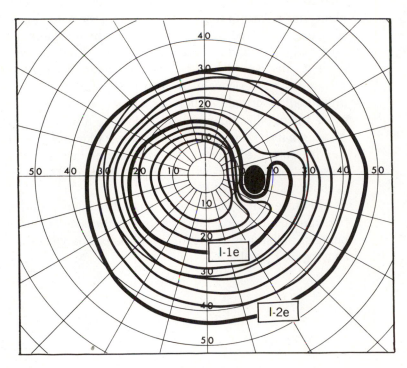

With intermediate isopters

FIG. 21-9

GENERALIZED DEPRESSION

A generalized depression is another situation requiring diagnostic interpretation. Usually a mild generalized depression is ignored because there is a certain amount of normal variation of visual threshold, and there is normally an overall decline in visual threshold (generalized depression) with age. Moreover, pathologic generalized depression is usually the result of preretinal factors that are very common, such as mild lens opacity (cataract), and usually the visual field examination is being performed for the detection and diagnosis of other conditions that may exist in addition to the mild cataract. For these reasons, one usually accepts as "normal" any mild generalized depression that might exist as a result of individual variations, age, and mild media opacity. The interpreter ignores the generalized depression and looks for hemianopias, scotomas, and localized depression based on a comparison of the visual threshold in the location of interest to adjacent thresholds. In judging the presence of a scotoma, the question is whether or not a visual threshold is reduced in a specific location compared to the immediately surrounding areas. In the case of upper nasal depression in glaucoma (pp. 114-116), comparison is made in the regions above and below the nasal horizontal meridian and a nasal step will be found. Similarly, in judging hemianopias, one side of the vertical meridian is compared to the other.

However, generalized depression should not always be ignored. For example, the early stages of optic nerve damage as a result of glaucoma can be manifested by generalized depression without localized defects. Therefore, when a generalized depression is found in a patient who may have glaucoma, the interpreter must decide if the depression is indeed the result of early glaucoma, is within the normal limits of variability, or is the result of factors such as age, media opacity, uncorrected refractive error, or small pupil size. Usually it is impossible to make such a distinction with certainty and therefore depression is only rarely considered to be the result of glaucoma. However, a depression can be attributed to glaucoma at least in those cases in which the field improves when the intraocular pressure is lowered. In other instances, the interpretation takes into account the presence or absence of other signs of glaucomatous damage, as well as the presence or absence of other causes of generalized depression, especially if the amount of depression in the two eyes is unequal. For example, if there is no preretinal abnormality (such as cataract) and the visual acuity is normal in both eyes, a generalized depression in one eye may be interpreted to be the result of glaucoma if that eye has a higher intraocular pressure and a larger excavation of the disc, provided there is no other asymmetry between the two eyes (perhaps anisometropia with accompanying amblyopia). The interpretation must take into account the entire clinical setting.

In any event, even if a mild generalized depression is ignored or dismissed as not significant, a moderate or severe depression should not be passed by without being sure that it is in keeping with the preretinal conditions present (age, media opacity, and pupil size).

GENERALIZED DEPRESSION PLUS

The more difficult phase of interpretation is to make a judgment of whether or not a glaucomatous visual field defect is present in addition to a generalized depression resulting from an age effect or a known cataract, perhaps aggravated by a small pupil. The presence of a cataract affects the center more than the periphery (p. 150), so that the field is not merely depressed, but flat, with areas of inconsistent responses (Fig. 15-3, *B*, p. 189) that may fall within the arcuate Bjerrum region. In this situation the presence of localized glaucomatous defects would be uncertain unless there are the typical defects—arcuate scotomas and nasal steps—that are sufficiently deep (0.5 log unit) that they are certainly not just shallow irregularities in a flattened hill of vision. A cataract can cause localized defects as well as generalized depression; thus, the examiner must equivocate in the interpretation unless the defects are undeniably typical.

OTHER DIAGNOSTIC PITFALLS

Sometimes one must call on other parts of the ocular examination to be certain of a cause of a given visual field defect. For example, ophthalmoscopy may reveal a choroidal scar that accounts for a scotoma rather than the suspected glaucoma. A branch retinal vessel occlusion can cause an arcuate defect. Similarly, macular disease may account for a decreased visual acuity and a central scotoma instead of the suspected optic neuritis.

Finally, one must be alert for artifactual defects caused by technical errors. For example, an arcuate scotoma inferiorly at 30 degrees, not connected with the blind spot, results when the lens holder is accidentally left in place while plotting the peripheral field. A field that extends to a full 90 degrees in both directions (both nasally and temporally) results when the opposite eye is not covered. In that situation a blind spot may not be demonstrated. There are many other artifacts; almost every day innovative perimetrists find new ways to produce false field defects.

PROGRESSION OF VISUAL FIELD LOSS

The greatest necessity for quantitated visual field examination is in deciding if the loss of visual function has halted or if it is continuing. Progression of visual field loss can be in the form of worsening of existing defects (becoming deeper or larger) or the development of new defects, or both.

It is obviously important to distinguish between a new defect and a newly discovered defect (that may have existed previously, but had not been detected). If a new defect is found, one must immediately look at the previous field diagram to see if the area in question had been adequately tested on the first occasion. For example, if a scotoma is discovered inside the I-3e isopter, it is very helpful to see that the previous field diagram is marked "OK to I-3e." Similarly, if a depression is found, it is necessary to look at the previous field diagram, noting whether or not an isopter was plotted through that region before and, if so, whether or not sufficient points were plotted in an appropriate place to uncover a defect if it had been present. It is not so much a question of whether or not the same isopter had been plotted previously, but whether or not the location now showing a depression had been previously examined with any isopter.

To judge the worsening of existing defects requires thoughtful analysis. First of all, it must be realized that there is a close relationship of some scotomas and depressions (pp. 82-83) and that the same defect may be represented in several different ways, depending on the way the test was performed. One must also take into account some amount of variability in the field from one time to another.

FIG. 21-10. Nonprogressive and progressive defects.
A, A nonprogressive defect. Note that the defect covers the same area and that, as far as one can tell, the threshold within the area is essentially identical in both diagrams, within the limits of variability in field testing.
B, Progressive defect. In contrast to diagram *A*, the visual threshold in the region of the defect is less than before. It is important to note that the threshold changed only in the defective area and not elsewhere, for example in the lower temporal quadrant.

In looking at the diagrams, it is tempting (and traditional) to look at the movement of isopters, and to say that the field defect has progressed because a certain isopter has moved inward ("become smaller"). Thus, in Fig. 21-10 the I-3e isopter became smaller superiorly, and this constitutes a worsening of the field defect in the upper arcuate region. The practice of looking at isopter movement suffices in simple examples, but one must remember that the amount of isopter movement for a specific amount of threshold change depends on the steepness or flatness of the hill of vision at that point. If isopters that differ by 0.5 log unit are 10 degrees apart in a region, then a 10-degree inward movement of an isopter represents 0.5 log unit loss of visual sensation in that region. If the hill of vision is flatter, there is more isopter movement with the same 0.5–log-unit loss (p. 148). It is best to compare representative points of interest in terms of threshold, as was shown in Fig. 21-10. The visual sensation at a specific retinal location is attributable to a specific set of neurons and progressive damage to the neurons is the underlying basis of progression. Isopters move when there is a change in visual threshold but it is the change in threshold at a specific location that is the relevant feature of progression.

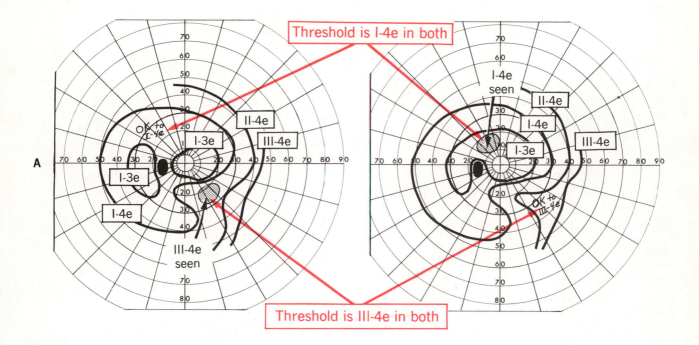

A

Threshold is I-4e in both

Threshold is III-4e in both

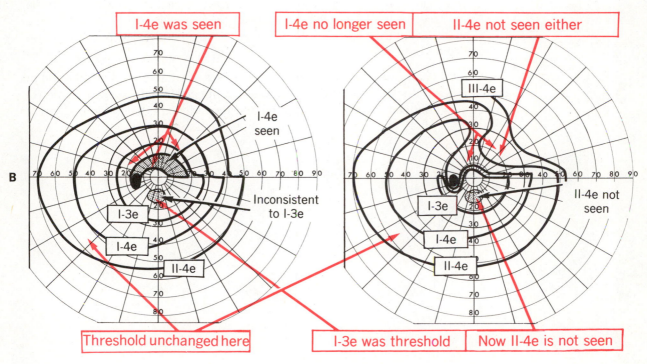

B

I-4e was seen

I-4e no longer seen

II-4e not seen either

Threshold unchanged here

I-3e was threshold

Now II-4e is not seen

FIG. 21-10

Interpretive analysis in terms of the threshold at points of interest is particularly helpful in complicated cases. For example, patients with glaucoma may also have cataracts, the visual effects of which are compounded by small pupils. The field must be analyzed carefully to tell if there is progression in glaucomatous change in addition to the declining visual threshold resulting from these pre-retinal factors. The reader should review p. 148 concerning the relationship between isopter movement and threshold change. Review also p. 150 to understand the reasoning behind the analysis of how much visual sensation is reduced.

FIG. 21-11. Interpreting progression. At the top is a hypothetical example of change in the visual field resulting from cataract. There is reduced visual acuity and the entire field is more depressed than before, varying in amount from 1 log unit at the center to 0.5 log unit at the periphery. (The approximate number of log units by which threshold is reduced is shown in the circles.)

The arcuate and nasal areas affected by glaucoma are no more depressed than before when compared to the amount of depression that occurred in the other regions. Throughout the field, the relationship of the threshold at any point to neighboring thresholds is unchanged. This kind of generalized progression might be the result of glaucoma but it is much more likely to be the result of media change (without the glaucomatous optic nerve damage being progressive) and would be attributed to glaucoma only if the media remained clear.

The lower part of the figure represents a hypothetical example in which there is progressive glaucomatous change in addition to cataract change. In addition to the overall depression accompanying cataract development (note declining acuity), both the upper and the lower arcuate regions suffer a 2–to 3–log-unit change in visual threshold, whereas the surrounding area suffered only a 1–to 2–log-unit loss. The change in the I-3e isopter in this example is exactly the same as in the top part of the figure; if only the I-3e isopter had been plotted as shown in blue one would not be able to distinguish whether the change was the result of progressive cataract, progressive glaucoma, or both.

Cataract can cause localized changes. In cases of cataract and small pupil in combination with the glaucoma with changes of uncertain nature, the situation is sometimes changed by dilating the pupil and repeating the field examination.

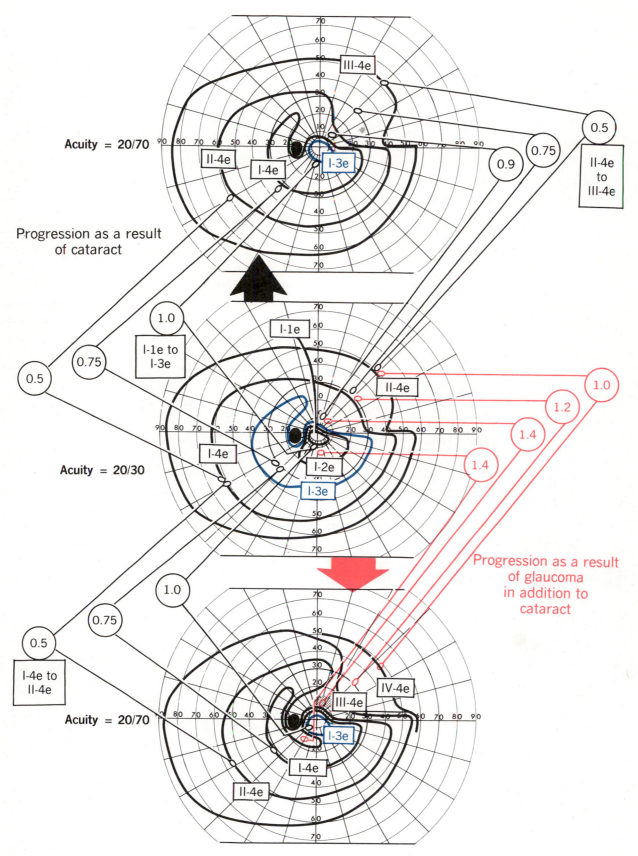

FIG. 21-11

Thus, the determination of visual threshold at pertinent locations is indeed the basis of visual field testing and interpretation. Because of this, it may not be necessary to plot isopters in the usual sense, but simply to determine visual threshold at several dozen representative points within the visual field. One does not necessarily need to visualize isopters, or outline precisely the boundary of each defect, or even to worry about any other locations within the visual field except the representative points. One can work on the assumption that any significant degree of progression will be reflected in some or all of these representative points. For example, if there is a decline in visual sensation at all points of approximately equal degree, a generalized depression is occurring. On the other hand, if there is a decline in visual sensation at those points that lie in the arcuate region, but not elsewhere, there is progressive loss of the glaucomatous type occurring. If all points are declining in sensitivity, the visual acuity test and the physical examination of the eye will be needed to distinguish cataract from glaucoma.

The Octopus operates by determining threshold at a selection of points, and doing only this may prove to be a most efficient method. In principle, this approach can be used also with the Friedmann analyser, the semiautomatic instruments, or any of the automatic perimeters that determine threshold by static presentations. However, determination of exact threshold at each point and recording of the results is cumbersome at present with many of the instruments.

Finally, when there is a progressive loss of visual function, one must always be on guard to be sure that the progression is resulting from the original disease (e.g., glaucoma) and not from some new condition such as retinal detachment, branch retinal vascular occlusion, or macular disease. Often the distinction will not be possible from the field examination alone but will require a complete examination of the eye. As another example, if declining acuity is associated with the development of a central scotoma but not with generalized depression in a patient with cataract and glaucoma, one may suspect that the declining acuity is not the result of progressive cataract. Clinical examination will be needed to confirm the absence of significant cataract and then to determine if the declining vision is the result of macular disease, optic atrophy, or a glaucomatous defect impinging on fixation.

APPENDIX A

Teaching perimetry

This book can be used as a textbook for a course in perimetry. The first phase is an intensive introduction over several days, which might be done as follows:

I.	Lecture 1	Chapter 1 (Introduction)
	Demonstration	Chapter 3 (Goldmann perimeter)
	Reading homework	Chapter 2 (Anatomy of the eye)
	Practical homework	Chapter 4 (Plotting isopters kinetically)
II.	Lecture 2	Pages 46-63 (Scotomas)
	Reading homework	Chapter 6 (The normal visual field)
		Chapter 7 (Scotomas)
	Practical homework	Pages 64-69 (Plotting scotomas)
III.	Lecture-demonstration 3	Pages 70-73 (Practical techniques)
	Optional demonstration	Pages 44-45 and 74-75 (Tangent screens)
	Reading homework	Pages 1-17 & 50-63 (Scotomas)
	Practical homework	Pages 76-77
IV.	Lecture 4	Chapter 9 (Localized depressions)
	Demonstration	Chapter 10 (Corrective lenses)
	Reading homework	Chapter 2 (Anatomy of the eye) and
		Chapter 9 (Localized depressions)
V.	Lecture 5	Chapter 11 (Visual field loss in glaucoma)
	Demonstration	Chapter 12 (Calibration of Goldmann perimeter)
	Reading homework	Chapter 11 (Visual field loss in glaucoma)
VI.	Lecture 6	Chapter 13 (Generalized depressions)
	Reading homework	Review Chapters 8, 10, and 12

The second phase consists of gaining actual practical experience—performing perimetry under supervision in a clinical setting. After a certain amount of practical experience, and while continuing to gain more, the student should review to be sure that no details of technique are being overlooked without realizing it. For this purpose, the following chapters should be read again, one or two per week, in the following sequence: Chapters 3, 8, 10, 12, 1, 6, 7, 9, 11, and 13. The idea is to review first the chapters dealing with practical points. Then the theoretical principles are reviewed at a time when they may have more meaning, after the student has some experience encountering field defects in the clinical setting. The outside readings cited in various chapters can also be tackled at this time.

At some point Chapter 16 on topographic classification of visual field defects should be introduced, either as a lecture or as a reading assignment. After several patients with hemianopias are encountered, this chapter should be reviewed and pp. 256-259 should also be studied.

Once the preceding material has been mastered, the third phase of formal teaching should include a review and a refinement of technique (Chapter 14), an understanding of technique selection (Chapter 17), details of glaucoma evaluation (Chapter 18), supplemental methods (Chapter 19), examination of the patient with poor visual acuity (pp. 254-255), and neurologic fields (pp. 256-259). These topics can be covered at weekly or biweekly intervals as lectures or as reading assignments with the opportunity for questions and discussion.

The subjects of static perimetry (Chapter 15), instrument selection (Chapter 20), and interpretation (Chapter 21) can be introduced when they are appropriate, depending on the nature of the group being taught. The basic principles in these three chapters should be studied by every student of perimetry, even if they will not be in a position to perform static perimetry, choose instrumentation, or be responsible for diagnostic interpretation. Understanding the principles involved will be important to anyone who wants to perform a high-quality perimetric examination.

Bibliography

GENERAL

This book has dealt in detail with the technique of performing the clinical examination of the visual field and the rudiments of diagnostic interpretation. Details about the characteristics of visual field defects in various diseases are described in the sources already given on p. 205 and in the following texts:

Dubois-Poulsen, A.: Le champ visuel; topographie normale et pathologique de ses sensibilités, Paris, 1952, Masson et Cie. *A lengthy and complete textbook and reference book for those who read French.*

Ellenberger, C., Jr.: Perimetry: principles, techniques, and interpretation, New York, 1980, Raven Press.

Harrington, D.O.: The visual fields: a textbook and atlas of clinical perimetry, ed. 5, St. Louis, 1981, The C.V. Mosby Co. *Current standard textbook by one of Traquair's first students on the uses of clinical perimetry based largely on the tangent screen examination. Much of the book deals with the characteristic field defects of various clinical entities.*

Reed, H., and Drance, S.M.: The essentials of perimetry, static and kinetic, London, 1972, Oxford University Press. *Another current primer on clinical visual field testing, briefer than Harrington. Drance was one of Traquair's last students.*

Scott, G.I.: Traquair's clinical perimetry, ed. 7, St. Louis, 1957, The C.V. Mosby Co. *Final edition of Traquair's classic; no longer in print.*

Traquair, H.M.: An introduction to clinical perimetry, ed. 6, St. Louis, 1949, The C.V. Mosby Co. *A classic, filled with valuable information; no longer in print.*

GLAUCOMA

Readers who want more details specifically about glaucomatous visual field defects and screening methods for glaucoma should see the references given on pp. 116, 218, and 226, and the following:

Aulhorn, E., and Harms, H.: Early visual field defects in glaucoma. In Leydhecker, W., editor: Glaucoma: Tutzing symposium, Basel, 1967, S. Karger, pp. 151-186.

Aulhorn, E., and Karmeyer, H.: Frequency distribution in early glaucomatous visual field defects, Doc. Ophthalmol. Proc. Series **14:**75-83, 1976.

Aulhorn, E., Durst, W., and Gauger, E.: A new quick-test for visual field examination in glaucoma, Doc. Ophthalmol. Proc. Series **22:**57-64, 1979.

Drance, S.M., and others: The early visual field defect in glaucoma and the significance of nasal steps, Doc. Ophthalmol. Proc. Series **19:**119-126, 1979.

Furuno, F., and Matsuo, H.: Early stage progression in glaucomatous visual field changes, Doc. Ophthalmol. Proc. Series **19:**247-253, 1979.

Greve, E.L.: Some aspects of visual field examination related to strategies for detection and assessment phase, Doc. Ophthalmol. Proc. Series **22:**15-28, 1979.

Greve, E.L.: Single and multiple stimulus static perimetry in glaucoma; the two phases of perimetry, Doc. Ophthalmol. **36:**91-93, 1973.

Greve, E.L., and Verduin, W.M.: Detection of early glaucomatous damage. Part 1: Visual field examination, Doc. Ophthalmol. Proc. Series **14:**103-114, 1977.

Kosaki, H.: The earliest visual field defect (II-a stage) in glaucoma by kinetic perimetry, Doc. Ophthalmol. Proc. Series **19:**255-259, 1979.

Krieglstein, G.K., and Andrae, K.: The screening of the central visual field, Albrecht von Graefes Arch. Klin. Exp. Ophthalmol. **193:**145-152, 1975.

Leblanc, R.P.: Peripheral nasal field defects, Doc. Ophthalmol. Proc. Series **14:**131-133, 1977.

Morin, J.D.: Changes in the visual fields in glaucoma: static and kinetic perimetry in 2,000 patients, Trans. Am. Ophthalmol. Soc. **77:**622-642, 1979.

Portney, G.L., and Krohn, M.A.: The limitations of kinetic perimetry in early scotoma detection, Ophthamology **85:**287-293, 1978.

Rabin, S., and Kolesar, P.: Mathematical optimization of glaucoma visual field screening protocols, Doc. Ophthalmol. **45:**361-380, 1978.

Shinzato, E., Suzuki, R., and Furuno, F.: The central visual field changes in glaucoma using Goldmann perimeter and Friedmann visual field analyser, Doc. Ophthalmol. Proc. Series **14:**93-101, 1977.

Werner, E.B.: Peripheral nasal field defects in glaucoma, Doc. Ophthalmol. Proc. Series **19:**223-228, 1979.

Werner, E.B., and Drance, S.M.: Early visual field disturbances in glaucoma, Arch. Ophthalmol. **95:**1173-1175, 1977.

Zingirian, M., Calabria, G., and Gandolfo, E.: The nasal step: an early glaucomatous defect? Doc. Ophthalmol. Proc. Series **19:**273-278, 1979.

PERIMETERS
Automatic perimeters

A variety of automated perimeters are being developed at the present time. Some of the recent articles describing the principles of automated perimetry, the instruments, and the first experiences with their use are:

Bengtsson, B.: Findings associated with glaucomatous visual field defects, Acta Ophthalmol. **58:**20-32, 1980. *Use of automatic perimetry in population survey.*

Bynke, H.: Krakau's computerized perimeter in neuro-ophthalmology, Neuro-ophthalmol. **1:**45-52, 1980.

Bynke, H., and Heijl, A.: Automatic computerized perimetry in the detection of neurological visual field defects: a pilot study, Albrecht von Graefes Arch. Klin. Exp. Ophthalmol. **206:**11-15, 1978.

Dannheim, F.: Clinical experiences with a semi-automated perimeter (Fieldmaster), Int. Ophthalmol. **2:**11-18, 1980.

Fankhauser, F.: Problems related to the design of automatic perimeters, Doc. Ophthalmol. **47:**89-139, 1979.

Fankhauser, F., Häberlin, H., and Jenni, A.: Octopus programs SAPRO and F: two new principles for the analysis of the visual field, Albrecht von Graefes Arch. Klin. Exp. Ophthalmol. **216:**155-165, 1981.

Fankhauser, F., and Jenni, A.: Programs SARGON and DELTA: two new principles for automated analysis of the visual field, Albrecht von Graefes Arch. Klin. Exp. Ophthalmol. **216:**41-48, 1981.

Fankhauser, F., Spahr, J., and Bebie, H.: Three years of experience with the Octopus automatic perimeter, Doc. Ophthalmol. Proc. Series **14:**7-15, 1977.

Gerber, D.S., and others: Automated visual field plotters vs tangent screen kinetic perimetry, Arch. Ophthalmol. **98:**930-931, 1980.

Gloor, B., Schmied, U., and Fässler, A.: Glaukomgesichtsfelder-Analyse von Octopus-Verlaufsbeobachtungen mit einem statistischen Programm, Klin. Monatsbl. Augenheilkd. **177:**423-436, 1980.

Häberlin, H., Jenni, A., and Fankhauser, F.: Researches on adaptive high resolution programming for automatic perimeter: principles and preliminary results, Int. Ophthalmol. **2:**1-9, 1980.

Heijl, A.: Computer test logics for automatic perimetry, Acta Ophthalmol. **55:**837-853, 1977.

Heijl, A.: Computerized glaucoma visual field screening, Doc. Ophthalmol. Proc. Series **14:**47-51, 1977.

Heijl, A.: Studies on computerized perimetry, Acta Ophthalmol. [Suppl.] 132, 1977.

Heijl, A.: Automatic perimetry in glaucoma visual field screening: a clinical study, Albrecht von Graefes Arch. Klin. Exp. Ophthalmol. **200:**21-37, 1976.

Heijl, A., and Drance, S.M.: A clinical comparison of three computerized automatic perimeters in the detection of glaucoma defects, Arch. Ophthalmol. **99:**832-836, 1981.

Heijl, A., and Drance, S.M.: Computerized profile perimetry in glaucoma, Arch. Ophthalmol. **98:**2199-2201, 1980.

Heijl, A., and Krakau, C.E.T.: An automatic static perimeter, design and plot study, Acta Ophthalmol. **53**:293-310, 1975.

Heijl, A., Drance, S.M., and Douglas, G.R.: Automatic perimetry (COMPETER): ability to detect early glaucomatous defects, Arch. Ophthalmol. **98**:1560-1563, 1980.

Jenni, A., Fankhauser, F., and Bebie, H.: Neue Programme für das automatische Perimeter Octopus, Klin. Monatblat. Augenheilkd. **197**:536-544, 1980.

Johnson, C.A., and Keltner, J.L.: Automated suprathreshold static perimetry, Am. J. Ophthalmol. **89**:731-741, 1980.

Johnson, C.A., and Keltner, J.L.: Comparative evaluation of the Autofield-I, CFA-120, and Fieldmaster Model 101-PR automated perimeters, Ophthalmology **87**:777-783, 1980.

Johnson, C.A., and Keltner, J.L.: In reply to letter to the editor on automated visual field plotters vs tangent screen kinetic perimetry, Arch. Ophthalmol. **98**:931-932, 1980.

Johnson, C.A., Keltner, J.L., and Balestrery, F.G.: Suprathreshold static perimetry in glaucoma and other optic nerve disease, Ophthalmology **86**:1278-1286, 1979. *Fieldmaster can do excellent screening if used with exacting care regarding the background illuminance, use of two stimulus intensities, rechecking missed spots, and appropriate criteria for what constitutes an abnormality.*

Krakau, C.E.T.: Aspects on the design of an automatic perimeter, Acta Ophthalmol. **56**:389-405, 1978.

Li, S.G., and others: Clinical experiences with the use of an automated perimeter (Octopus) in the diagnosis and management of patients with glaucoma and neurologic diseases, Ophthalmology **86**:1302-1312, 1979.

McCrary, J.A., III, and Feigon, J.: Computerized perimetry in neuro-ophthalmology, Ophthalmology **86**:1287-1301, 1979.

Schindler, S., and McCrary, J.A., III: Automated perimetry in a neuro-ophthalmic practice, Ann. Ophthalmol. **13**:691-697, 1981.

Younge, B.R., and Trautmann, J.C.: Computer-assisted perimetry in neuro-ophthalmic disease, Mayo Clin. Proc. **55**:207-222, 1980.

Projection perimeters

The original description of the bowl perimeters of Goldmann and Harms and the original scientific studies that form the basis of quantitative perimetry with these instruments are found in these articles:

Goldmann, H.: Lichtsinn mit besonderer Berücksichtigung der Perimetrie, Ophthalmologica **158**:362-386, 1969.

Goldmann, H.: Demonstration unseres neuen Projektionskugel-perimeters samt theoretischen und klinischen Bermerkungen über Perimetrie, Ophthalmologica **111**:187-192, 1946.

Goldmann, H.: Grundlagen exakter Perimetrie, Ophthalmologica **109**:57-70, 1945.

Goldmann, H.: Ein selbstregistrierendes Projektionskugelperimeter, Ophthalmologica **109**:71-79, 1945.

Harms, H.: Die Technik der statischen Perimetrie, Ophthalmologica **158**:387-405, 1969.

Harms, H.: Die Bedeutung einer einheitlichen Prüfweise aller Sehfunktionen, Ber. Dtsch. Ophthalmol. Ges. **63**:281-285, 1960.

Harms, H.: Entwicklungsmöglichkeiten der Perimetrie, Albrecht von Graefes Arch. Klin. Exp. Ophthalmol. **150**:28-57, 1950.

Sloan, L.L.: Area and luminance of test object as variables in examination of the visual field by projection perimetry, Vision Res. **1**:121-138, 1960.

PERIMETRIC TECHNIQUE

Readers who want more practical hints for the performance of field testing or brief reviews of basic principles may be interested in the references cited on pp. 182, 183, 184, and 238, and the following:

Burde, R.M.: Static perimetry. In Thompson, H.S., and others, editors: Topics in neuro-ophthalmology, Baltimore, 1979, William & Wilkins, pp. 30-45. *This chapter is instructive reading as a brief introduction for anyone who is contemplating performing static perimetry with the Goldmann perimeter. It covers the principles, technique, and examples of its usefulness.*

Ellenberger, C., Jr.: Perimetry international, Int. Ophthalmol. Clin. **17:**85-113, 1977. *Short, didactic, general review emphasizing static perimetry with examples of its use, especially in a neurology practice.*

Frisén, L.: The cornerstones of perimetric strategy. In Thompson, H.S., and others, editors: Topics in neuro-ophthalmology, Baltimore, 1979, Williams & Wilkins, pp. 5-19.

Frisén, L.: Kinetic perimetry: techniques and strateges. In Thompson, H.S., and others, editors: Topics in neuro-ophthalmology, Baltimore, 1979, Williams & Wilkins, pp. 20-29. *This and the previous article by Frisén contain considerable information about details of very compulsive quantitative field testing technique and contain a nice list of references. Many of the details are valuable technical hints that will sharpen the skills of those who have mastered the contents of this book, but some details are nit-picking for the usual clinical purpose and will be of interest mainly to specialized perimetry centers. The information is difficult to find elsewhere and every person who will perform perimetry in a clinical setting will find these two articles instructive.*

Havener, W.H., and Gloeckner, S.L.: Introductory atlas of perimetry, St. Louis, 1972, The C.V. Mosby Co. *This manual was written for the training of an ophthalmologist's office assistant. It contains many practical hints, particularly for the tangent screen. It is no longer in print but may be found in some libraries. A somewhat revised version is being printed by the Continuing Education Department of the Ohio State University School of Medicine, Columbus, Ohio, for use in their visual field course.*

PSYCHOPHYSICS

For readers who want more details on the psychophysical basis of visual field testing, the variables (e.g., stimulus size and density, pupil size, time of stimulus presentation, and stimulus movement) that go into making a test stimulus visible or not, the following will be of interest:

Aulhorn, E., and Harms, H.: Visual perimetry. In Jameson, D., and Hurvich, L.M., editors: Visual psychophysics: handbook of sensory physiology, Vol. VII, no. 4, New York, 1972, Springer-Verlag, pp. 102-145. *Authoritative encyclopedia of information about the psychophysical basis of perimetry.*

Aulhorn, E., and Harms, H.: Early visual field defects in glaucoma. In Leydhecker, W., editor: Glaucoma: Tutzing symposium, Basel, 1967, S. Karger. pp. 151-186. *An unusually lucid presentation of the underlying considerations in perimetry with glaucoma as the example. This article is well worth the hour it will take to read and absorb.*

Greve, E.L.: Single and multiple stimulus static perimetry in glaucoma: the two phases of perimetry, Doc. Ophthalmol. **36:**1-355, 1973. *A major thesis on many details of modern perimetry.*

National Research Council, Committee on Vision, Assembly of Behavioral and Social Sciences: First interprofessional standard for visual field testing, Report of Working Group 99, Adv. Ophthalmol. **40:**173-224, 1980. *Detailed discussion of variables that influence clinical visual field testing and their standardization.*

Tate, G.W., Jr., and Lynn, J.R.: Principles of quantitative perimetry: testing and interpreting the visual field, New York, 1977, Grune & Stratton, Inc. *This general clinical visual field text book concentrates on the physiology and psychophysics underlying visual field testing, and the technique of performing visual fields. It is worth reading in order to become better acquainted with the various basic and technical factors that influence visual field testing.*

Index